MISEDUCATED

MISEDUCATED

A MEMOIR

BRANDON P. FLEMING

New York

Copyright © 2021 by Brandon P. Fleming

Cover design by Terri Sirma
Cover photograph © Ranta Images/Shutterstock
Cover copyright © 2021 by Hachette Book Group, Inc.

Hachette Books
Hachette Book Group
1290 Avenue of the Americas
New York, NY 10104
HachetteBooks.com
Twitter.com/HachetteBooks
Instagram.com/HachetteBooks

First Edition: June 2021

Published by Hachette Books, an imprint of Perseus Books, LLC, a subsidiary of Hachette Book Group, Inc. The Hachette Books name and logo is a trademark of the Hachette Book Group.

The Hachette Speakers Bureau provides a wide range of authors for speaking events. To find out more, go to www.hachettespeakersbureau.com or call (866) 376-6591.

The publisher is not responsible for websites (or their content) that are not owned by the publisher.

Print book interior design by Amy Quinn.

Library of Congress Cataloging-in-Publication Data
Names: Fleming, Brandon P., author.
Title: Miseducated : a memoir / Brandon P. Fleming.
Description: New York : Hachette Books, [2021]
Identifiers: LCCN 2020054279 | ISBN 9780306925139 (hardcover) | ISBN 9780306925122 (ebook)
Subjects: LCSH: Fleming, Brandon P. | College teachers—United States—Biography. | School failure—United States.
Classification: LCC LA2317.F54 A3 | DDC 378.1/2092 [B]—dc23
LC record available at https://lccn.loc.gov/2020054279

ISBNs: 978-0-306-92513-9 (hardcover), 978-0-306-92512-2 (ebook)

Printed in the United States of America

LSC-C

PRINTING 1, 2021

To my students—the reason for my second chance.

I, too, sing America.

I am the darker brother.
They send me to eat in the kitchen
When company comes,
But I laugh,
And eat well,
And grow strong.

Tomorrow,
I'll be at the table
When company comes.
Nobody'll dare
Say to me,
"Eat in the kitchen,"
Then.

Besides,
They'll see how beautiful I am
And be ashamed—

I, too, am America.

—Langston Hughes, 1926

CONTENTS

FOREWORD

BY DR. CORNEL WEST

As I enter the last stage of life, one of my great joys is to be inspired by those of a much younger age who plan and pledge to pick up the blood-stained and tear-soaked banner of truth and justice. I first met my dear brother Brandon in the hallowed halls of Harvard University. His brilliance, charisma, and commitment were undeniable as he visited my lectures on Frederick Douglass, W. E. B. Du Bois, Lorraine Hansberry, and other Black scholars.

It became clear to me that his heart, mind, and soul were on fire for truth. We broke bread and I learned about his painful past, I learned of his resilient present, but he primarily focused on an ebullient future—one that held a commitment to his scholars and the plight of American education at the center. It was infectious, his deep delight and genuine glee at reflecting on the great talent and grand victories of his brilliant students. I was elated to greet them upon their arrival in Cambridge, but our plans were thwarted when the coronavirus lockdown set in and university programming shifted to distance learning. But on the virtual platform, I had an opportunity to spend time with them and share rich and wonderful dialogue. And I can attest to their magic.

Fleming stands in the great tradition of Black writers and fighters who unite thought and action, reflection and execution, based on a deep love of people—especially for young Black people who grow up on the kicking fields of America's hoods. Like those who helped Brandon turn his life around, he has now taken the lead in transforming the lives of so many young brothers and sisters by means of paideia: a deep education rooted in truth, justice, and love.

Miseducated is paideia. It is power and insight wrapped beautifully in prose. It is art that touches the heart, incites the mind, and reaches deep down into the depths of the soul. It is poignant the way Fleming's formation unfolds—from a life of drugs, violence, and hoop dreams to a quest for intellectual and spiritual excellence. The way he cultivates critical thinking in young people puts a premium on academic debate, joyful learning, and the transformative power of language. And his journey in finding self and helping others do the same is both heart-touching and soul-stirring.

In *Miseducated*, the upward climb is not about making it to the top, it is about pulling others up when you get there. And Fleming's fight to moral greatness and societal significance is boundless. The following pages lay bare the stages of failure, of triumph, and the discovery of a special calling that will lift us all in such a grim moment in the history of this country.

MISEDUCATED

CHAPTER ONE

GOLDEN TICKET

I could not seem to die. I opened my eyes in a hospital bed, the faint beeping of a monitor signaling I had been given a second chance I did not want. I was still here. Forced to see, hear, feel, and face the reality I had desperately tried to flee. I did not want to feel anymore, but I felt. I felt cold. I felt pain. I felt alone.

I scanned the room searching for the culprit, the one who was no friend of mine for dragging me back to the life I was desperate to leave. How could they? I did not want to be saved. I wanted to be free. And if they could feel, see, or sense my anguish, they would not have thwarted my exit, barring the door to my escape. They would have opened it. They would have let me through.

"Mr. Fleming?" My rush of angry, frustrated thoughts was stilled by a gentle, compassionate voice. "Mr. Fleming, how are you feeling?"

I averted my eyes from the infusion pump to a petite woman dressed in white. Her blonde hair was backlit and luminescent. She looked harmless enough, but I felt vulnerable, exposed, weak. Surely she would take one look at me and see everything, all the insecurities that fueled my cowardly desire to run. Surely she would see I had no reason to be alive. I felt ashamed to be here, in this room, receiving this attention. It took a while for me to gather the courage to look at her. At her soft gray eyes that made me somehow feel safe. Her smile was perfectly appropriate. It was subtle enough to respect my circumstance yet assertive enough to assure me that everything would be okay.

"Here, drink this." She gently braced my neck as she held a bowl of gritty black liquid to my lips. "This is activated charcoal. It will help to dissolve the drugs you took."

I grimaced as I gulped the elixir. It tasted like cement mixed with the castor oil my aunt made me drink as a child. As I gagged through the last swallow, the nurse dabbed the corners of my mouth and carefully nestled my head back at rest. She promised to return to check on me and disappeared through the veil that separated me from other patients.

I did not want her to leave. She was all I had. My feeble hand lifted and beckoned her to stay, but I did not have the strength to speak. Wide-eyed, I lay back and gazed at the ceiling as tears welled in the gutters of my eyes and streamed slowly down the contours of my face, dissolving in the stubble on my chin. I was alone—with my thoughts, my feelings, and the life I did not want.

Lying there, I thought about the day before. It was my last shift on the assembly line of Vitamin Manufacturing. I was an eighteen-year-old college dropout dating a girl whose mother insisted that I try to earn a living. My girlfriend had not yet developed a radar for detecting low-lives, so her mother had intervened with a passive-aggressive introduction to the local temp agency. In this way, she'd avoided challenging her daughter's taste in men while also demonstrating her distaste for jobless suitors. I had no education, no resources, and no skills, so menial labor was my only hope for making a decent living.

The agency had assigned me to a vitamin plant in Anderson, South Carolina, about twenty miles from Greenville, where I'd finished high school almost two years prior. Mom's deployment to Iraq had separated and scattered my siblings and me. Sierra was twenty-two and had gone to live with her boyfriend. Barry was a year older than me and had gone to live with his father in New York. I'd moved to Greenville, where I temporarily stayed with my aunt. Ben, the youngest of us, was the only one with nowhere to go. So he'd gone with me until Mom's return.

Mom was away in Iraq for a year. She was now back home in suburban Washington, DC, settling into civilian life as a retired veteran. She, too, had no job, no education, and limited resources. And she did not have the emotional capacity to take me back in. She was tired, and getting older. Raising us took everything she had, between Sierra's teenage pregnancy, Barry's street fights, and my drug peddling. After all that strife, she was still not yet an empty nester, watching my little brother—now at home with her—be kept back in school while he followed my footsteps into delinquency and danger. Instead of intervening and imposing strict rules like she'd tried with us, she raised her hands in surrender because she had nothing left to give. The chances that she would take me in, after I'd gone off to college and dropped out my first semester, were unfavorable. "When you turn eighteen," she'd always said, "you're on your own." And she'd meant it. Now I jumped from house to house, sleeping on couches and floors belonging to friends whose parents were kind enough to shelter an unemployed boy who was barely a man. But even those kind parents had a threshold.

One of those friends was Kevin. His family allowed me to make a pallet on their living room floor. The floor was much more comfortable than their derelict sofa, whose yellow cushion seeped through the abrasions in the aging leather. They gave me six months, but under one condition: I was to maintain a job or be out of the house looking for one during business hours. For a few months they had kicked me out and banned my reentry until 5 p.m. each day. But instead of job searching, I spent most of that time with my girlfriend. Until her mother self-aligned with Kevin's parents in trying to pressure me into responsibility. That's when I'd started at the temp agency.

Once I began work at the vitamin factory, my old-fashioned tabletop alarm clock blared at 5 a.m. each morning. I despised the dreadful sound. I swiped blindly at the clock, my face still buried in the pillow, hoping to hit snooze, or I yanked the cord from the wall to silence the damn thing. New days were nothing to look forward to. Sometimes I would lie there in the dark contemplating my options, which were few. Reluctantly, I rose, donning my blue long-sleeved coveralls and boots, remembering the imposed conditions of my stay.

I was out the door by 5:30 a.m. In my Honda Accord, I'd blaze down a dark freeway as day was breaking. I'd lower the windows and blast the music to fight back drowsiness. I tried coffee. I tried Red Bull. But my heavy eyelids and grizzly yawns never acclimated to the early rise.

The factory was a dystopia. No one laughed. No one smiled. No one hugged in the morning. The first-shift workers filed into the factory like androids, punching our time cards and fastening our goggles, assuming our positions on the assembly line, where we'd slave for the next ten hours.

I was there to collect a check, like everyone else. But I had never labored so hard in my life. The assembly line was about twelve feet long. I'd start on one end of the machine, where the forklift drivers delivered endless boxes. The towering stack nearly rose to the ceiling whenever I fell behind. The forklift man would grow increasingly irritable and growl, "Pick it up! You're slowing me down!" I'd be going as fast as I could, but sharp spasms would shoot through my spine from the bending and rising and bending and rising to break down boxes and load bottles into the machine. Then I'd sprint to the middle section of the line, where another forklift operator piled bins of vitamins that had to be poured into the machine. But the vitamins were gelled and stuck together. To break them up enough for the machine to ingest, I had to deadlift each twenty-pound bin, lofting it over my head and slamming it on the floor. I'd reach my hand into the bin to loosen the capsules that were stuck together, gagging as I inhaled the abysmal stench. I'd do an overhead press with a bin as I climbed a ten-foot ladder to the mouth of the machine. After dumping the vitamins, I'd climb back down and dash to the end of the line to help screw caps on the bottles. Then I'd run to the front of the line to start all over—for ten hours a day, six days a week.

On this day, I was supposedly unpacking boxes of bottles and lining them up on the conveyor belt when Rita, my line leader, caught me day-dreaming. Every chance I got, I stopped and leaned against the machine to catch my breath while thinking, *I can't do this shit*. But I was quickly reminded that I had no choice. On this occasion, I was imagining the life I wanted—one where I didn't have to sacrifice my sanity and my body while toiling like a cotton picker in high August for a measly two dollars above minimum wage.

"Watch out!" Rita screamed from the end of the line, snapping me back to my miserable reality.

I rushed to organize bottles on the belt, but it was too late. The timer opened the valve that dispensed vitamins into waiting bottles, but no bottles were in place. Pound after pound of gelled capsules spilled onto the conveyor, quickly building a mountain that became an avalanche onto the factory floor. Another coworker slammed the emergency button and the entire machine jerked to a halt. I stood in shock, breathless and ankle-deep in pills. I felt laser beams of anger from my coworkers' eyes hit me like the red dot of a sniper's sight.

"What the hell are you doin'?" Rita shouted. Her voice was a thunderstorm. She looked like her grandchildren might call her Big Mama. She was as large as Tyler Perry and she was channeling Madea in a towering, dramatic rage. Her voice was so terrifying that, at first, I could not raise my eyes to see the expression on her face. I flipped through a mental index of excuses that might break the tension but came up empty. Finally, I looked at her and said nothing, hoping she would somehow take pity on my youth.

A few seconds of awkward silence was broken by her sigh. Hands on her hips, she rolled her eyes as if she felt sorry for me. We were all dressed in the same coveralls, face mask, and elastic nets on our head and shoes. The place felt like the contemporary hotbox version of a plantation. This one was filled with industrial workers tending robotic machines and looking as busy as possible when "Massa" strolled by our stations with his checklist and clipboard. I was tired. Tired of the same steps, same movements, same people, same routines. Every minute. Every hour. And every single day. It was a living nightmare of drudgery on an endless loop.

Rita grabbed me by the arm and whisked me off to the side. Once out of the other workers' hearing range, she released my arm and returned her hands to her hips. She looked carefully over both shoulders and pulled down her face mask. "The hell you doin' in here anyway, boy?" I didn't understand why she was whispering so aggressively. "You ain't got no damn business being in this factory." Her tone sounded like she was telling me a secret—like she wasn't mad anymore. She seemed sympathetic and loving. But this was that hard love, like when Mama says, "I'm doing this because I love you" before she swings the belt across your hind. For a moment it felt like she knew me. Her voice sounded like she loved me, like she knew something that I didn't. It felt like she was begging me to get out.

"I dr-dropped out of college," I muttered. I flinched as her hands flew from her hips. Her arms folded across her chest, she leaned forward and hissed, "You did what?" Her tone had shifted toward the one she used when the pills hit the floor. I was confused by the sound of rage layered with disappointment and a touch of love. I barely knew her but, in that moment, I felt like her son.

"Look around this room, boy." With one hand she gripped my arm and with the other she made a sweeping gesture. Instantly, I knew what she wanted me to see. I saw a warehouse full of blue bodies moving as fast as foot traffic in Times Square. I saw hundreds of intense faces moist from labor. I saw dozens of backs hunched with soreness and fatigue. I saw drudges sneak tiny moments of relief each time their machines were temporarily inactive. That's what I saw: a seemingly endless cycle of heaviness and hopelessness. And I couldn't bear to look anymore. I wanted to run back to the dream where I had been before I screwed up with the bottles. Those daydreams were often my only fleeting moments of escape. Sometimes nostalgia made the hours pass quicker. My mind left the factory in those moments and traveled back in time to relive basketball triumphs. I replayed championship wins. I reenacted game-winning shots by counting down, "Three . . .

two . . . one" and making a buzzer sound as I held my arm arched in the air after shooting bottles into the mouth of the machine. It made me remember the time when I once had a purpose. And I smiled. But then Rita's desperate voice yanked me back into reality.

Rita's voice quivered through her gritted teeth. "Do you understand what the people in this shithole would have done to trade places with you? Don't you know you threw away your golden ticket?" Her grip got tighter. "Don't you?" she exclaimed.

I didn't. But I would soon.

I sat in the cafeteria during my lunch break, turned to stone by Rita's words. I held a sandwich in my left hand but couldn't raise it to my mouth. I could only stare straight, paralyzed by the image Rita had forced me to confront, and overwhelmed by a truth I carried inside me but had somehow ignored. There was no one else my age. They were all older, two and three times my senior. I could see their sullen faces in my sleep. Temp workers were overjoyed when the factory switched their employment to permanent jobs. They celebrated the announcements, cheering, "I got on!" in the cafeteria when they won the coveted positions like they were grand prizes. I could not understand it, because it seemed like we were all just stuck in sinking sand.

My anxiety soared at the thought of getting such an offer, and of being there forever. Rita's voice echoed in my head: I had thrown away my golden ticket, she said. My golden ticket. It sounded so beautiful, so liberating, yet so far from reach. And here I was, in the factory lunchroom, wondering if I could ever get it back.

I laid my head down on the table for the last few minutes of my lunch break. Moments later, I was jolted awake by the commotion of people being herded back to work. I did not want to go. Before I could rise from my seat, my eyes caught the movement of the third-shift workers clocking out. I watched them punch their yellow time cards and disappear into the blinding sunlight breaking through the doorway, wishing that I, too, could be cast into that emancipating glow.

Above the door was a bright red EXIT sign.

"Come on, son," said Rita. "Break is over." Rita touched my shoulder as she passed by, but I did not move. I was captivated by the sign I had seen a million times but never like this. Those four boxy letters spoke to me in a way they never had before. The sign was summoning me to leave, to get out, to seize my one and only chance. So I listened. And I left. I got up and walked straight through the door into the parking lot. I got in my car, I drove away, and I did not look back.

I felt liberated, but only for a moment. I was at a portentous crossroad, having no idea what to do next. I had walked off the job without notice. There was no way they would keep me or hire me back. I was officially unemployed, with no money, no real home, and no plan. But I was finally free, it seemed. But freedom without hope is like living in a black hole.

I was tired of going to the cash advance store to get payday loans, parking all the way down the street and creeping in with a hood and sunglasses to hide my identity. I was tired of going to the gas station for daily five-dollar fills, which I probably wasted driving miles in search of a gas station displaying a price that was just a couple of cents cheaper per gallon. I was tired of sorting through the items I owned, conducting a cost-benefit analysis to see which I could do without and which would be most valuable at the local pawn shop. I was tired of cup noodles and beans-and-weenies and stretching one serving of Hamburger Helper to last three days. I was tired of being broke. I was tired of being needy. I was tired of the weight of simply being.

The full punch of what I had done didn't hit me until I was parked in the driveway. When I got inside, the first thing I did was dump my blue coveralls in the trash can. I fixed a grilled cheese sandwich and sat in the dark, hypnotized by the shambles that was my life. I wanted to watch TV, but I couldn't. I wanted to call somebody, but I couldn't. I sat in the still house and descended into a depressive abyss, accepting that what everyone had said about me over the years was obviously and painfully true.

I heard the voice of my stepfather as he palmed my head and told me I was ugly, pressing my face against the mirror until I agreed. And his enraged voice when he beat me with any inanimate object within reach. I heard the screams of my sister as he smashed her bloodied face into the table, daring her to try to save me again.

I heard the voice of my mother, crying and asking where she went wrong as she cupped her hand full of Vaseline and polished the welts on my back.

I heard the voice of my father call me a thug, a reject, and a disgrace to his family before walking out of my life.

I heard the voice of my eighth-grade teacher call me a piece of shit as she kicked me out of class and slammed the door.

I heard the voices of administrators discussing my ten-page disciplinary record and devising a plan for my expulsion.

I heard the voices of coaches say, "He's too short. He can't play at the next level." And I heard the voice of the coach when I'd made it to the next level as a collegiate athlete say, "He's injured. We don't need him."

I heard my college advisor say it's not too late to withdraw.

I heard my mom say I couldn't come back home.

I heard Rita say I threw away my golden ticket.

I heard the EXIT sign say I could just run and be free.

So I ran.

And when I made it to the medicine cabinet, I reached for the pills that promised relief. The ones I remembered hearing were meant for numbing pain and sleeping with peace. I needed both. So I took one, then two, but the pain was still there.

I saw the EXIT sign again. And I just wanted to ride the rays of that emancipating glow right through the doorway. I could feel the drugs coursing through my veins. My heart started pounding against the cage of my chest, telling me I was almost there. And I filled my mouth with another handful, desperate to make it to the other side.

I closed my eyes and lay back, embracing the peace I had only hoped to find.

I was ready to let go. I was ready to die. Ready, I was, to just be free.

CHAPTER TWO

THE DEVIL PREACHES

When people imagine the devil, they picture him in different ways.

In *Paradise Lost*, Milton saw the devil as the most beautiful of the angels, until he wasn't.

In his painting *The Last Judgment*, Fra Angelico saw the Renaissance version with horns, scales, cloven hooves, and an arrowhead tail.

Generations of cartoonists have drawn him as a puckish red figure perched on a person's shoulder, with an angel standing on the other.

This is how some envision the devil.

But not me.

When I imagine the devil, I see a man that few people would recognize as Satan, the Prince of Darkness.

I see Lucas.

I watched him creep into our home at night—slippery, angry, high. We suspected it was the alcohol or cocaine that stained his eyes as red as blood.

But on Sundays, he preached. I watched him lead worship at church. Like heaven's minister of music—Lucifer the archangel—he preached

God's word, played the guitar's melodic strings, and aroused the parishioners until they quickened and quivered in a Baptist convulsion.

After church, I watched him disappear into the night. Sometimes alone. Sometimes with my baby brother. And it was Ben's recollections—confided many years later—that filled in the details about my stepfather's whereabouts. How he had sex with prostitutes in the back seat of our minivan as his toddler son sat silently in the passenger seat, forever marked by what he watched in the rearview mirror.

My mother had no idea that she funded these exploits. Or maybe she did. But there was nothing she could do. When duty called, Mom had to answer. Roughly every month, the army sent her on temporary duty assignments that lasted for weeks at a time. This was when we were left in Lucas's care, or rather at his mercy. He owned us. And we wore his wrath like metal collars clinched around our necks.

We gathered at the front door to say goodbye. It was our custom. Mom knelt and wrapped her entire wingspan around her children, hugging our necks and planting kisses on the crown of our heads. Sierra and I cried—partly because we'd miss her, and partly because we knew what would happen when that door closed behind her. With short breaths and hearts filled with fear, we waited. Counting the seconds until our safety ended. Clinging to those final moments before the dark clouds opened and brimstone rained down. Searching for a reason that would make her stay. Hoping she could see the infrared signal of distress radiating from our eyes.

She saw it.

She always saw it.

But it did not matter.

Because she still had to go.

"I left money on the counter," she said. "This is for food and food only. You hear me?" She gripped my cheeks and lifted my chin to make sure that I paid heed.

We didn't have time to go grocery shopping before she left. On the table was enough money for two weeks' worth of pizza, Chinese, and our standard Sunday dinner at Western Sizzlin.

She rose to her feet, our four tiny bodies entwining her legs and arms and waist. "You're in charge," she said to Sierra. She hugged us one last time. It was long and tight and full of remorse. She looked him in the face with tearful eyes. She did not say a word to admonish him or plead, though her fraught expression said it all. She tilted back her head and looked upward, as if petitioning God and fighting back her own tears. She made no sound. She said no words. But her lips trembled as she silently mouthed something that looked like "Please" and turned away as if she could look no more.

"Shut that noise up!" he yelled after the door closed behind her. We stood still, frozen by his rolling rage. He hated when we cried, especially for her. Affection didn't live here. He barely even seemed to like my mother. I never saw him hug her or kiss her. Not a word of affirmation. He only used his words to malign her as a mother and to defame her as a wife. He called her stupid and dumb. "She don't know nothing," he always said. Everything that went wrong, he attributed to her lack of knowledge and overall unfitness. He shamed her. And we listened, because there was nothing else we could do.

"If your mother wasn't so dumb . . . ," he said when it pained her to punish us. Like the time we were caught accepting candy from a stranger at the grocery store. Going to the grocery store was like a trip to the amusement park for us. Sierra fastened Ben in a cart and pushed him down one aisle, while Barry and I were in another lane cruising on carts like scooters. "Faster, Barry! Faster!" I begged. Barry was at the back, kicking and steering, while I rode on the front of the buggy, smiling from ear to ear and yelling, "Woohoo!" as we darted down the aisle. Customers gaped and snatched their children from our path. But we didn't care, we were having the time of our lives—until Mom seized us by the ear and dragged us away. The fun was over.

All four of us followed Mom through the exit, trailing like a line of pups. She always made us boys dress identically from head to toe: same gold cross necklace, same matching outfit and shoes, same haircut.

An older white man approached us on our way out. He complimented us on our outfits and kneeled to offer us lollipops. Our faces lit with excitement as we reached for the candy. Mom was heading for the car when, suddenly, she glanced behind her and saw that we were missing. In a panic, she rushed back into the store, snatched the candy from our hands, and roared, "Get away from my children!" Then she whisked us away, dragging us on her heels like tin cans on the back of a wedding car. She slammed to a stop when we got outside, like she couldn't wait another second to explode. She popped us in the head and wagged her finger in our faces. "What I tell y'all about talking to strangers?" These situations were difficult. We never knew when she actually wanted an answer. Sometimes, we'd start responding to her question and she'd yell, "Shut up!" When in doubt, we looked at Sierra to follow her lead. Our sister was muted by fear. "Wait till we get home," Mom hissed, "I'ma tear y'all behind up."

No one spoke during the ride home. Ben wasn't old enough to get fullfledged whoopings. But the three of us were as silent as prisoners passing death row cells on their way to the chamber. I admired Sierra, because she knew how to maintain a look that said she didn't care, she was untouchable. I'd try to harden my face to look like hers, but an expression of dread overtook my features when I thought about the last whooping we got. Mom always gathered us in one room. We stood in a line as she spanked us one by one. There are different types of whooping-getters, and we each had our own style. There are stoics—the ones who stare straight and stone-faced like a protester who refuses to budge: that was Sierra. There are runners—the ones who make Mom run laps around the room, chasing and swinging and missing: that was Barry. Then there are thespians—the ones who dramatically cry and fall out before Mom even takes the first swing: that was me. And Mom would leave the room, but not before yelling, "Stop crying before I give you something to cry about," as if she hadn't already fulfilled that promise.

These scenes played through my mind on our ride home. Suddenly, Mom's tension started to wane as she cruised to her gospel music, crooning ballads that conjured up the Holy Spirit. She occasionally lifted one hand, the other still clutching the wheel, and gently cried, "Thank you, Jesus." I knew that she was spiritually stirred and her heart was softening when she passed frequent glances in the rearview mirror. She was checking to see if we were okay, showing remorse that she might have overreacted. To Hezekiah Walker and Helen Baylor, I am indebted—for they often saved our asses, quite literally.

The car slowed to an unexpected stop. By this time, we had all fallen asleep. "Wake up, y'all," she said. My heartbeat instantly accelerated because my first thought was that we had reached the end of death row. I just wanted to get it over with. The wait was the most painful. We stretched and yawned and wiped our eyes and realized that we were not home.

"Reach back there and grab the bread," Mom directed. I was in the back row of our seven-passenger minivan so I strained and contorted to reach into the storage area. I dug through the heap of grocery bags to unearth a loaf of bread. "Hurry up before I change my mind," Mom added, as if there was a time limit on her kindness. I retrieved the loaf and she told us to get out of the car.

At our feet was a picturesque lake with dozens of ducklings nibbling at the shoreline. The air was clear and the sun's rays were gentle. The water was still. And I'll never forget the sounds, as if Mother Nature welcomed us with song. The ducks quacked and the birds chirped and the wind whistled gently in the willows, which swayed like they were dancing.

"Go ahead," Mom said. "They don't bite." But Ben didn't believe her. We tossed our share of bread crumbs and gave him the rest. Once he overcame his initial fear, he discovered that he had found new friends. "Be careful!" Mom yelled as his confidence grew. He looked so innocent, so free, so safe.

Ben suddenly became the food bank. A flock of fully grown and baby ducks thronged him at once. Ben laughed and ran away. It was fun at first, until he glanced back and saw a mob of determined waterfowl charging him like villagers with pitchforks. Ben's chortling ascended into a siren's scream. He cried for help and ran while we stood by, laughing and teasing him. Finally, Ben dropped the remains of the loaf and jumped into my mother's arms. We laughed and hugged and grinned, as if our world was so perfect. But it wasn't. Because the titan of terror was waiting at home for our return.

Our home was no home while Mom was away. It was a callous crypt where fear and darkness loomed. It was an eerie penitentiary where we barred our rooms like stony cells. We thought we were safe as long as we pretended not to exist. We would have starved rather than tell Lucas we were hungry.

We enjoyed more freedoms when Mom was home. We enjoyed the most freedom when Lucas wasn't. When Mom was away on duty, he sometimes disappeared for days at a time. His abandonment pained Mom, but it brought us so much peace. We were safe in Sierra's hands. She taught herself how to cook so we were fed. And when there were no groceries, she hiked for miles to reach the nearest food pantry. She once stole Mom's keys and drove, with her head barely peeking over the wheel, so we wouldn't go hungry.

Our rooms were in a row along the second-floor hallway of our house, and the devil's chamber was across the hall on the opposite end. When Lucas was home, we kept our bedroom doors locked and our televisions low. We tiptoed to the bathroom for emergencies, so as not to awake the angry beast of Babylon. Even when he did not force us, we stayed in our rooms where we were sometimes safe from his capricious explosions.

It was safest to stay hidden, though it grieved us to be apart. Especially Barry and me. We were best friends. Mom made sure of it. Anytime Barry wanted to go somewhere or do something, he couldn't make it out the door before Mom yelled, "Don't forget your little brother!" He never grumbled or griped when I joined him. We took the long way to the corner store and turned those trips into outdoor adventures. We played basketball in the front yard, and he hugged me when I cried out of frustration because he would not let me win. We watched endless cartoons. And when we weren't doing that, we played with Hot Wheels or G.I. Joes, making sound effects for every weapon, from rifles to grenade launchers. Or we pretended to be WWF wrestlers, performing dropkicks and Stone Cold stunners and Rock bottoms and jumping off the bed doing dangerous elbow drops. Or we yelled, "KAME HAME HAA," pretending to be Goku and Vegeta from Dragon Ball Z as we stretched our hands to blast each other with our superpowers. We could do none of those things when Lucas was home. But

I was determined to outwit Lucas and the drywall partition that kept me from my brother.

While locked in our rooms, I got an idea from a kids' TV show, but putting it into action would require a potentially perilous trip downstairs. I cracked the door enough to poke my head through. Barry's room was to my immediate left and Sierra's to the right. I crept down the stairs like they were beds of nails. Descending slowly, planting one foot at a time, I froze if I heard a creak. When I reached the final step, I could hear the television in the living room. I paused, reluctant and considering the danger. I took a deep breath and resolved that the risk was worth reuniting with my brother.

Just as I leaned in to turn the corner, I heard Lucas shout, "Are you kidding me?" I jerked back quickly and closed my eyes. "Come on ref, that was bull!" he continued. My chest was pounding. I was scared to breathe because he might hear it. Finally, I just went for it.

I walked quickly but not too fast because I didn't want to appear a running target. My eyes were fixed on the kitchen but in my peripheral vision I could see him eating chips and jeering at his losing Steelers. I retrieved four red plastic cups from the cabinet and darted back toward the stairs. I made it safely, this time, courtesy of *Monday Night Football*.

When I got back to my room, I poked a hole in the bottom of each cup and connected them with shoestrings. They were telephones, like the ones I had seen in the cartoon. I peeked my head in the hallway and tossed one pair to Barry's door. I rushed to the wall that divided us, thrilled that I had devised a solution. I pressed one cup to the wall and the other to my mouth. "Barry, you there?" I whispered into the plastic. Then I held it to my ear anxiously awaiting his response. "I repeat, Barry are you there?" It did not work. After several minutes of silence passed, reality set in. Obviously, these cups must have been defective.

When that plan fell short, we pushed boundaries by lying on the floor with our doors cracked and our heads barely peeping out like whack-a-moles. Sometimes we talked in whispers. Other times, we simply took comfort from being able to see each other. We made faces to see who would laugh first. Then we had staring contests, eyes watering while we squinted, trying desperately not to blink. Then we busted out in laughter and slapped our hands over our mouths, horrified that we'd made a sound. "Shut that noise up!" Lucas yelled from downstairs. Then we closed our doors and went back into hiding.

Of our cells, Barry's had the best view. His room was in the front and from his window he could see other kids playing outside. My window faced the vinyl siding of the house next door. Rarely did I get a chance to see the sun.

There was one last hope before I'd give up. The wall that divided our rooms had a vent at the bottom. I crawled on my stomach to the foot of the wall and placed my ear against the vent. I thought I could hear sound from the other side. I put my mouth against the vent.

"Pssst," I whispered through the air duct. "Barry, can you hear me?"

I was desperate to hear my big brother's voice.

"Barry? Barry, you there?" I said again. But I got nothing in return.

I was saddened by another failed experiment. I retired to my bed to kick my feet up and watch the day fade away.

Suddenly, I faintly heard something near the vent. I flopped back on my belly and crawled with lightning speed. I put my ear to the air vent to listen. "Barry, is that you?" I whispered into the air vent. But I heard nothing. "Barry, are you there?" I asked once more. Before I could crawl back to my bed with my face dragging on the floor, I heard his voice reach through the air duct and hold me the way he did when I was frustrated because he never let me win: "I'm here, little bro. I'm here." Once we figured this out, it was how we communicated for years while in confinement.

Barry has always been my best friend. Sierra has always been my protector. It didn't matter that we had different fathers, though it often incited what we call "daddy wars." During these lively disputes, Barry and Sierra—who shared a father—would tag-team against me, taunting, "Our daddy is better than yours." But I would strike back, "No he isn't!" and fervently defend my father. Ben, the youngest of us, was fathered by Lucas and was far too young for verbal jousting. But even if he could have joined in, his nefarious father's drug use, domestic abuse, infidelity, and frequent abandonment would have left him nothing good to say.

As a boy, I couldn't have asked for a father more perfect. Mom had a unique type of "baby-daddy drama." Instead of deadbeat men who skipped visits and missed child support payments, she had two overcommitted fathers and a series of custody battles where she and her former partners traded charges of unfit parenting. Failing to gain full custody, they fought incessantly over visiting rights. Lucas fought against them.

Mom was adamant about keeping her children together, so it pained her to see us whisked away in different directions for weekends or holidays. Barry and Sierra went with their dad in New York, Ben remained in his two-parent home, and I went with my dad to North Carolina, Arizona, or wherever the military had stationed him. Although he and my mother had never legally married, nothing could keep him away. He drove thousands of miles, survived accidents, and weathered storms to keep his promise to his little boy. He didn't seem to care, at first, how poorly I fit into his second family. Anyone who knew him knew that there was nothing he treasured more than his only son.

In the '90s, Dad was what they called a "man's man." He stood five foot ten and was a star athlete with burly shoulders, veiny biceps, and a chiseled chest. His bald head was immaculate and glistened like bronze. He was a valiant soldier who had survived foreign wars and climbed military ranks. He was a competitive boxer who had contended with the best in Golden Gloves bouts. He was that and more. But above all, he was my hero. And together we turned every idle moment into a sport.

When we visited my paternal grandmother in South Carolina, our roughhousing scared her. Lying on the floor, my dad with his legs bent and upraised, I planked on the soles of his feet. He grabbed hold of my hands, straightened his legs, and boosted me high into the air with my hands free and my arms outstretched. "Superman!" he yelled as Grandma closed her eyes and shrieked in fear.

I woke him up in the mornings by turning the bed into a trampoline. He stretched the blanket over his drowsy face, no doubt wishing his hyperactive son had a snooze button. Then I flopped onto his belly, demanding that he come to life.

We played football in the yard, where he'd allow my meager 85 pounds to topple his 200-pound mass with a tackle.

In parking lots, he'd suddenly call out, "Bet you can't beat me!" and take off running toward the car at far less than his actual speed. When I bolted past him, he'd yell, "Slow down! You're too fast!" and he smiled as I left him trailing on the asphalt.

We played one-on-one at the basketball court. I once delivered my best crossover combo to get around his wide frame when, suddenly, he grabbed me from behind and hoisted me on his shoulders for a slam dunk.

We arm-wrestled at the dinner table, where his face would twist with anguish as he hissed through his gritted teeth, "I can't win. You're too strong."

And when we weren't competing in some sport, he was affectionate. In private and public, he'd say, "Come here" and plant wet kisses on each cheek. I squirmed and wiped them off, but he wouldn't stop until I allowed his love seal of saliva to dry on my face.

Most vivid, however, are the scenes when our visits ended. The cross-country drives in his blue Dodge truck didn't last long enough. He steered with one arm, and with the other he stretched his calloused hand to wipe the tears pooling in the corners of my eyes. He sang to me until I fell asleep. And when I dozed off, or when he thought I had, I could hear soft sniffles as he cried, too.

By the time I had awakened, I was home—back to the hellish place ruled by my demon stepfather. Dad knew something wasn't right, but he lacked proof of what was happening to me inside that house. During custody hearings, the judge always asked for evidence of maltreatment. Dad would pull me aside and coach, "Come on, son, it's okay. Tell us what's going on," pushing me to validate his suspicions. But I couldn't. At that age, I had no true concept of abuse. It was an abstract term that my ten-year-old brain could not yet comprehend, and an experience that my elementary vocabulary could not capture.

Besides, the devil brainwashed me to believe that my beatings were deserved. I will not be the bad child that I am is what he made me write a thousand times a day, seven days a week, for nearly five years. That message was encoded in my mind. I dreaded coming home from school because I knew what awaited me. The sentences were top priority. Homework often went undone, and dinner was a luxury—permitted only if I had finished. I'd spend hours writing, legs crossed, hunched over on my bedroom floor. My neck cricked and my fingers would blister, bleed, and burn with splinters from shabby wooden pencils. The pain crippled my right hand and forced me to become ambidextrous. The labor begat "Wow, your writing is so neat" from schoolteachers who hadn't a clue. But the cost wasn't worth those fleeting moments of praise. And the writing was only the beginning of his rage.

When I'd finished the one thousandth line of the script, I delivered the stack to his bedroom. His chamber felt like the underworld, his bed a throne shrouded in darkness and despair. I'd hand over the parcel, eyes fixed on the discolored carpet as my body stiffened in fear. He'd examine the packet to verify the sentence count. I had tried to outsmart him a few times, but I did so at my own expense. So I employed other strategies, such as writing *I* a thousand times, then *will*, then *not*, and so on. After shuffling the pages for a few seconds, he'd shove the sheets into my chest and say, "Now rip it." I'd begin tearing through the dense stack, but I never moved fast enough for him. His rage simmered, then boiled and rose into a violent eruption.

"I said rip it!" he'd roar as he snatched the papers and angrily tore them to shreds. My hands would tremble as he stormed to the closet. He'd retrieve a wad of tangled belts and carefully study the weapons. When he couldn't settle on one, he'd hold them all in the palm of his hand and grip them into a bundle. He'd examine it like a bullwhip—but, still, he was unsatisfied. He'd turn the belts upside down so the metal buckles dangled at the end, clanging like lepers' bells. With one hand, he'd cock back the metal batch and then slash across my torso, rip across my legs, my head, or wherever the iron might land—until I'd crumple to the floor, swollen, bleeding, beyond reach of mercy. The gut-wrenching sounds of lashes and ghastly screams echoed through the hollow place that I called home. Helplessly I'd lay, my body mangled, my knees tucked into my chest, and my forearms frantically guarding my face. But he'd continue swinging the belt buckles, thrashing and striking me like I was his slave.

One time when my father and I pulled into the driveway, there Lucas stood, guarding the gates of hell, looking far scarier to me than Maalik or a three-headed hound. But I wouldn't get out of the truck. I couldn't. Dad unloaded my luggage and stood impatiently, beckoning through the window. Sorrow gathered in my eyes and fell in a silent, steady stream. I hoped for divine intervention or for Dad to read the fear that drove my tears. He reached for the door, but I barred it shut. After a brief tug-of-war, he grappled me out of the truck. But I resisted. "No, Daddy! No! Please!" I yelled. He was so much stronger than me, but I kicked and hollered and roped my arms around the headrest. Half of my body dangled outside the vehicle. I held on tightly and screamed for my life. "Son, please, you have to stop," he said, embarrassed as neighbors observed the dramatic scene. "No! Please! No!" I continued, hoping he would give in. I threw my weight to the ground, desperate to break free.

"You need some help?" the devil said with an ominous grin as he watched us tussle. His evil chuckles portended the dark amusements he had in mind.

"It's okay, I got him," Dad responded. He tugged on my legs, trying to drag me as gently as possible toward the house while I clawed and dug my fingernails into the earth, dirt filling in my cuticles.

"Son, please. Don't do this," he begged.

Eventually, I surrendered to exhaustion. When we finally made it to the door, Dad planted a last wet kiss on my cheek and said, "I love you, son" as I begged him not to go.

I pressed my face against the screen door as I watched him fade into the distance. He was gone. My heart sank to my stomach and contracted in an agony so unbearable that I collapsed to the floor. I was fatigued—and stricken with grief. Suddenly, the devil yelled, "At ease!" He nearly yanked my arm out of its socket as he snatched me to my feet and barked, "Shut that noise up, boy!" This, I understood, was his sinister way of saying "Welcome back home."

Five years we survived him. And it might have been longer. Until one day, Sierra decided that enough was enough. She devised a plan to get rid of Lucas. He had to go. Even if it meant that he would die.

It was a Saturday and Mom had to work. Most mornings like this, Sierra sat us down and fixed us breakfast like wheat toast and Cap'n Crunch, the cereal du jour. She loved pretending to be our mother. It was beautiful at times and embarrassing at others. Like when she once cut my eyelashes because she was jealous they were longer than hers. Or when Barry and I would be slap boxing or wrestling in our rooms and she would barge in to interrupt and force us to play house instead. She pretended we were her children. I was prettier than Barry, according to her, so I always had to play the daughter. She put the mouth of a white undershirt over my head and used the sleeves and body to make a single long braid. Then she chose the finest makeup from Mom's bathroom to dash my lips with Ruby red and decorate my face with rosy blush. It was torture. But we had to comply because she was still bigger than us.

Lucas made breakfast this particular Saturday. He did this sometimes when he was in a decent mood. He yelled from the kitchen, "Get down here and eat!" We sat on stools at the kitchen counter, eating wordlessly, because we did not like to talk in his presence. He was steps away in the living room. Barry and Ben finished their food and went back upstairs, but I stayed for an extra bowl or two of cereal. This was a mistake.

As soon as I took my bowl to the sink, he came back into the kitchen. I flinched and quickly moved out of his way, tightening my body as if he might swing at any moment. I wanted to run, but I did not want to leave my sister behind. I looked at her, trying to give a subtle signal for us to leave. But Sierra stayed on her stool. I scrambled to collect my spoon and cup. Still, Sierra did not move. She sat gracefully eating her meal. I looked at her in deep concern. She looked back at me like things were going to change today.

I went and sat next to Sierra. As small as I was, I thought somehow I could protect her. I was terrified of him. We all were. But judging by Sierra's expression, she was not scared this day.

"That woman can't do nothing right," Lucas said as he slammed the fridge. "Not one damn thing."

I looked at Sierra, who was still looking at him, like something was getting ready to happen. My heart felt like it was beating two times its normal speed. I looked to my right at the hallway where I could run, considering the option once more. But I had to stay with my sister. I had to keep her safe.

"She don't know nothing. She can't do nothing," Lucas continued. "I gotta do everything for my goddamn self."

That's when Sierra snapped.

"Stop disrespecting my mother!" Sierra yelled, standing to her feet. My heart nearly stopped. Lucas turned his attention toward her. I looked at him and saw a fire burning in his eyes. I tried not to cry, looking at Sierra and thinking, *No, what have you just done?*

"What you just say to me?" Lucas said, slowly closing the space between them.

Sierra's face was clenched as tight as her teeth.

"I said stop disrespecting my mother!" she repeated.

He rushed toward her and yoked her by the arm. "You better watch your goddamn mouth!" he growled and tossed her toward the back door.

"Now go out there and get me a stick!" he said. He got great satisfaction in watching us fetch weapons he would use on us. He'd send us back time and time again until we found one to his liking.

Sierra screamed back into his face, "No!"

He looked at her like she had lost her mind. I stood immobile, thinking the same thing. Lucas flung open the door with Hulk-like strength. He went outside and grabbed the first stick with a suitable girth. When he returned, Sierra stood there as fearless as I had ever seen. He swung the stick like a baseball bat, aiming toward her head. I heard a big *CRACK!* as it slammed against her neck and snapped in half. But Sierra did not budge. She tightened her hand into a fiery fist and struck him in the face. His glasses went flying as he stumbled backward. I could not believe my eyes. My sister had suddenly transformed into Amanirenas, the Queen of Kush. Then Sierra wound up and swung again. But this time, she missed. I covered my eyes and my stomach clenched because something terrible was about to happen. Lucas's arm shot out and he palmed the entire left side of Sierra's head and slammed it against the counter, pounding and smothering and smushing her face into the granite. I stood in shock as she struggled to yell, "Brandon, run! Go get help!" She was suffocating under his grip. Thick streams of blood were pouring from her nose and into her mouth as she tried to breathe. Her face was a paste of blood and tears as she choked out a scream: "Brandon, go!" But I could not move. I stood wide-eyed, and my entire body was frozen. My feet were bolted to the floor. My legs and arms were paralyzed. My sister's face was being battered, bruised, and crushed under Satan's claw. But I could not move. I could not save her.

Sierra kicked her leg back. Lucas stumbled and she broke free. Her fearlessness had been replaced by terror that she would be killed. She bolted down the hall toward the front door, screaming, "Help! Help!" She made it halfway before Lucas clutched the back of her shirt and tugged her backward. She stretched both hands toward the door, pushing and lunging with all of her might. Her face was sweating blood. Suddenly, Sierra's bra strap snapped under her shirt and Lucas lost his grip, allowing her to break free and charge ahead with all she had. She wrestled the lock and yanked the door open, but before she could thrust her head outside to call for help, Lucas jerked her back, slammed the door, and threw her to the ground. Then he stood, towering over her tattered body. Sierra had no fight left.

Having busted my sister's face, Lucas fled the scene. We did not know where he went, but we guessed that neighbors might have heard the commotion and contacted the authorities. As we waited for Mom to get home, the four of us huddled together in Barry's bed. Sierra was shaking, but she still held us tight. The last thing Lucas said before he slammed out of the house was "Now go upstairs and wipe that blood off your face." But Sierra refused. She left her blood-soaked shirt and face untouched until Mom returned to witness what he had done to her.

Mom arrived home in a rage. We knew she had had enough of him assaulting her children. She stormed up the steps calling, "Lucas! Lucas, where are you?" She'd thought he was still home when they'd spoken on the phone but quickly discovered that he was nowhere to be found. "Sierra, Barry, Brandon?" she called. She opened and closed each door until she found us in Barry's room. She was panting and frantic.

"Sierra, what happened?" Mom asked. Her hands were clutching her hips and she was breathing heavily.

Sierra told her the full story. How he was disrespecting Mom like he always did. How she finally stood up for her. How she was tired of him hurting us. How he battered and bloodied her face. How she tried to run and get help. Mom listened to it all. But none of us were prepared for her response. Of all the scratches and punches and kicks, Mom's reaction was the most devastating blow of the day.

"Well, that's not what he told me," Mom said. "Lucas told me that y'all were disrespectful and tried to jump him."

"What?" Sierra yelled. "Mom, he's lying—"

"Shut up, Sierra!" Mom cut her off, refusing to listen.

"Please, Mom, he hit me in my—"

"I don't give a damn! I said shut up!"

We stared in shock. The entire world stopped moving. Mom didn't use curse words. Not even the small ones. So when she said "damn," we knew whose side she was on.

"That is my husband," she continued, "and y'all are ruining my marriage!"

Our hearts broke instantly. Mom saw him creep in and out, coming home reeking of distant fires. She watched us lose our last house to foreclosure because he failed to pay the mortgage. She watched our car get repossessed because he spent our money on drugs and hookers. She nursed the wounds and welts and sores that scarred my back because of him. All of this, because of him. And still, to her, we were the problem.

Mom left the room in a fury. She slammed the door behind her and a wail of agony broke from Barry's room. Sierra could not hold us anymore. This time, we held her. The realization that our mother was never going to choose us flattened us like a ceiling collapse. Mom wanted to be a godly wife. The one her husband used scriptures to describe. "The Bible says to submit yourself," Lucas often charged. "And it says I rule this house like Christ rules the church." When he opened the Good Book and pointed with his yellow-pigmented fingernail, she believed him. She was wrapped in a garb of oblivion and oppression. But her husband defined it as the cloak of a virtuous woman.

Lucas returned home later that evening. We stayed in our rooms. Sierra spent most of the night on the phone, confiding in her best friend. At first, I'd later learn, they talked about the incident. Then they moved on to their usual topic: boys.

"Girl, I gotta tell you about what happened the other day with me and Dame," Sierra said. "We did it."

"Shut the fuck up," her friend responded in surprise, eager for the juicy details.

"Well not *it* it. But we did stuff," Sierra said. They went on to talk about "stuff" that, as her brother, makes me uncomfortable to think about.

The conversation lasted hours into the night before she hung up the extension. Sierra went downstairs to get a drink of water, not knowing that Lucas was in the living room. He was lounging and his eyes were as scarlet as usual. Sierra walked past calmly, ignoring his presence. But Lucas was determined to invade her space. He looked at her and said, "How did it taste?"

Sierra stopped.

"Excuse me?" she asked, scowling in his direction.

"I said how did it taste? What you did to Dame?" His demonic laugh was imposing. It was haughty and baritone and wicked. Sierra saw the handset for the landline sitting beside him. She suddenly felt her stomach turn like she was going to gag. Lucas continued to laugh as Sierra walked away in shame.

She poured a cup of water and leaned against the counter trying to gather herself. She would have rather stayed in the kitchen forever than to cross back through his line of sight. As she stood there, her eyes caught the knife block on the counter. She picked up a butcher knife, a steak knife, and every other knife that she could handle at once. Then she tucked them under her shirt and headed back to her room to think.

She planned to kill him. And she spent all night imagining different scenarios. As soon as he went to sleep, she would sneak into my mother's room and slit his throat while yelling like a madwoman. Or maybe she would do it quietly, like an impassive assassin. Or maybe she would stab him in the heart. Or maybe she'd slit his throat with the butcher knife and stab him in the heart with the steak knife concurrently and watch him bleed. And when my mother shrieked and screeched and screamed, she wouldn't care. Because Mom would never have the opportunity to choose him over us again.

After Sierra considered her options, she slid the knives under her pillow and closed her eyes to wait a few hours until he was sound asleep. She rested in peace knowing that he would go to sleep this night and never wake up to terrorize our family again. Our mom would be sad at first, but eventually she would acknowledge the truth of what he did to us while she was away from home. Sierra might spend years in juvenile detention, but it was okay as long as it meant that her three little brothers were safe. She was ready to take the fall. She slept until everyone was sound asleep, when her mission would begin. But by the time she woke up, it was already dawn. And she was angry that she had not seen it through.

The next day, Sierra returned all of the knives but one. Having failed to kill her tormentor, she turned to a different plan. She sat on her bed with the blade in hand, her eyes toggling between the knife and her wrist. Maybe she could not end the pain for us. But there was one sure way that she could end her own. She grabbed a pencil and a sheet of paper, and with tears dripping on the thin blue lines, she wrote a one-page note that ended with the words *I can't do this anymore.*

Before pressing knife to flesh, Sierra decided to break her silence. She called her father to tell the truth. Mr. Barry later told me about this moment and what happened afterward. It was the first time he'd heard of the horrors. He calmed her down and assured her that everything would be all right. He called my mom and the phone in her hand was smoking: "Liz, if he puts his muthafuckin' hands on those kids one more time, it'll be the last time he breathes!" Mom tried to keep the exchange private, but Lucas was listening to every word.

"Hang up that phone," Lucas yelled. "The Bible says I'm the man of this house."

But Mr. Barry would not let up. "Tell that scripture-quoting, crack-smoking husband of yours that if he ever touches Sierra, Barry, or Brandon again, I will drive to Richmond from New York to kill and bury him myself."

But Mom defended her husband. She denied that he was beating us. She denied any allegations of abuse. She said she had never seen him do such a thing and she did not believe it.

"What the hell you mean, Liz?" Mr. Barry barked back. "My daughter's face is busted and Brandon is walking around with welts all over his body." But she protected Lucas. She wanted to be a godly wife. The threats did not matter, because Lucas didn't stop beating us. Mom didn't stop defending him. But Mr. Barry kept the pressure on and fought for us when no one else would.

Months later we were summoned to court for a custody hearing. Mom dressed us to look like proper preacher's kids and loaded us in the minivan. Lucas drove. We sat woefully in the back, suffering under his gospel quartet cassette tapes and his tiresome lecturing about what it means to be a man and how he fulfilled every requirement.

In the courtroom, Mr. Barry argued for custody of my sister and brother on the grounds that our well-being was in danger if we stayed where we were. He wanted to take me, too, if they would let him. The judge brought the three of us into his private chambers for questioning. Barry and I were too young to be interrogated. Sierra's recollection is that the judge asked her a question that seemed to have no relevance to the custody dispute at all. One question only. No follow-up. Sierra was confused when he patted our heads and we were ushered back to the courtroom. Then the judge ruled in favor of my mother and Lucas, saying that allegations of abuse had not been corroborated by any evidence.

Mr. Barry was a changed man. He was honest about his past life in the streets. But Lucas always found ways to use old charges against him. We were unable to convince the judge or other authorities that Mr. Barry had mended his ways and was now the father that we all dreamed of. One who did not miss a holiday. One who drove for hours to be with us. One who treated me like his own. One who was determined to fight for us, emotionally and physically.

Mr. Barry descended the courthouse steps with his head down and his heart broken. He unfastened his tie and walked a sorrowful path toward his car, his feet dragging. He could barely watch as we were herded into our van to be shuttled back to hell.

"Daddy!" Sierra cried out. Her father passed one more mournful look in her direction to remind his baby girl that he was still there. Mom closed the van door and we pressed our faces against the window, our mute expressions begging Mr. Barry not to go, begging him to keep fighting for us.

Lucas made his way down the opposite side of the broad steps, wearing the same sadistic smirk he wore when tormenting us. He stared Mr. Barry down before his face widened into a victorious grin.

As the two men passed each other, Lucas turned in Mr. Barry's direction and said, "I'm the man of this house."

Mr. Barry stopped in his tracks. "What you just say to me?" he asked. From the car, we could see the tension brewing as their shoulders squared toward each other.

"I said I'm the man of this house."

Mr. Barry stepped in closer. They were faced off like gunfighters in an old Western movie. Mom stepped out of the car like she knew things were about to get serious. "Lucas, let's go!" she shouted. "Get in the car." But by now the men were close together, yelling and cursing and pointing in each other's faces. Bystanders were gathering around them.

"I tell you one thing," Mr. Barry said. "You touch those kids again and it'll be your last day on earth." Their noses were nearly touching. Mom kept shouting for them to stop and for Lucas to get in the car. But they were oblivious to everything except the hate burning between them.

Lucas leaned in and said, "I'll beat them as much as I want." And Mr. Barry exploded in an uncontrollable ferocity. Their bodies crashed to the ground and they scuffled and tumbled on the pavement, punching and flipping and rolling.

"Lucas, stop!" Mom yelled. But the fight was on. When Lucas tried to pin him, Mr. Barry tossed him to the side. He grappled Lucas's legs into a figure four. He stretched one arm across Lucas's windpipe, latched on to the other arm, and locked the chokehold so tight that Lucas's eyes nearly popped out of his head. Lucas could not breathe, but Mr. Barry squeezed tighter. Lucas's body flapped like a dying fish, but Mr. Barry squeezed even tighter. Suddenly, Lucas's arms stopped moving. His eyes were rolling backward, and Mr. Barry clenched his teeth like someone who did not plan to let up. In Mr. Barry's eyes was pain and love and desperation for his children. It was as if he saw nothing but the bruises on our faces and our bodies. So he squeezed tighter, as if our freedom depended on it.

"Sierra, go get help!" Mom yelled. "Run, go get the police!"

Sierra obeyed. She jumped out of the car and sprinted toward the courthouse. "Help! Somebody help!" Sierra screamed in panic. "My daddy is killing my stepdad!"

The police officers rushed to the scene, yelling for Mr. Barry to let go. But he couldn't let go. He was almost there. He was almost finished. He was almost at the point of saving us like he had promised by doing what no one else was willing to do.

Lucas was limp and still, but Mr. Barry was not letting up. The officers grabbed Mr. Barry by his arms and pulled him off his enemy. He didn't release his grip immediately but finally lifted his arms in a gesture of surrender. Lucas rolled over on his knees, coughing and holding his throat. The officers stood Mr. Barry on his feet and pulled his arms behind his back.

"You're under arrest," the officer said, clamping the cuffs on his wrists. We watched our protector's chin drop to his chest as the officers carried him away. Mom ran to comfort Lucas and help him to the car. It was all over. There was no one left to save us now.

We were all hopeless and deflated. This felt like a devastating defeat for Sierra, Barry, their dad, and me. But we had no idea how that event would change everything. Our home became a lot quieter for the next several weeks.

When Mom left for duty at Fort Irwin, California, she put enough cash on the kitchen counter for two weeks' worth of food. As usual, we stayed in our rooms and out of Lucas's way. Later that evening, when he hadn't brought home take-out food like we expected, Sierra went to retrieve some money and order us dinner.

But the money was gone. She looked around the house, and Lucas was gone. She checked outside, and the van was gone. We called Mom and she panicked. She was on the other side of the country and powerless to help.

"He said he was going to get us Chinese food, but he never came back," Sierra told her. "Nobody can know about this," Mom said. If the authorities found out, she and her husband could be charged with child abandonment. She told us to stay home and not to talk to anyone or go anywhere besides school. Sierra put us on the bus in the mornings and she picked us up from the bus stop in the afternoon. We survived on spaghetti and meals Sierra had taught herself to make.

Two weeks later, on the day before Mom returned, Lucas came back. There was a dent on the side of the van and he looked like he hadn't bathed or changed clothes for weeks. His eyes were as scarlet as they'd ever been and he seemed incoherent. In his hand was the Chinese food he'd promised two weeks earlier.

"Get in here and eat," he yelled, placing the food on the counter. It was green and moldy and smelled like sewage. Sierra dumped it in the trash as soon as he went upstairs. Shortly after, he came down with bags in his hands. "Tell your Mom I'll be back," he said. But he did not come back. Lucas was gone. We never saw him again. When Mom got home, she grieved. She didn't understand why her husband had left. But we knew why. It was because he had learned, on the pavement of that courthouse, that another man was willing to fight for us.

CHAPTER THREE

MIDDLE SCHOOL MENACE

Although Lucas was no longer present in our daily lives, he lingered in our nightmares. Each of us had been marked by his relentless cruelty. Mom was emotionally, spiritually, and physically abandoned. Sierra was a beautiful and popular girl but she had a hair-trigger temper, ready to throw a punch at any person she distrusted. Barry felt sorry that, as the oldest boy, he could not protect any of us. As the youngest, Ben's memories were not as distinct as the rest of ours. But it seemed that I had been impacted the most. Forced by Lucas to write that I was a bad child, hundreds of thousands of times over, I eventually believed it. When I looked in the mirror to brush my hair for school, sometimes his specter reared up behind me, telling me I was ugly and shoving my face against the glass until I conceded. At a time when surging hormones make all preteens question who they are and what their place in the world will be, my answers had already been supplied by my sadistic stepfather and the toxic environment he'd created.

My maternal and paternal sides of the family were diametrically opposed. Mom's New York side of the family was a wide-screen, large-cast version of our own household: my siblings and I were like Bébé's kids. Dad's southern family was the opposite. They reminded me of the Huxtables from *The Cosby Show*: educated, successful, and ultra-conservative. My dad idolized his father. Papa was a Renaissance man: deeply religious, dexterous, and widely regarded for his achievements. He led community revitalization projects in the poorest neighborhoods of his community, where he demolished and built houses for families in need. He held a doctor of divinity and once served as the president of a seminary. He was the chaplain for the local sheriff's department, he chaired and served on numerous boards, and he pastored a small church for over forty years. My father was Papa's namesake and always wanted to make him proud.

The firstborn of three sons, Dad was Papa's expected heir. He wanted my father to follow the path he blazed in academic and civic achievement. But Dad took a different path by enlisting in the army after graduating from high school. And Papa's disappointment was heightened when Dad revealed that he was expecting a child out of wedlock with my mother, an uneducated immigrant woman who was a decade his senior, a lifer in the army, separated but still legally married to a drug dealer, and the mother to two children, one of them only sixteen months old. This was not the dream Papa had for my father. Their relationship soured and ultimately left Dad feeling that he had to prove his worth over and over to measure up to his father's legacy. In terms of being a father to me when I was young, he more than measured up. Dad was everything that I wanted him to be, until he wasn't. And that happened when the tables turned, placing him in the seat of disdain and me in the position of a prodigal.

By the time Lucas disappeared, my demeanor had already changed. The crescent smile that once made people want to pinch my cheeks had settled into a permanent grimace, as though I was angry at the world. Because I was.

When I visited my paternal grandparents, Grandma nudged me to fix my face when people asked, "What's wrong? Is he okay?" But I couldn't, because I wasn't. Five years of abuse had left physical wounds that scarred and emotional wounds that might never heal.

She was especially upset when my scowl drew attention at church. "Fix your face," Grandma said while preparing me for Sunday school. "You're always frowning. God is too good for you to be frowning like that." As far as I could see, God hadn't actually been all that good to me. She went on and on about how I used to smile more when I was younger. "You had the prettiest little teeth," she said, "and the cutest little smile." But I wasn't that affable kid anymore. It felt like Lucas had buried him alive.

Social propriety was everything to my dad and grandparents as the first family of their church. When I did not live up to their expectations, they blamed my mother for every inappropriate word or deed. They didn't like the way Mom let me talk, so they scolded my northern accent, asked me to call them Grandmother and Grandfather with a hard er, and demanded that I over-enunciate vowels like the white people that Papa always wanted to impress. "You're embarrassing me," Grandma often growled through her dentures, leaning close enough for me to smell her peppermint breath. They hated the way Mom dressed me. "Ugh, this is a ghetto mess," Grandma said as she unfastened my gold necklace and patted down my Afro while complaining that only hoodlums wore their hair like that. She had a conniption one time when Mom dropped me off with cornrows.

I was my father's firstborn and my grandparents' only grandchild for much of my childhood. I never questioned their love for me even though they criticized my mother, my world, and thought I would have been better off in theirs. And maybe they could have saved me from some of my misfortunes at home. But in their world, I was a misfit, a miscreant. And their condemnation of my appearance only confirmed that I did not belong in the land of the bourgeoisie.

I do not believe that this was how they intended to make me feel. I believe their hearts were pure, but they were incredibly disconnected from Black culture. They did not dislike Black people, because their church was full of them. But there was no hand-clapping and foot-stomping at this church. Papa would have none of that. He did not allow gospel music or drums or any instrument other than the grand piano. "God doesn't like all that racket," he said. He preferred softly sung songs from the red and the blue hymnal books that didn't remind anyone of Negro spirituals or our history of oppression.

They loved me so much that they wanted to adopt me. They wanted to keep me safe. But it wasn't because of what Lucas did to me. They knew nothing about that because I had never confessed it. They only wanted to rescue me from a culture they loathed. From the "hippity-hop thuggery" they associated with my mother's side of the family in New York. But that wasn't all. They wanted to save me from my mother, whom they still presumed to be an unfit parent. She had her challenges, but I hated when anyone bad-mouthed my mother. I never believed that she was unfit. She was broken. She was vulnerable. But she was hopeful. It was just that her faith was misplaced in the wrong men. A cycle that her children continued to bear the brunt of. Especially me. And her next relationship took me to a dark place of no return.

It was less than a year after Lucas disappeared. The divorce was not yet finalized. Mom was resistant toward the idea of dating any man. Mom told me about one day when she was making a deposit at the bank and she recognized someone who looked incredibly familiar.

"Wilson, is that you?" she asked as she approached him. Wilson had been a dear friend of hers from back in the day. It had been more than a decade since they'd seen each other in New York, when Sierra and Barry were tiny and I wasn't yet born.

"What in the world are you doing here?" he said as he turned in surprise. They spent hours catching up. Those hours turned into days. Those days turned into an unexpected relationship before either was officially divorced. They bonded over old stories and shared struggles, including their failed marriages.

Their relationship had always been platonic. Never did they think they would be together, until their paths crossed by chance. Wilson was the answer to her prayers. He treated my mother well. He was a family man. And, most importantly, he professed to be a man of faith. Things moved quickly and it was beautiful to see my mother swept off her feet. I had never seen her smile so much. She was suddenly nicer and more affectionate than usual. He had two daughters. One was Sierra's age and one was Ben's age. We would occasionally spend the night at their house and they would sometimes spend the night at ours. We were spending a lot of time together and becoming like a blended family, and Mom was caught up preparing for her next marriage before we had really healed from the last one.

I always looked forward to the sound of the doorbell. It brought a rush of joy, because it meant that it was time to play. The doorbell sang as it reverberated throughout our two-story home around noon every Saturday, announcing that our friends were here to ask if Barry and I could come outside. We were the only ones with a basketball hoop. For hours, we played in the searing sun, taking an occasional break to sip the most delicious water from the spigot on the side of the house, or to run inside and grab Kool-Aid Popsicles and other snacks until Mom yelled, "Do your friends pay any bills in this house?" or "Stop running in and out of this house!" or "Come in this house one more time and you ain't goin' back out!" She hated when we "smelled like outside," though we never understood what outside smelled like. We kept playing until the streetlights came on, marking the end of our fun.

The precious sound of the doorbell eventually changed. It lost its meaning. It still signaled that it was time to play. But not in the innocent way I once desired. The once happy chimes of childhood became ominous when Renae, Wilson's teenage daughter, was scheduled to babysit me. Now when the doorbell rang, I would close my eyes and press my palms to my ears to shut out the sound that signaled the end of my boyhood. I'd run to my room and lock my door the same way I hid from Lucas. Mom and Wilson went out on dates. Sierra left with friends. Barry stayed outside to play. Renae situated Ben in his room with toys and cartoons. That's when she came for me. She took what she wanted. She made me become a man.

It first happened one night when my mother and Wilson left for an evening of what she called "grown folks' business." Renae, my siblings, and I were crammed in my room watching my old twenty-inch Philips television.

Barry and Sierra usurped my twin-size bed and I sat at its foot on the floor next to Renae. How I ended up on the floor in my own room is a mystery. But I sat on the carpet as they lounged in comfort. We all fought sleep until 3 a.m., trying to catch a glimpse of something salacious on *BET: Uncut*. Nelly's "Tip Drill" music video was the closest we could get to soft porn.

"Aight, y'all, I'm going to bed," my sister mumbled as she climbed to her feet. Barry followed only a few minutes later, leaving Renae and me alone with the television softly glowing in the dark.

We sat there without speaking for a few minutes. My eyelids were getting low when, suddenly, I felt Renae's hand rest on top of mine. "Are you sleepy?" she inquired so gently. Her tone was tender. Her nurturing touch made me feel safe. I yawned and nodded innocently.

"Come closer," she beckoned. I slid toward her and nuzzled my head in the pocket between her shoulder and neck where she had always let me rest. But this time felt different. "Look at me," she commanded. I raised my eyes as her fingertips lifted my chin. My eyes were drowsy, but hers weren't. Hers were wide, beguiling, ambitious. She used her hand to guide my lips toward hers. Before I could recognize what was happening, she shoved her tongue in my mouth. It tasted slimy and sour. She started breathing heavily. She unbuttoned her jeans and grabbed my hand and told me what to do in husky terms that left me no choice. I did not know what I was digging for. "Stick it in," she said. But I didn't know where or how. She adjusted her body and angled my hand to go deeper. That's when I felt it. It was warm and gooey and felt like putty. It scared me and I jerked my hand out. I bolted for the bathroom and slammed the door and locked it. I looked at my hand and there was slime all over it. I turned on the hot water, emptied the entire bottle of soap on my hands, and nearly scrubbed the skin off of my fingers for about thirty minutes straight. Then I fell asleep on the bathroom floor. Because I did not want to go back out there.

Each time that doorbell rang, I knew she was here. I knew what she wanted. She always waited until no one was around. I was scared at first, then I was confused the first time that my body responded in favor of her advances. For some time, she trespassed against my impubescent body.

But nothing happened when she fondled me, so she guided my hands and mouth to the places that brought her the most pleasure. One day, I got an erection. I was so confused. In my mind, I did not like it. I did not want it. But my body disagreed. Her touch sent blood rushing to the place that I was not yet proud of. It was wrong, but it felt good. "You want me to stop?" she asked. But I could not utter words, only gasps as her hands and mouth performed some sort of dark and beautiful magic on my body. The first time I climaxed, I felt so ashamed. Everything about it felt wrong. But my would-be stepsister held me and chuckled and said, "It's okay. It means you're a man now." But I didn't want to be. I wanted to go outside and play with my brother and my friends, but she held me captive in my bedroom and made me do things that I did not want to feel good. But they did. Every day. I fought back the eruptions in my body that she triggered. I tried to think about my favorite shows on Nickelodeon and Cartoon Network. But it did not work. My body kept betraying me.

This went on for over a year by the time my mother broke off her relationship with Wilson. She had no idea what had been happening to me. I tried to tell Sierra once. I must have downplayed the details because Sierra sucked her teeth and said, "Boy, she is too old for you." I never tried to tell anyone again. Partly out of shame for what Renae did, and partly because of the craving that it created.

If Lucas left me with a permanent scowl, Renae's disappearance left me with a yearning emptiness and a raging sexuality that I didn't understand at age eleven. What we did together began as abuse, but it ended as an appetite. She called it love, and it became my only understanding of the word. I wanted love again. A craving seized my mind and body and blotted my capacity for telling right and wrong. I would go to any lengths to find a fix and fill the lustful void that Renae left. It consumed my body and commandeered my conscience. I was wounded. I was angry. I was sexually charged. And that's when a menace was born.

I had just turned twelve and was entering the sixth grade, but I did not like the girls at school. They did not know what I knew. They did not want what

I wanted. This became clear when I was written up for flashing girls on the school bus and suspended for asking them to flash me at school.

Three girls lived on our street. They were best friends and loved to reenact music videos with a boom box in our shared driveway, where they often performed entire Destiny's Child albums. From the window of our home, I could hear them arguing over who would star as Beyoncé. The honor was usually bestowed upon the most fair-skinned girl. One day, I convinced them to take a break and meet me in a secluded spot behind our houses where no one could see.

"Follow me, I got something to show you," I said. We ran around to the back of the house. "Come closer," I said. They were eager to see my surprise. I whispered softly, "I'll show you mine, and you show me yours."

"Show you what?" they asked, confused.

I looked in all directions to make sure the coast was clear. I unzipped my pants and pulled them down with pride, as if a fluorescent glow was emanating from my privates. Two of them screamed and ran away. But one of them stayed and stared in shock.

"Your turn," I encouraged. She looked uncertain at first, but reluctantly lifted her shirt and quickly yanked it back down.

"I couldn't even see anything," I grumbled. She sucked her teeth and closed her eyes as she gave me another three-second peek at her breasts before hastily covering up. We exchanged awkward, silent stares, clueless about what to do next. Then she wheeled and ran off. And I walked away with a grin, convinced that I had finally found love again.

That was the most I could get out of girls my age. Then my lustful compass shifted toward girls who were significantly older. Sierra's friends were the most accessible. They always came over to hang out and stay the night. I tried everything I could to win their affection. I gifted them with bouquets of the finest dandelions I could pick from the lawn. When that approach failed, I set out to learn more about their interests and appeal to them.

After school one evening, we were watching *106 & Park* on BET. Cartoons were a thing of the past. We were grown now, so we watched grown television. And Mom was never home to stop us, so we thrived on hypersexual BET shows and hood movies like *Belly* and *Paid in Full* and *Don't Be a Menace to South Central While Drinking Your Juice in the Hood.* For us, this was both entertainment and education.

There was nothing like seeing Funkmaster Flex on the ones and twos and hearing "Welcome to *106 & Park,* the hottest show in the universe! I'm Free," "And I'm AJ!" from two of BET's most legendary hosts. For us, the daily top ten countdown each evening was as sacred as a table dinner with fine china in a bougie family. We wouldn't miss it for the world. Especially when Jin, the Asian sensation, shocked all of Black America on Freestyle Friday. This was our Black-ass tradition: gathering in the living room with Sierra and company commandeering the couch while Barry and I basked in their nearness, despite being uncomfortable on the hardwood floor.

During the top ten countdown, the girls waited on the edge of their seats for one video in particular. They shrieked at the first notes of the electric guitar, but grew wide-eyed and breathless as a close-up focused on the back of D'Angelo's cornrows, then circled around to his face, capturing his tongue licking his lips, before the camera pulled back to reveal his naked body down to his pelvis.

"Untitled (How Does It Feel)" was one of D'Angelo's biggest hits. He didn't dance and the camera stayed in one place for the entire four minutes and thirty seconds. He sang nude in a dark room. The girls were enamored. I watched them squirm in their seats as the camera focused on the sweat beads falling down his body. They fanned themselves as if the temperature in the room had risen several degrees. I looked at D'Angelo. I looked at the girls' reactions. Then I looked at the television again, and it all made sense. I realized what I needed to do.

Sierra's friends stayed over that night. The next day, the girls were doing girl stuff in Sierra's room. Barry and I were playing basketball in the front yard with our friends. The heat peaked in midafternoon so we took off our shirts and played bare-chested. We took a break after someone, likely Barry, won a game of 21. Panting in a patch of shade, I looked down and realized that rivulets of sweat were running down my body. Then it dawned on me. I was D'Angelo.

"I'll be back, y'all," I said to the guys, knowing that I had business to take care of. I walked toward the house as if I had a rose clenched in my teeth and Sinatra's "Fly Me to the Moon" was playing on cosmic speakers. I climbed the stairs toward Sierra's room. I could hear the girls laughing inside. I examined my chest, disregarding its lack of definition, and decided that I needed more sweat. I ran to the bathroom and splashed water on my chest, then topped that off with a few squirts of baby oil. I was ready.

I took a deep breath at Sierra's door and opened it slowly. I crossed the threshold with my head bowed, then raised my chin slowly for dramatic effect. Then I closed my eyes to serenade them with passion. But before I could let out the first "Hooow does it feeeeel?" Sierra yelled, "Get out of my room!" She rushed me like a tackle and threw me back across the threshold. The door slammed in my face. From the other side, I could hear that Sierra was angry, but her friends were laughing. I decided they liked it.

Sierra radiated a force field that repelled my attempts to get close to her friends. I had to find a way around her.

Selena was the one I loved, Sierra's best friend. I pulled back the bow and shot Cupid's arrow a number of times, but my love darts fell short. "Sierra, get your little brother," Selena said when I sat too close for comfort. "Take yo lil ass on somewhere," she'd retort when I begged her to marry me. She laughed it off, until I went too far.

This was the era of compact discs, which had album art on one side and a reflective film on the other. At some point, I discovered that this could be repurposed as a mirror. One night when Selena was staying over, I had an idea while she was showering in the bathroom. I reached for one of my CDs, blew my hot breath on it, and cleaned it with my T-shirt until I could see my reflection crisp and clear. Then I used rubbing alcohol and a cotton ball to polish it more. When it was ready to go, I crossed the hallway flat on my stomach like a soldier traversing a swamp. There was a half-inch crack between the door and the floor and I slipped part of the disc under the door and tilted it just enough to catch a glimpse of the other side. I was mesmerized. She was so beautiful. Her crinkly wet hair fell down to the small of her back, and I watched as she dried herself off and tied her curly hair into a headwrap.

Selena took a step and her foot was only inches from the disc. I should have retreated but I couldn't. The sight of her was spellbinding. She was wrapped in a towel, and I angled the disc to get a better view when, suddenly, it slipped from my hand.

"What the fuck," she said from the other side. I could not reach to retrieve the disc. Before Selena could open the door, I jumped to my feet and dashed to my room and locked the door. I dove into my bed and threw the covers over my face, pretending to be asleep.

When I wasn't harassing my sister's friends, I found other trouble to get into. I was a lover boy at first, with my dandelion-picking and D'Angelo-singing. Even not-so-romantic acts like flashing girls, I thought, was in the name of love. I equated love with sex because that was what Renae had showed me. And sex is what the R&B singers sang about. I wanted to be D'Angelo, Donell Jones, or Jaheim, because they were who my sister's friends loved. So if I could be like them, then maybe they would love me, too. But that changed when I discovered that what women really wanted was a *real nigga*.

I learned about *real nigga shit* as an impressionable twelve-year-old boy, visiting the Bronx, where my family is from, for weekends and holiday breaks. It all went down at my maternal grandmother's house on 227th. It was a single-family home, but multiple families lived in it: my aunts, uncles, cousins, just about everybody at one time or another. The house was big but it was old. So old that the water pipes got confused when one person flushed the toilet while another was showering. This happened to me when I was three years old. My big cousin was bathing me when Barry came in to use the toilet and flushed it. Scorching-hot water gushed from the showerhead and I was rushed to the hospital with second-degree burns on my back.

I attended school in the kitchen with my grown cousins. This was no ordinary classroom. This was the school of hard knocks where I learned about *real nigga shit*. Eating together was not a thing in our household. You ate if you were around when someone happened to be cooking. And when it's gone, it's gone. If we missed meals, we were told, "You better take yo ass to the corner store." But I had to wait until someone felt like taking me, because walking alone to the end of our street was too dangerous for someone my age. The corner is where my other cousin was hit in a drive-by shooting and almost lost his life.

I was always hungry and could not bear missing another meal. So I'd camp out in the kitchen until the men cousins came in to make hot wings, a house specialty. One cousin would pull out the saucepan and drop a full stick of butter in the pot. Then he'd take a big bottle of Tabasco and pour and pour and pour until the ancestors said stop. Then he'd slap the wings in there and let them bad boys soak and simmer for about fifteen minutes. Then we'd devour them like it was our last meal, because chances are it was for the day.

Five of us would hold down the kitchen like a Union fort, the men talking about life while I listened to my portable CD player. One time, a cousin overheard the song and snatched the headphones off my head.

"What the fuck you listening to, nigga?" he asked, his tone loud and aggressive. "Is that Ja Rule and fucking J.Lo?"

He was obviously disgusted, and I had no idea how to respond. I didn't see the problem. Girls loved this song. So I loved this song. Because I loved girls.

"Man, if you don't get that soft shit out of here," he continued. The men guffawed, then sang the tune in high-pitched, mocking tones. I tried to defend the song but that only made it worse. I explained that I liked it because it made me think about a girl that I wanted to make love to named Selena. And that's when they schooled me.

"We don't make love to these hoes," he said, as if the idea was ridiculous. My cousins explained the difference between making love and *fucking bitches*. I then learned that we only care about two things: *fucking bitches and getting money*. There were no talks about being a man, only what it meant to be a *real nigga*. And if I wasn't a *real nigga*, then I was nothing but a *bitch nigga.* I tossed the two terms around in my head. I sat pensively, like there was a *real nigga* on one shoulder spittin' hardcore gangsta rap and a *bitch nigga* on the other singing softly.

I felt like a *bitch nigga* at the moment, and I hated it. I wanted to run from the laughing and heckling, but I had nowhere to go. Outside the house, my life was at risk, but inside the house, my *bitch ass* pride was being flogged. So I decided that this would be the last time I'd feel like a *bitch nigga.* I was ready for the *real nigga* life course.

There was no kids' stuff at Grandma's house; no books, no games. Spending an entire summer there, I had all the time needed to ponder this *real nigga shit.* I watched closely with my pen and pad as my cousins went about their daily *real nigga* lives. I watched what they said and how they said it, what they did and how they did it. I learned that *real niggas* don't smile when they greet people; they act unenthused even if they are internally excited. I learned that *real niggas* don't wear tighty-whities; they wear boxer briefs. I learned that *real niggas* don't wear their pants on their waist; they let them sag so the boxer briefs will show and everybody can see that you're not a tighty-whitey-wearing bitch. I learned that *real niggas* don't listen to R&B; they listen to Ruff Ryders and Wu-Tang and Dipset. I learned that *real niggas* don't wear collared shirts and off-brand sneakers; they wear long white tees and Timberland boots with their baggy jeans double-cuffed at the bottom. I learned that *real niggas* don't take no shit; they stay strapped and never walk away from a fight. I learned that *real niggas* don't snitch. I learned that *real niggas* smoke and sling dope. I learned the way of the streets: the codes, the culture, the mentality. I studied. And I was ready to be a *real nigga* connoisseur. I was ready to graduate summa cum laude in *real nigga shit.* By the end of that summer, I was ready to go back home—not as a new man, but as a *real nigga.*

We lived in Richmond, Virginia, at the time. I never hung out with kids my age because I was always with Sierra's friends. She was popular in high school. She was tall and beautiful and physically developed. She wore big hoop earrings with her nickname, "Sie Byrd," inscribed across the middle.

She was loud and chewed gum and popped bubbles all the time. She had attitude, and she was not afraid to fight girls or boys. The girls wanted to be her friend because she was cool, charismatic, and slightly intimidating, which made her a great ally. She attracted the roughest boys in school and several boys who had already graduated. They wanted to be her friend because they either liked her or thought she was *the homie*. Barry and I became affectionately known as "Sie's lil brothers," a moniker that we wore with pride. Like us, most of Sierra's friends were transplants from places up north like Jersey, Philly, and New York. They reminded me a lot of our cousins back home. They, too, were *real niggas*.

Sierra's boyfriend at the time was equally popular. His best friend, Rell, was a leader of a well-known gang. They ran our side of town, and everyone knew that if you dared to cross them, they would make an example of you. Like the time a brawl broke out at our bus stop. The high school bus always dropped Sierra off first, then the junior high bus dropped Barry off, and the elementary school bus dropped me off last. I was in the sixth grade. As my bus pulled up, a full-blown gang fight had already erupted in the street. Rell and his crew were jumping some boys from a rival gang.

"Everybody, get down!" the bus driver yelled, trying to shield us from the violence and worried that somebody would start shooting. Kids screamed and the bus driver kept the door shut as the bus stood still. The hard seats had lacerations in the brown leather and bits of yellow cushion seeping out. All the kids ducked down between them. But not me. That's not what *real niggas* do. I stood atop my seat and pinched the levers on either side of the window, lowered it, and stuck my head out, yelling, "Fuck them niggas up!" with utmost pride.

My first thought was that this was like a real-life version of *Power Rangers*, but that was a *bitch nigga* reference. Barry and I used to love playing Power Rangers; I liked the white ranger because he seemed super elite, and Barry liked the black ranger because it was played by the only Black guy— which all seems quite questionable in retrospect. That aside, I had to ditch the *bitch nigga* reference and come up with some *real nigga shit* to compare this street brawl to. When Rell's men caught the last opponent standing, they ganged up and stomped his body and face until the guy stopped moving. It was like watching Caine and O-Dog stomping out that one nigga in *Menace II Society*.

The gang gathered at our house after their victory. They wore wifebeaters and colors representing their set, bandanas wrapped around their heads or hanging out of their pockets, durags on their heads or draping from the neck, and wheat Timberlands or icy-white Forces.

Mom was never home, so on any given day our house might look like a block party. After watching the beatdown in the street, I realized that this was the *real nigga shit* that I had been waiting for. So I decided to approach Rell.

"Ayo," I said to him. "I'm tryna be down." It seemed like the ideal time. Three 6 Mafia blared from the boom box in my mother's garage where fifteen to twenty of our friends gathered, brown-bagging bottles of beer and liquor and rolling and passing joints. This was my village. My family. I had people who would protect me and a place where I belonged. I wanted to fight with them.

Rell didn't respond the way I had hoped. "Get yo lil ass outta here, nigga," he said and turned away with a condescending chuckle. I was tired of everyone dismissing me and treating me like I was a little kid: Sierra's girlfriends, my cousins, and now Rell. I let a few minutes pass as I tried to keep control of my feelings. I felt like he had just called me a *bitch nigga*, and I wasn't going to stand for that. I confronted him again.

"What I gotta do?" I asked. My face was stone. "I'll do whatever to prove to y'all niggas that I'm down."

"Fight me, then, nigga, if you really 'bout this life." His challenge caught me off guard. Never would I have even considered such a thing. He was twice my size and his chest protruded through his ripped wifebeater. His biceps looked like he did curls with dumbbells and then ate them for lunch. He looked mean and tough and fierce and hardcore. With half of his hair cornrowed and the other half picked out, he looked exactly like the *real nigga* I aspired to be.

"I'm not gon' fight you, Rell," I responded as confidently as I could.

"That's what I thought, nigga," he said, sizing me up. "Now sit yo lil ass down somewhere." He turned back toward the crew and said, "Puff, puff, pass, nigga" as he laughed and took another smoke.

I faced a life-defining quandary. I could man up and bark back or I could walk away. It was like choosing which type of dog I was going to be: a pit bull or a baby Yorkie. So I made my choice.

I stepped toward Rell and yelled, "Nigga, I ain't no bitch!" with all the bass my untuned vocal cords could muster. Before I could process his response, Rell turned his body with all of his momentum wound into a right jab that landed directly in the center of my chest. I stopped breathing. My barely hundred-pound body went tumbling to the ground as I gasped for air. Before I could get up to fight back, the rest of our friends rushed toward me. I was grateful that they were coming to restrain Rell, so I thought. But instead they began kicking and stomping me while I lay curled on the ground. I guarded my face and chest and stomach as best I could for what felt like an hour but was probably one minute. Then they stopped and stepped away. "Yeah, bitch!" Rell yelled as he towered over me. Everyone stared to see if I would get up.

I stayed down for a couple of seconds as I caught my breath. I uncovered my face just enough to see them all scowl in my direction. I slowly stood to my feet, ignoring the sharp pain shooting through my rib cage, and I stared back at them. Then I lifted my chin.

"Lil nigga got heart," Rell said and chuckled. This time, his tone was not condescending.

"All right, lil nigga," he continued. "You're in." I sighed in relief. Those words were music to my ears. "But there's one more thing you have to do first."

My initiation was only halfway complete. The gang walked me over to our nearby park. It was clear that I was being hazed like a fraternity pledge. The basketball courts were to our right and the community center and pool were to our left. I hated walking near this pool. One of my close friends had nearly drowned there a few weeks earlier. We were horseplaying and he'd hit his head on the diving board and went under. I'd screamed for help, but it took the lifeguard nearly five minutes to realize that we were not playing. My friend narrowly survived.

"Him. Right there," Rell said, pointing at a kid walking away from the pool. He was my age. The kid wasn't bothering anybody, just as innocent as a twelve-year-old kid could be. I knew what they wanted me to do. I did not want to do it. But I had no other choice. I was in *real nigga* training. And I was willing to pay the price to see it through.

Walking toward my target, I realized that I recognized him from the bus. His was the last stop on our side of town before the bus took us to school. He was one of the good kids who made good grades and tried to act and dress hip to fit in, but it didn't quite work for him. He wore off-brand shoes and his use of slang was laughable. He looked like T.J. Henderson from *Smart Guy*, except with baggy jeans and a durag on his head with the strings hanging down and a headband like Nelly. He looked exactly like the type of *bitch nigga* I didn't want to be. So I shoved my moral compass back into my pocket and did what needed to be done.

"Aye, nigga," I said. He greeted me by name, and with a smile. His kindness threw me off for a moment. He looked at me as if I were a friend. Remorse started to creep into my conscience, until I glanced back at my squad. I saw their gang colors and their stares holding me to task.

"I heard you was talkin' shit," I growled, stepping closer to confront him. To my knowledge, he had never said a bad word about me, or anyone else. He was just a corny-looking kid minding his own business. "What do you mean?" he said. His concern was genuine as he assured me that he had no idea why anyone would accuse him of such a thing.

Then I yelled, "Shut the fuck up, bitch nigga!" and punched him in the face. He stumbled backward and I grappled his legs and scooped him off his feet and slammed him to the ground. "Get that nigga!" my team chanted in the distance. I kicked and kicked and kicked as he cried and covered his face and begged me to stop. After I gave him a few good stomps, Rell yelled, "Aight, nigga, let's go," and we all took off.

As I ran away, I felt conflicted. I couldn't get the image out of my head of him lying on the ground, fetal and helpless. I had been there before, in that same position. My mind flashed back to Lucas and the times I lay feebly after enduring beatings that I did not deserve. I'd curled up the same way he did. I'd pleaded the same way he did. When I saw him lying there, I saw myself. I never thought I would become the monster inflicting such pain on another person. I wish I had listened to those inner doubts. I wish I could have kept my heart from turning cold. But it was too late. I was officially down. The only caveat was that I could not tell my sister. But I think she knew, because she repeatedly asked, "Why you wearing that bandana on your head like you in somebody's gang?" I had a crew of *real niggas*. This meant that it was time for me to move up to the next level of *real nigga shit*. It was time for me to do drugs.

In the early 2000s, weed was not as accessible as it is today. Getting caught was a serious offense, so you had to know somebody who knew somebody that could get it. But I did not have that kind of patience, so I decided to act on my own impulse.

I was looking for salt one day when I opened the kitchen cabinet. There were rows of herbs and spices. One caught my eye because it looked exactly like the weed I saw the guys pouring out of a little baggie. I examined the bottle, labeled PARSLEY, and I figured it could not be much different. I was excited by the idea of smoking my first joint, but I needed something to roll it in. I could not recall what the guys were using to twist their blunts, but I remembered overhearing, "Yo, pass me the rolling paper." So I figured paper was what I needed, but I did not know which type. That's when Big Pun's lyrics came to mind from his song "How We Roll." He mentioned "rolling ganja in Bible paper," so I shot upstairs to Mom's room and dug through her belongings to find one of her Bibles. I ripped out a page and ran back downstairs to finish the mission. I dashed parsley in a straight line, like I had seen others do. I wrapped it like a fruit roll-up, but I did not know how to keep it from falling apart. I had to keep starting over because my first attempts were too loose and the contents spilled. I finally decided to secure it in the middle with a piece of Scotch tape. It looked more like a flimsy bow tie than a blunt. It wasn't pretty, but it worked.

I went into the garage and closed the doors for privacy. I'd learned from observance that smoking required the right tunes to complement the weed. I flipped through my sister's leather CD book filled with gangsta rap. It had everything from northern rappers like Biggie, Nas, and Mobb Deep to southern rappers like Mystikal, Project Pat, and Gangsta Boo. This was before mix CDs, so it was important to pick the right album that you could play all the way through. Otherwise, you'd be swapping discs like old-school records to find the right songs. I popped in *Eternal* by Bone Thugs-N-Harmony and got ready to smoke counterfeit weed for the first time. I held one end to my lips, used a lighter to spark the other side, and took an overly ambitious inhale. I thought I was going to die. It did not work for me the way I'd seen it work for others. The entire roll of paper caught fire. I coughed and wheezed and threw it to the ground and stomped to put it out. I ran inside to the kitchen holding my throat and reaching for a glass of water. I decided that smoking was not for me.

My *real nigga* evolution took a toll on my relationship with my upright, storybook father and his ultra-conservative family. I became a hoodlum in their eyes and his love for me seemed to fade like a siren in the distance. Reputation, to him, was everything. Reports of my transgressions and school suspensions had reached his parents and other law-abiding relatives, and he saw my new image and identity as the enemy of his own. He needed to distance himself from me to save face and avoid disgracing his family's name.

"This is your mother's fault," he said to me. "You would've never turned out this way if I'd had custody of you." And that might have been true. With his family, I once colored and read books like *Clifford the Big Red Dog* and watched *Barney*, *The Magic School Bus*, and *Reading Rainbow* on TV. But at home, I was edutained by BET, *Jerry Springer*, and hood films. On my visits with his family, we ate breakfast and dinner around a table and talked to one another. But in my mother's home, we ate meals on an uncertain schedule and spent half the month with her gone and us getting up to no good.

There were two conflicting versions of me. As a child visiting my paternal side of the family, I was one version—the one where I enunciated my vowels and said "Grandfather" and "Grandmother" with a hard *er* and was forced to dress like a Huxtable child. That little boy had died. The other me was born. The me who was full of mischief and rage after kicking and screaming and clawing at the dirt, begging my dad not to send me back into the hands of Lucas. The me who was brutally beaten for five years until the only father who intervened was not even my own. The me who wished that my father and his high-sadity family had a little bit of gangsta in them, so if they had the slightest sense that something was wrong, they would have gone to hell and back to fuck shit up until I was safe. The other me prevailed: the one who no longer felt like a misfit because I dressed, walked, and talked too hood. The one who finally had a place and a purpose and people who would have my back.

Dad didn't know what had heated and hammered me into a new form, only that I had changed. And he looked at me the way his father had probably looked at him when he blew off college and enlisted in the military, and again when he decided to be with my mother instead of the type of woman they imagined for him. He saw the opposite of what he had worked hard to build, the opposite of what he had planned, the opposite of what he had hoped I would become. Dad stopped calling me his beloved baby boy. Instead, he started calling me a thug and a hoodlum. There was no more singing as he drove me home. There were no more love seals drying on my face when he dropped me off.

The life that I wanted and the life that Dad wanted for me were opposites. He wanted to show me a different life, a better life. One with stability and family gatherings with his wife and other children and a nice house and a fenced yard. But it wasn't my style. It wasn't my taste. Not for a *real nigga*. Stability felt parched and stuffy, like a G-rated movie, devoid of drama and explicit thrills. Strange, I know. But dysfunction was my normal. Delinquency, second to basketball, was my favorite sport, and I thrived on creating chaos. Orderly environments made me feel like the black sheep. I became the little devil my father wanted to fix. The heathen he wanted to convert. The rebel he hoped would conform. Eventually, my actions showed him that I was a reprobate beyond redemption.

The home he shared with his wife and other children was like another planet to me. The hallways and living room walls were decorated with Bible quotes and Christian keepsakes. The backyard had a trampoline and the kids would invite friends to play and hold picnics in the grass. His two daughters talked properly, the way he and my grandparents forced me to talk when I was their age.

He wished that I was more like his stepson, judging by the frequent comparisons. We were the same age but polar opposites. Kelton was smart, soft-spoken, and respectful. He made straight As in school and his record was blameless. I, on the other hand, spent more time in the principal's office than in class.

Kelton loved shit like Kidz Bop and boy bands and singing along to Dad's gospel music. But I was inspired by gangsta rappers like Jadakiss, Sheek Louch, and Styles P. I walked around with my bandana on, repping my new set, aiming my index finger at imaginary people and pretending I was pulling a trigger while chanting explicit lyrics about shootin' mothafuckas. I didn't know how to adapt to my dad's suburban life, so I proved myself to be a rebel.

"You can't be a thug and a son of mine," he said as he snatched the bandana from my head. I hated being there. The comparisons drove me insane. The way he would extol my stepbrother's accomplishments and scold me for not doing as well. The way he would honor his wife with words of affirmation and demean my mother as unfit. I came to see their whole whitewashed family as my adversaries. And I knew that by targeting his stepson, I could hurt them all.

My father was big and strong, so there wasn't much that I tried in his presence. But he eventually had to go to work. And during those eight hours of the day, I became a household terrorist. I destroyed Kelton's *bitch ass* toys, punched him in his *bitch ass* face, spit in his *bitch ass* food, everything imaginable. And I dared his mom to do something, like, *Touch me, and my big sister will whoop your ass.* But when Dad returned home after my eight hours of tyranny expired, I paid the price in whoopings. But I was immune. He couldn't hurt me. His blows were love taps compared to the vicious beatings I'd endured from the man he did not save me from. All of the adults in my life either wanted to expel me from school, cast me out of the family, or beat me.

Then came a day when all seemed to be well. I hadn't caused any trouble and I was playing nicely in the backyard, jumping on the trampoline with Kelton and two of his white friends from the neighborhood. It was the last day of my weekend visit with Dad before he took me back home, and I wanted to go out with a bang.

I came up with the brilliant idea of breaking into homes in their subdivision. There was one home in particular that hadn't had any cars in the driveway for the past several days. I figured the family was out of town or on vacation. To pull it off, I recruited Kelton and his friends as my accomplices, because they knew the neighborhood better than me. Kelton immediately said no. I called him a *bitch nigga* and then looked at his friends like I was Deebo and they were Smokey and Craig.

The three of us set off on our mission. We had no camouflage, no tools, and we walked stealth-like down the middle of the street in broad daylight. When we arrived at the house, I gathered my gang and devised a plan. We identified four possible entry points: the garage, the front window, the side door, and the back window. I commanded the troops, "Y'all go that way, and I'll go this way."

I sent them around the back, and I tackled the garage door, which I was able to pry open at the bottom. I called the others and we squeezed through into the darkened garage. Only one more door stood between us and the inside of the house. I tried to jimmy the lock with an ID card, but it didn't work. The only option left was the drop-paneled ceiling. But there was no ladder.

"Here's what we'll do," I said. "Lock your arms together and lift me up."

The plan worked. They bolstered me like a cheerleader as I struggled to gain balance. I reached up, pushed aside one of the panels, and was about to hoist myself through when there was terrifying pounding on the garage door and a voice bellowed, "Police! Open up!"

I would have tried to improvise an escape, but one of my accomplices panicked and pressed the button to open the garage. There we stood, two white boys abetting a Black boy and cops ready to take us away. One of the cops was a Black man. Lucky for us, he threw us in the car and decided to return us to our respective homes. Nothing was damaged and nothing was stolen. Plus, the home we had broken into was vacant. Nobody even lived there.

At that age, I was still learning how to be gangsta. I eventually stopped visiting my dad for holiday breaks, which suited us both. New York is where I wanted to be. I was eager to go back and show my cousins how much of a *real nigga* I had become. They seemed to be proud. But then I started getting ahead of myself. I was testing boundaries, leaving the safety of our street, going to the corner store alone. I even met an older girl one night while hanging out on the corner. She said there was fun happening at her house, so I followed. This was a dangerous indiscretion. On the next block, Barry and my cousin were once lured to a girl's home. When they arrived, they were ambushed, beaten, and robbed by a gang of men.

I did not have enough street knowledge to anticipate that something like that could happen. My twelve-year-old ego was inflated by the fact that I had a new crew and a few misdemeanors under my belt.

The girl's home, if it was really her home, looked like a trap house. The place was dark, the lights were dim, and the house was filled with smoke. We walked past a group of guys playing cards; they were smoking weed and drinking forties. On the table were other types of drugs that I had only seen in hood films. A few bodies were sprawled on the couch like they were lifeless. They gave me a wary, faraway look as if I were suspicious. The girl grabbed my hand and said, "Come on, this way" as she led me toward the steps. The stairs creaked as we climbed them. I could hear indistinct moaning in the distance. There were three rooms upstairs and the doors were all open. When we walked past one room, I saw pornography on the television screen. We walked past another doorway and I was stunned. There were multiple men taking turns on one girl. "Come on," my girl said as she nudged me to keep moving. I could not un-see it. I glanced back to confirm that what I saw was real. But by that time, we had made it to the third room. This one was ours.

I was no longer a kid. Kids aren't supposed to see what I saw. Kids aren't supposed to do what I did. I was something else now. But I was not a man either. I only knew that I was born into circumstances that I did not choose. I conformed to the identities and lifestyles of people that were accessible to me. I needed their acceptance. I learned their values and mindsets and traumas. I became their likeness. This is how the cycle goes.

Back home, I was almost thirteen and finally graduating from elementary school to join my big brother in junior high. Then Mom came home with news right before the school year began. She sat us down in the living room to make the announcement.

"We have to start packing," she said. "We're moving to Washington, DC."

Mom was excited for the fresh start. She was done trying to find love. She was ready to be the mother that she wished she had always been. But I had gone rogue. And she had no idea that I was on the brink of becoming everything she wanted to save me from.

CHAPTER FOUR

DRUGS & HOOP DREAMS

It sucked being the new kids in the DMV, a place we had never heard of until Mom moved us there. Washington, DC, lower Maryland, and Northern Virginia are lumped together for their shared culture and proximity. The area has its share of rough neighborhoods, and we lived near a few of them.

When school started, Sierra was in eleventh grade, Barry was in eighth grade, and I was in seventh grade. On that first day, we hit cultural barriers that we didn't expect. Kids took one look at us and knew we were New Yorkers, even if we had just relocated from Richmond. Being the new kids can be challenging: we wanted to make new friends, but we didn't want to seem desperate. And we were contemptuous of the DMV lingo, culture, and style.

Even our attempts to say hello were awkward. We opened New York style: "Yo, what's good, son?" But their greeting was "What up, moe?"

Moe? Barry and I looked at each other like, *What the fuck is a moe?* Granted, they could have also sneered at our use of the word *son*, which might sound demeaning to someone unfamiliar with the term.

That wasn't our only difference in dialect. When someone said or did something outlandish, we said, "Yo, you wylin'!" or "You buggin'!" But they said, "Young, you lunchin'!" Barry and I looked at each other like, *What the fuck is lunchin'?*

We used the term *mad* for emphasis, as in *This food is mad good*; but they used *jah-like*, as in *This food is jah-like good, moe.* It was all confounding.

And their fashion sense—it was seriously contorted. We wore long white tees and Timberland boots and durags. They wore skullcaps and Nike boots with rubber bands clinching the hem of their jeans above the shoe. But our odds did not end there.

We even danced differently. Up north, we Diddy-bopped like Bad Boys and we could break out in a Harlem Shake battle at any given moment. But in the DMV, the hallway dance battles between classes involved a strange set of moves called Beat Ya Feet. Barry and I looked at each other like, *Beat your what?* and broke out in childish laughter.

I was willing to adapt to get along. Barry, on the other hand, was not. He came across as standoffish and supercilious, which put us at odds with our new community from the start.

One day during our first week in our new place, I was hitting it off with a girl who rode our bus. We were in the back row vibing. I leaned into every word she said and occasionally licked my lips like LL Cool J. Every time a speed bump or a pothole jolted us off the seat, I landed closer to her. I finally closed in enough to finagle my left arm around her shoulder and whispered in her ear all the *real nigga shit* I'd done back in New York and Richmond. "You lying," she said. But in a soft, smooth voice I cooed, "Nah, girl. You can ask my brother." Barry was sitting in front of us. I had reached first base, and I was aiming for an RBI when, suddenly, our romance was interrupted by a guy across the aisle.

"That's Dre's girl," he said. "You better watch it."

Before I could turn to address him, Barry rose from his seat and yelled, "Nigga, fuck Dre!"

It seemed that the entire back of the bus fell silent. Everyone swiveled and looked at Barry as if he had just screamed the Lord's name in vain during a revival. Dre was like the neighborhood Kimbo Slice. He was tall with big hands and knuckles that looked like boulders. There were tales about him beating up kids for looking at him the wrong way; when one kid had tried to escape, Dre had chased him into his home and thrashed him in front of his parents. Junior high was his kingdom and no one challenged him.

None of that mattered to Barry. So he drove the point home: "And tell him that I said it!"

Word got back to Dre. The next day on the bus there were oohs and aahs and hoopla around the news that Dre wanted to fight Barry.

"Tell that nigga to meet me on my street," Barry said. "He know where I'm at."

I was against this idea. Dre had the one thing that we did not have at the moment: friends. Our gang was back in Richmond. Here, we had no crew to support us, and I feared that we would be mauled like the kid who was stomped by Rell's gang back in Richmond. Barry did not care.

The next day, people rode our bus who did not even live in our neighborhood. Everyone anticipated the brawl between Dre and the new guy. The bus was rowdy and they ignored the bus driver's demands to sit down. Amid the chaos, Barry did not say a word.

When the bus doors opened at our stop, everyone waited and let Barry out first, like he was a heavyweight boxer making his grand entrance from the foyer. I was either his trainer or his tag-team partner, depending on how the event would unfold. If Barry was winning, I'd stay on the sideline screaming, "Fuck that nigga up!" But if he appeared to be losing or if Dre's friends piled on, I would have to jump in and we would go down together.

I felt like Barry was Adonis and I was Rocky in *Creed*, entering the ring with Tupac's "Hail Mary" blaring. I walked by my brother's side, rubbing his shoulders and giving pep talks. Barry stood five foot ten and I was five foot seven. We were both laced in Timbs like they were combat boots, prepared for whatever was about to go down, surrounded by naysayers who wagered on Barry's demise.

We waited for almost an hour at the rendezvous. Dre never showed up. His fans were shocked. They had never seen Dre back down from a fight.

Some said that he was shook because no one had ever been crazy enough to challenge him. Some said otherwise. But whenever they saw each other at school, Barry fearlessly scoffed in his direction. And Dre never dared to look Barry in the eye.

We got respect from that moment on. Barry was the new neighborhood Kimbo Slice, and I was Pepé Le Pew, reaping the benefits in girls. I dated Dre's girlfriend and her best friend as well.

Eventually, Dre moved away and the neighborhood acknowledged and respected our gangsta. Only one other person tried to cross my brother. Barry nearly beat him into a coma. The most savage part is that my brother did not even flee the scene. Instead, he called the ambulance for his victim. When the police arrived, Barry said unapologetically, "Yeah, I did it" and handed himself over to be cuffed and taken away.

But there was one other crown to claim: we wanted to leave our mark as *real niggas* as well as superior athletes. That would mean beating Marquel, one of the best basketball players for miles around. This would be up to me.

Years had passed since Barry outscored me in our old front yard. He and our New York cousins had taught me well and made me tough. I'd go for a layup and Barry would knock me to the pavement and yell, "Get up, nigga!" During our backyard battles in New York, I'd call foul and my grown cousins would tell me to stop my *bitch ass* crying. So I learned to keep playing with blood dripping down my face. I'd go for a layup and they'd push me in midair. I'd crash hard to the ground, but if the shot was good, I'd pop up and yell in their faces, "And one, bitch!" I became obsessed with the physicality of the game.

The AND1 streetballers were my idols, and Mom used to take us to parks in the Bronx and in Harlem where they played. I'd watch playground legends like Skip to My Lou, Half Man Half Amazing, and Hot Sauce and mimick their every move on the court.

Barry was proud when my skills surpassed his. He pushed me to be better than him. The basketball cage near our new house was a major gathering place. This was the era when guys wore basketball shorts under their jeans because a game of 21 could happen any time someone started talking shit. I had beaten nearly everyone in the neighborhood while Barry yelled, "Fuck that nigga up!" from the sideline. After an especially intense game where I emerged victorious, one of the guys said, "Brandon might be nice, but he can't beat Marquel."

In true Barry fashion, his chest flared and he balled his fists as he stepped to the guy's face and barked, "Nigga, fuck Marquel!" I knew where this was heading. But this time, the fight would be mine.

Word reached Marquel on the other side of town. He accepted the challenge. Although we had never met, I had seen him at school a couple of times and heard people talk about him in worshipful tones. He was the Jesus Shuttlesworth of local basketball. He was expected to be one of the best players to come out of the DMV, and time proved this true. At age thirteen, his ability so far exceeded his years that he was even better than most of the high school's varsity players. But I was unfazed. We played the same position and we were headed to the rec center for an epic Battle of the Point Guards.

We caught the REX bus across town. Stepping out this time, I was Adonis Creed with Barry at my side like Rocky. I had all the entourage I needed. Marquel was in the middle of a game when we arrived and it was impossible to watch anyone else. The way he handled the ball was like a wizard, and his jukes looked like he danced with feet as light as feathers. It was artful. But I was ready to topple him from his throne. I called next.

As soon as I touched the court, I could hear Barry yelling from the sideline, "Fuck that nigga up!" Marquel and I glared at each other, but we did not speak a word. No greeting. No handshake. No sportsmanship.

The game began and we went after each other like pit bulls in a ring. Our intensity drove our teammates to pass us the ball on every play. It was as if they cleared the court as the entire gym watched us at each other's throats. I scored, then he scored. He blocked my shot, then I crossed him over. We went back and forth and back and forth as chants and cheers rose to a deafening level. Then it came down to one final moment. It was game point. Marquel was up, and he had the ball. I crouched low on my toes in defensive stance with my arms outstretched, and our eyes locked. I knew that he wanted to slash toward the basket, so I pivoted one foot in anticipation of his next move. He sprung into a rapid combination of jukes and ball fakes. He started slashing toward the hoop, then suddenly yanked back midway from the basket, creating enough distance between us. He pulled up for a mid-range jump shot. It was nothing but net.

His friends jumped and ran around the gym yelling, "I told you! I told you!" I stood there, gassed and wallowed in defeat. I felt bad, mostly because I had let Barry down. But before I could approach my brother, Marquel approached me with his hand out. "Much respect, bro," he said as we dapped each other and hugged. Then he dapped Barry, and we laughed at how serious we took it all. We spent the rest of that day—and most of our high school years—playing together as teammates. Barry, Marquel, and I—along with many of the other guys on the court that day—went on to win championships together. Marquel and I became our own version of Michael Jordan and Scottie Pippen from middle school to high school. The difference between Marquel and me was discipline. Basketball was his lifestyle; it was only my hobby. I was a *real nigga* first, and a basketball player second. I played the game and played it well. But at the time, basketball was not enough to pull me off of the streets. And it couldn't keep me from getting in trouble in school. Especially when I turned thirteen and entered the eighth grade.

"I want him out of this school."

The principal didn't care that his door was open and I could hear the fiery words he shot at Mrs. Pearson, the middle school's overworked guidance counselor. I'd been thrown out of class for the second time that day and now sat, frowning with arms folded defiantly across my chest, in an all-too-familiar seat in Mr. Johnson's outer office.

Mr. Johnson wasn't the only one who was fed up. Teachers had no idea what to do with me, the menace of junior high. The school resource officers knew my name and kept a wary eye on me, and when I was ejected from class or busted in the hallways, I was passed like a hot potato between the principal, the in-school suspension lady, and Mrs. Pearson.

There were only a few things that I did not hate about school. Like passing notes to girls in class. I enjoyed watching and waiting as they opened them. A slight smile let me know that I had the green light. I enjoyed treating our five-minute trips from class to class, racing against the tardy bell, like they were adventurous excursions or destination dates. I enjoyed treating the aisle like a runway when I took trips to the pencil sharpener just to flex my new outfit as I looked upon the class with a smirk, thinking, *Yeah, y'all see it, don't you?* But there was nothing I enjoyed more than the provocative power I had over the teachers I despised.

My list of disciplinary infractions was nearly ten pages long and the offenses varied. I touched a teacher in an inappropriate, sexual way. Ordered to leave class and stand in the hallway, I repeatedly jerked open the classroom door and slammed it with demonic force while the teacher was trying to teach. Between classes, I broke the rules in quieter fashion by selling T-shirts and mixtapes out of my locker. More kids were catching on to the knee-length white T-shirt look that Barry and I had brought from New York. When Barry and I made weekend visits to family in the Bronx, we caught the 2 train to Dr. Jays on 125th Street and purchased them in bulk. Back then, they were five dollars each. We brought them to the DMV and sold them like hotcakes for ten dollars a pop. I also sold the mixtapes I recorded at a friend's house in his makeshift garage studio. He made rap beats on FruityLoops as we ripped off verses about *real nigga shit.* I was Killa B, and our group name was Royal Fam. We were ready any time another rap group at school wanted to challenge us to a freestyle battle. "Kick the beat," we'd say to any bystander who could beatbox and drum two pencils on the cafeteria table or hallway locker. Our performances drew crowds of rowdy kids who ignored the bell commanding us to class. We kept rapping until one of my friends ripped a verse about fucking somebody's mom and a fight broke out, which turned into yet another trip to the principal's office.

"I've had enough." I could hear the fury in Mr. Johnson's voice. "He belongs at Bryant." This was not good: Bryant was an alternative school, essentially purgatory for teens who seemed to be heading for GEDs at best, or jail at worst.

"You can't kick him out," Mrs. Pearson insisted. "Give me time to figure out what's going on with him." She was the only person who cared about what made me this way. Mrs. Pearson talked him down, my sentence was reduced to a suspension, and my mother was once again summoned to retrieve me. Her boss was intolerant because she left work so often for drama that I created. She was livid and embarrassed by it all. Before Mom could yank me away by the ear, Mrs. Pearson asked to have a word.

They stepped into the counselor's office, but I could hear their exchange.

"I'm concerned about Brandon's mental health," Mrs. Pearson said. "He's exhibiting behaviors that just don't seem right." Her instincts as a counselor and a mother told her that there was a deeper issue. My apathy was unusual to her. It told her I had nothing to lose, and that I inflicted pain on others because there was a deep-seated pain in my own heart. Mrs. Pearson kept after my mother: "Is something going on at home?"

Mom was in no mood for psychologizing. "Brandon is just being rebellious," she said. "He needs to learn how to follow the rules."

Mrs. Pearson pressed on. "Well, you know basketball means the world to him. I think it might help if you could attend some of his games."

Mom snapped brusquely, "Listen, Mrs. Pearson, I'm a working mother with four kids that I am raising by myself. I appreciate your concern, but Brandon will be fine."

"Well, what about his dad? Where is he? Can I talk to him?" Mrs. Pearson asked, still seeking a solution.

"No," my mother said, turning on her heel.

Despite all the drama, I managed to complete the eighth grade and move on to high school. I earned a spot on the summer league varsity team as a freshman, and I became part of a legendary team that drew massive crowds. Our gym was one of the newest and largest gymnasiums in the DC metro area. The ceilings were as high as a cathedral's. Championship banners adorned the walls. The lofty stands looked too big to fill, yet they were always packed.

When we played T.C. Williams, Wakefield, West Potomac, and other rivals, the gym overflowed and hundreds of people stood to watch. Most came for the high-level competition, but some were doubtless hoping for a brawl. No matter how crowded the stands were, they always seemed empty to me. None of the parents there were mine. Mom was always out of town for work or at home too exhausted for a weekday game. I envied DeMarkus for having a dad who heckled the refs. When Marquel rolled an ankle, he was mortified because his mother swooped to the rescue like Wonder Woman. I was jealous. I yearned for that paternal passion and motherly concern—but I had neither. The stands were full—but to me, they were empty.

That changed one night when I looked up from my spot on the bench and saw Mrs. Pearson enter the gym. She was the one person who would not let me down. I had left middle school, but she had not left me. The year before, she'd traveled hours to follow my AAU travel team no matter where we played. My heart filled at the sight of her and she was no longer my counselor; she was the living embodiment of someone who loved me. My eyes followed her from the door to the front-row seat she chose, so I'd know exactly where to look. Adrenaline coursed through my veins and I could not wait for Coach to put me in the game so I could make her proud.

"Brandon!" Coach yelled. "Pay attention or you gon' stay on that bench. I said go get Shameek." My time had come. I threw off my warm-ups and dashed to the score table, eager to enter the game. To me, Mrs. Pearson was the only person in the gymnasium, and I could hear her croaky voice rise above the masses.

"UConn! Run UConn!" Coach shouted. But the minute I touched the ball, everything I knew about the play evaporated. I launched a shot from wherever I stood. And I missed. Then a second, third, and a fourth shot— all missed. I looked in Mrs. Pearson's direction, fearing disappointment, but she was still smiling. So I kept shooting, and I kept missing. After a final shot fell short, I spiked the ball to the floor and yelled, "Fuck!"

This triggered a technical foul, Coach summoned me back to the bench, and I didn't reenter the game. Overwhelmed with shame, I held my head down and shielded my face with a towel. I couldn't bear to look at my one-woman cheering section.

"You did such a good job," she said to me afterward. Her words of comfort temporarily filled the chasm in my heart.

By the time I started high school, I was already knee-deep in the drug game. I sold dope at school. I went to basketball practice. Then I went home and sold dope in my neighborhood. Once again, it was my sister's older friends who put me on. Except this time I wasn't a twelve-year-old kid; I was fourteen. I had two years of quality *real nigga* experience. I had put in time and earned my stripes. I loved being a hooper, but I fully embraced the thrill of hustling.

Real niggas smoke dope, fuck bitches, and get money is what I was taught. I was now checking all the boxes. Before I started selling drugs, my merchandising career began with bootlegging. Barry and I sold everything that we could get our hands on. We came to school with backpacks loaded: pirated albums, underground rap tapes, and mix CDs we burned on LimeWire. Throwback jerseys for boys and jersey dresses for girls were major status symbols, and on our weekend trips to New York, Barry and I snagged pirated Mitchell & Ness jerseys on the streets of Harlem. We brought them back home to the DMV and sold them at school for $150 a pop. We advertised by wearing our supply to school and would literally sell shirts off our backs. "Oh, you like this?" I asked when given compliments. "Hundred fifty bucks and it's yours." A friend robbed us one time, but he paid his debt after we threatened to kill him. It didn't take long for us to realize that high schoolers are not the most affluent consumers, so we moved away from selling high-end items to shallow-pocketed teens. We needed to sell something more accessible. Something that everyone wanted and could reasonably purchase. That's when we entered the drug game.

Marquel and I had been playing together since seventh grade, so I was furious when Coach tapped him to play regular-season varsity but left me behind on the JV team. I thought it was an insult to my ability. But Coach wanted to prove a point, demanding that I get my act together. Coach had low tolerance for players that seemed too hood. He thought they were trouble and lacked discipline. Some of the best hoopers in our school were denied positions on the team for this reason. Coach favored the student athletes: ones who were college-bound like Marquel and others. Marquel and I were better than most of the guards on the varsity team, and if he deserved to be there, so did I. My AAU coach had even moved me up to the highest level of elite summer travel ball when I was only thirteen years old. But my regular-season coach held me back because my behavior did not match my potential. Even when I played backup point guard for one game on varsity and outscored every player on the team, Coach still sat me back on the bench.

I was barely academically eligible and Coach received frequent misconduct reports from teachers. Once when I was kicked out of class and sent to the main office, Coach barged into the principal's study pleading, "Let me deal with him, please. This won't happen again." I slouched with my flaccid body draped over the hot seat in the principal's office, incoherent because I always went to school high. The principal reluctantly agreed, and Coach had a firm grip on my arm when we left the office. "Look at me," he commanded. "Do you want to throw your damn life away?" he asked, staring into my hazy red eyes. "You keep this up and you'll become another statistic. You hear me?" But I was impervious.

He tried talking to me, talking to my mom, and he even tried taking me to church as a last recourse. None of it worked. I loved being a hooper, but I was passionate about being a hustler. And it almost cost my mother her job.

Dishonorable discharge from the military was my mother's greatest fear. Time and time again, disgrace had come so close that she'd felt its stony breath on the back of her neck. Yet at the last minute, she'd escape dismissal as if some spiritual protector had bent the barrel of a shotgun that was pointed at her.

Mom's ex-husband had once been the biggest threat to her job and our family. Now it was turning out to be me. Her own children—and especially me—constantly threatened her sanity and her career. Her hard work, diligence, and sacrifices could be undone in an instant. If news of my misdeeds reached her commanders and she was discharged, she'd have nothing to fall back on—no formal education, no professional network, no extended family support. The military was our only safety net, and it was becoming severely threadbare.

Most of our friends were out of school. Sierra's popularity drew crowds of guys from the DC who drove hoopties and slang dope. Our house became the hang-out spot because Mom was always away on temporary duty assignments. Our home became an underground saloon full of loud music, drugs, and drinking. Sierra's friends—Que, Keem, Ramel, and Deuce—had already graduated high school a few years ago. They were in their early twenties and they took Barry and me under their wing, calling us "the lil niggas" as a term of endearment.

One night, we were at Que's house up the street. We were in the garage and the guys were playing spades and swapping stories about *real nigga shit*. With each sip of cognac, Que became more oblivious to the fact that we were minors. "Try this, lil nigga, it'll put some hair on that bare chest of yours," he said, pouring my first cup of Christian Brothers. I took an ambitious gulp and grimaced in disgust, and the men laughed hysterically and said, "Slow down, lil nigga. That's gon' make you a man."

Que held the 750 milliliter up in the air and looked at it lovingly. Then he took a swig straight from the bottle, looked at it again, and exhaled from the depths of his chest, "Ahhgg, that's some good shit," then he poured more into my cup and told me to stop babysitting my drink.

I hated the taste. But I dared not show it. They would've said "Get your young ass outta here" like I was told when I used to be a *bitch nigga*. Not today. I had come too far to go back now.

I remembered overhearing that chasers were for bitches, so I drank the liquor straight. Two cups later, I blacked out. Barry towed my deadweight a quarter mile to our house, his right arm wrapped around my waist and my left arm slung around his neck.

Everything would have been fine, except on this occasion, Mom was home. It was after midnight and Barry dragged my unresponsive body into the house. He peeked around each dark corner to ensure the coast was clear. He laid me on the couch and tiptoed halfway up the stairs, then craned his neck to confirm that Mom's door was shut. By the time he returned, I was face-planted in a pool of undigested brandy and hamburger meat. Barry grabbed the mop and bucket and cleaned it all before Mom had a chance to see. Then he carried me upstairs and put me to bed, hoping that Mom would not suddenly emerge.

Barry was always the more cautious one. I was careless, fully disregarding all potential consequences of my actions and how they might affect the people around me. My decisions became a threat to everyone within proximity.

Sierra's boyfriend Peanut was a drug dealer, and he introduced us to "the game." High school girls had a thing for adult men with cars and money, which Peanut had. It didn't matter that he worked at Target and drove a Pontiac—to a seventeen-year-old girl, he was the equivalent of a Wall Street banker.

Peanut wasn't the best influence for any of us. He was the reason why my sister eventually got kicked out of our house, and the reason I almost ended up in jail. He did not want me to sell drugs for him at first, but not for any noble reason; he was just afraid that Sierra would break up with him if she discovered that he'd appointed her little brother as his corner boy. But I begged and swore I'd be smart about it, and he reluctantly agreed. "Man, I shouldn't even be lettin' yo lil ass do this shit," he said, sucking his teeth with apprehension.

I promised him that I was good for it. "Trust me," I said, "I'm gonna move this shit quickly and bring the cash back to you. How much do I get to keep?"

His response made it clear that I had put the cart before the horse.

"Keep?" he exclaimed. "Slow yo happy ass down, lil nigga. Just don't get caught."

We were in Peanut's empty apartment. There was one couch and a television stand with no television. We sliced a pound of weed into nicks, dubs, and dime bags for distribution. I stuffed it all in a black trash bag and took the pound home after I promised to flip it and report back within a week.

"Yeah, aight," Peanut said grudgingly. "Yo lil ass better not get caught."

I understood Peanut's concern. But he did not realize that I had a master plan. I concealed it, however, because I wanted to let my actions speak. Also because he would have beat my ass for making such an audacious and absurd proposition.

Finally, my chance had come. Mom was driving us to South Carolina for a basketball camp hosted by Southern Wesleyan and Furman Universities. College coaches would be there hoping to find future recruits. The camp was held in a gymnasium located in West Greenville, one of the most drug-infested neighborhoods in upstate South Carolina. I saw this as an opportunity. We loaded luggage in the trunk as Mom waited patiently in the driver's seat, sifting through her gospel CDs as usual. I waited for Barry, Sierra, and Ben to drop their bags at the foot of the trunk.

"Y'all go ahead. I'll get it," I said.

I watched everyone settle into our Dodge Caravan. When no one was watching, I slipped back inside to retrieve a black trash bag from the back corner of the garage. I buried it beneath the mountain of luggage, closed the trunk, climbed into the back seat, and braced myself for the eight-hour haul.

Two hours down the highway, a not-so-gentle backhanded slap on the chest jerked me out of sleep.

"Yo," Barry hissed. "What the fuck is that?"

I didn't answer. His eyes flecked with fury. A pungent scent was spreading through the passenger compartment. Barry's expression mixed anger with fear.

I didn't know what I was thinking. I had put us all in jeopardy. My entire body tensed with anxiety, frightened that the skunky smell of contraband would reach my mother in the driver's seat. I was focused on what she'd do to me. But considering the circumstances—a sergeant first class and a criminal amount of weed in a minivan full of minors—I should have been frightened of something far worse. If the police stopped us for any reason—speeding, expired tags, or the smallest infraction—a whiff of the weed would put my mother, who was completely innocent, at grave risk. She would have taken the fall.

My body tensed each time a cop drove past. I tried not to keep looking back when one followed closely behind us. I held my breath as if that somehow helped. Maybe I thought that if I did not inhale the trace of weed, I could pretend that it was not buried there beneath our luggage. I closed my eyes and promised God that if he got me out of this, I would never sell drugs again. He made good on our deal. I did not.

The basketball camp made my hooper-versus-hustler conflict even worse. I excelled at both, but I only saw myself having a future at one. After a long day of training, I told some of the other players in the locker room, "Ayo, I got that if you need it." I could tell a *real nigga* when I saw one. The *real niggas* are the ones who exchange banter in the locker room and randomly shout, "Where da hoes at?" Then everybody would start bragging about their body count as if women were units of wealth.

During that week, I befriended a few players at the camp who lived nearby. "Give me a bag and I'll give you some customers," Jay said. "I know where they be at." It sounded like an even exchange. But I knew enough to know that this was not the way Peanut wanted me to do business. So I struck a deal. "How 'bout I let you smoke one with me?" I proposed. I violated a street precept: you don't get high on your own supply. But I justified it as a client courtship. And I sold about an ounce of weed by week's end.

The last day of camp flew by and it was time for the closing award ceremony. I was confident in my performance, but it seemed that everyone except me was being recognized. Coach Stevens from Furman University men's basketball team was the final presenter. We all moved closer to the edge of our seats as he took the stage.

"This final award goes to a young man who has displayed exceptional talent for his age," the coach said. "He has been a human highlight film and joy to watch." All of us looked around the room to wager on whom he might bestow such words upon.

"The camp's MVP trophy goes to . . ." He paused briefly for dramatic effect, then trumpeted, "Brandon Fleming!"

After I accepted the award, Coach Stevens pulled me aside. "I know you're only a freshman," he said, "but I want you to make me a promise."

He told me that I was one hell of a player and that I had a promising future in the game. I wasn't taking his words too seriously, because I knew he'd feel differently had he known about my other life. "When your senior year comes," he continued, "I want you to call me."

I could never forget that conversation, because I had never considered college before. It was not a thing in our family. Hardly anyone on my mother's side had gone to college. Lofty words like *SATs* and *transcripts* and *admissions* were not in our vocabulary. Mom talked about God more than she talked about grades. Her expectations for us were not too high. She was grateful to see Ds and Cs on our report cards. As long as we were on track for graduation as opposed to jail, that was enough for her.

I could not imagine being a college student. The idea of suffering through more school sounded horrific. Success to me was becoming a playground legend like Skip to My Lou and the other AND1 superstars who played in Rucker Park. "Ball is life" was our philosophy. It meant playing streetball from sunup until sundown. Then we all sat on the blacktop watching night descend and someone said, "Spark that shit up" as we lit a blunt and shot the breeze. That was my idea of a perfect life. Not that lame-ass college boy shit.

On our long trip back north to the DMV, I thought about Furman University and the idea of being a Division I college athlete. I thought about what I had seen on TV: the arena and the Jumbotron and the crazy college fans, yelling at the top of their lungs, bodies painted in Furman colors. I imagined hearing Dick Vitale's iconic voice during March Madness as we competed in the Sweet Sixteen. It didn't sound half bad. The Furman coach was one of the first to suggest that I could play at the next level. But I digressed from the thought, because *real niggas* don't go to college.

When I wasn't smuggling weed across state lines in my mother's car, I was smoking it at the park behind our house. Every evening after practice, the gang waited for me to arrive at our usual spot: a derelict playground in the middle of a vacant field. When the wind blew, the rusty chains of broken swings screeched. One arm of the seesaw was missing, the slide's undergirding was obviously unhinged, and the monkey bars were the only intact feature of the playscape.

The isolation of this place made it our headquarters for smoking and selling weed. It's where Que, Keem, Deuce, and Ramel imparted wisdom to their fourteen-year-old apprentice.

They taught me how to roll a joint in a matter of seconds, a speed drill I embraced as fervently as a soldier breaking down and reassembling a rifle. I surgically parted the body of a Dutch Masters cigar, emptying the tobacco on the ground, then sprinkled the weed in a delicate straight line and rolled the bundle like a pig in a blanket. After sealing it with saliva, I roasted it with the lighter and raised it triumphantly in the air.

"You freaked that shit, lil nigga," my tutors would say, laughing and admiring my work.

Weed turned us all into pseudo-intellectuals. Each wheezy inhalation raised our discourse a notch; passing the joint awakened us spiritually and made us scientifically astute. One minute, we were theologians; the next, we were philosophers. At other times the smoke turned my companions into patriarchs, like a ghetto version of Don Vito Corleone.

"When I was your age," Keem said, "the streets was all I had. You feel me?" He spoke in short breaths. The smoke oozing from his mouth rose and was whisked away by a gust of wind. Keem handed the joint to Que, as if passing a microphone.

"Yeah, lil nigga," Que pontificated as he took a pull. "You got choices. You got time to do some shit we ain't never done. You can get ya muhfuckin' education, keep hoopin', and go to college and do something with your life." Que inhaled another smoke and looked lovingly at the joint pinched between his fingers. With each pull, the embers glowed like the tail of a firefly.

"Hell yeah," Ramel said, joining in on the homily. "You got this basketball shit going for you. You need to get out these damn streets and get your shit together. Be better than us."

I simply looked at them and marveled at the irony of it all. They had spent years teaching me the skills of *real niggas*, and now they were urging me to take a different path? I ignored their grandiose, weed-driven advice, laughed to myself, and said, "Y'all gon' pass that blunt or nah?"

Suddenly the ground rocked beneath us as we spotted a flashlight beam, sweeping from side to side and heading straight for us.

"Yo, who the fuck is that?" Ramel said, squinting to gain a better view. Two human figures and a large dog took shape in the distance.

"Five-O. Put that shit out. Put that shit out," Que hissed anxiously. I threw the joint to the ground, snuffed it with my foot, and scooped up the remains. "Let's walk," he said. But the moment I pivoted to walk away from our visitors, the powerful beam hit me like a spotlight.

"Stop right there," one of the cops commanded. They'd be on us in thirty seconds or less and I had a blunt in my hand and nowhere to discard it.

Dusk had settled and the air was thick. Perspiration gathered in my armpits and my heart was hammering. The hourglass that measured my freedom had been turned on its head, and the sand was running with each step the officers took. I had been in similar situations, but there had always been an obvious escape route. Not this time.

"What the fuck should I do?" I asked Que, desperate as the cops closed in on the playground. Everyone discreetly patted their bodies to ensure they were clean. Fortunately for them, we had smoked up all the weed. Except for the incriminating evidence nestled in my hand. If I ran, the cops would surely catch me. If I tossed the blunt, the dog would find it immediately. My brain fast-forwarded through the coming attractions: I would go to juvie for drug possession, the cops would get a search warrant for my home, they would find the stashes under my mattress, Mom would be charged with possession and kicked out of the army. Life as we knew it would be over. And it would all be my fault.

I turned to Que with a look of complete panic.

"I'ma tell you what to do," he said, "but you ain't gon' like it."

"I don't give a fuck, nigga," I responded. "Just tell me."

Que eyed the cops approaching, then swung his gaze from side to side, like someone about to deliver bad news.

"Listen," he said, "you gotta put that shit in your ass."

"Nigga, what?" I was appalled by the idea.

"Nigga, we ain't got that much fuckin' time. Either you do that shit, or we're all fucked." Everyone stood wide-eyed, nodding in agreement. I couldn't believe this shit.

I had seconds left to choose between my life and my pride. My first impulse was toward pride. But I changed my mind when the cops were only a stone's throw away. I reached one arm behind my back and into my pants—the worst possible posture for a Black boy—when the cop yelled, "Put your hands where I can see them!" But I hadn't quite secured it yet. I knew I had to get it in there, pull my hand out, and raise both hands in the air—or else the cop could perceive that I was reaching for a weapon.

"I said get your hands where I can see them!" the cop shouted once more. And both of my hands shot to the sky.

The officers seized our playground. They were both white. They were wearing army fatigues and black bulletproof vests with MILITARY POLICE stitched across the chest. The panting K-9 had already started sniffing around the vicinity. The officers knew what was going on. The dog wasn't the only one who could smell the skunk in the air.

Que looked the cop up and down. "How can we help you, officer?" he said in what could be heard as a defiant tone, squaring his body with his hands still raised. I had the most to lose. Now wasn't the time for Que to be acting hardcore. I tried to make eye contact to beg him to relax. But he ignored my silent plea.

Then it all escalated so quickly. The officer stepped closer to Que until they were facing off like two UFC fighters weighing in. Their toes were barely touching. Their noses were nearly kissing. And Que dropped his arms in defiance.

"I didn't tell you to put your hands down, boy," the officer said, his vehement glare burning a hole into Que's eyes. But Que chuckled at the officer's words. My face, once again, pleaded for him to chill. The faces of our friends also said that Que was taking it too far. It seemed that Que knew there was nothing the cops could do—they'd witnessed no illegal activity, they had no cause to search us, and even though marijuana perfumed the air, there were no remains to be found. Que took for granted that the officers would be law abiding. And his rebellious chuckle had sparked a firestorm.

"You think you're funny, boy?" the officer yelled, his spit misting Que's face. He pressed the brim of his hat into Que's forehead, causing Que to stumble backward.

Que regained his balance and squared off with the officer again. Showing no fear, Que scowled at the man and asked, "What you gon' do?"

In a rage, the officer pressed forward with his fists clenched and shouted, "You think you're tough? I'll put your dick in the dirt, boy! You hear me?"

I couldn't tell whether he was military police or a drill sergeant. The rest of us stood, helpless, with our hands still in the air. It felt like I was watching a tragic movie unfold. It was a scene we'd seen many times before, and the outcome was never good.

"Search them," the officer instructed his partner. One by one, the K-9 frisked us with its nose. Nobody seemed concerned—except for me, because I knew the truth. And the truth was: I hadn't quite followed Que's instructions for stashing the blunt. Instead of actually putting it *in* my ass, I clinched it with my cheeks. I was scared to talk, scared to move, scared to breathe.

When the dog reached me, I closed my eyes and stood breathless—wondering if God would still hear my prayers and promises while I was high. The dog started barking, alerting the officers, who came at me aggressively.

"Empty your pockets," one officer commanded.

I explained that they were empty. Then he demanded a second time, "I said empty your pockets, dammit!"

I followed his instructions and withdrew my wallet and a lighter, which cranked up their suspicions. If I had a lighter, we must have been doing drugs. I fumbled to explain its presence.

"It's for Newports," I said as he looked at me incredulously.

The officers could see at a glance that I was likely underage. Fortunately for me, the cigarettes were not in my possession. I explained that I had brought the lighter for my friends.

The dog never stopped barking during the search, and he circled me repeatedly. The animal sniffed around the front of my pants, then he sniffed my behind, where the blunt was nestled tightly in my crack. I stood as still as humanly possible, tensing my rear like I was holding on to life itself. My feet were tight together to keep my legs from trembling. I spoke as little as possible so that breathing wouldn't cause my cheeks to part. I knew that if I coughed or had to take a single step it would all be over, because the slightest movement would let the remains of the blunt fall down my pant leg and onto the ground. I was still high and getting light-headed from not breathing. I tried not to contort my face.

After patting me down, the officer looked at his partner and said, "We're done here." They walked away, and I exhaled the most gratifying sigh of relief. Then I bent to retrieve the joint that fell to my feet.

I went off the rails fast with drugs. All I cared about was getting high. So much so that I stole product I was supposed to sell for Peanut. If he hadn't been my sister's boyfriend, he would have had my head in a swift medieval-style execution. Cannabis was a gateway drug, and my pursuit of higher highs reached levels that frightened even those who'd introduced me to drugs.

Lacing was an especially dangerous discovery. Friends recall me hallucinating that I could fly, then jumping from the top of a jungle gym while flapping my arms and squawking like a bird. I don't recall the event. But I do remember waking up with a battered, throbbing face that looked like I had gone a round with Mike Tyson.

People who had been my accomplices became concerned and stopped supplying me with drugs. It reached a point where I was willing to do anything to get my fix, even if it meant stealing from my own mother. I stashed the $2.50 she gave me each day for school lunch and used it to buy drugs. I embezzled from a coin jar that Mom kept in her bedroom. While she was at work, I emptied the jar and spread the change across her bed, plucking quarters from the mass of pennies, dimes, and nickels and taking them to the Coinstar converter up the street at Food Lion for enough cash to pay my drug debts or reup. When there was nothing left but pennies, I went after Mom's jewelry box and pawned her least favorite pieces in exchange for a few dollars. It was not long before she noticed that her jar was in the wrong place and several gems had mysteriously disappeared. All she could do was cry, thinking about two marriages destroyed by drugs. Now the same curse had befallen her son.

Each morning I went to school with the stench of weed hanging on to my tail. I sold the drugs at school lockers and took bathroom breaks to replenish my own high. As hard as I had worked to build my athletic career, my hoop dreams took second place. My coaches caught on to my scarlet eyes and my unusual wheezing while running laps. I was losing myself and risking my future. I was stumbling into the locker room late. Coach eventually discovered that I was getting high and having sex with girls right before our games. In a desperate attempt to protect both me and the team, Coach threatened the girls who were ruining his key player, and he lectured me about ruining myself. He demanded that I change my ways and benched me to prove a point. But nothing worked.

Barry had more sense than me. We defied rules together but he was far less reckless and spent most of his time covering my ass. He smoked and sold a little dope and we did dumb stuff like run up Mom's dial-up internet bill with $500 worth of porn purchases. But Barry only wanted to get his feet wet with mischief, while I went deep. Barry would yank me up and say, "Yo, chill the fuck out. You're gonna get us caught." But I didn't care about anything and Barry realized that he could not save me. Clearly I was destined for juvenile detention despite his attempts to talk sense into me. He and all my friends said that basketball could be my salvation, but it was too late. I was too far gone. I was a ticking time bomb and didn't care who was nearby when I exploded.

Not even Bre, my girlfriend, was safe. One weekend, we had been watching hours of TV in my living room and I was ready for my next hit. I went upstairs to fetch the baggie usually hidden between my mattress and box spring, but it wasn't there. I phoned Barry because only two people knew about the stash. He didn't have it, which left only Bre.

I stormed downstairs to confront her. She was smiling and singing to music videos when I raged into the living room.

"Where's my shit?" I said in a thunderous voice.

She kept her eyes on the screen and continued dancing to the music like nothing was wrong, like I wasn't there towering over her. I repeated the question, but all I got from her was a shoulder shrug. When she reached for the remote to jack up the volume, I snatched it from her hand and launched it at the wall. The remote shattered into pieces.

"I said where is my shit?"

She gave me a long glare.

"I know you better calm the fuck down and watch who you're talking to," she said.

"Give it back!"

"No!" she yelled.

I wrapped my arms around the television, jerked it off the stand as the cords pulled loose from the wall, and threw it across the room. The crash left Bre with an expression of sheer shock.

"I'm gonna tell you one more time," I said. "Give me my shit." Her facial expression went from anger to worry to fear.

"Brandon, you need help," she said, hoping to defuse the tension. She tried to reason with me, explaining that this was the same path my stepfather had gone down. "You are not him," she said.

It triggered me. How dare she compare me to that monster? She meant well, but those words were like gunshots that tore through my chest. She might as well have called me by his name. My hands tightened into fiery fists. With all of my might, I cocked back my arm and punched the wall beside me, my hand plowing through the drywall. I punched and punched and punched until blood-stained debris fell to the floor. Bre yelled, "Brandon, stop!" then pulled my stash from her purse and threw it to the floor. I retrieved it. I rolled it. I smoked it.

Mom tried to save me a couple of times. She even tried to get me on one of those reality TV shows that isolated misbehaving teens into a boot camp and tried to frighten them into being good. Unfortunately for her, the producers only accepted kids who agreed to cooperate, and I wasn't about to go along with that corny shit. With that off the table, she decided that maybe church could save me.

One Sunday, Mom dragged us into a nearby middle school cafeteria for a church service. I hated school and church, and I couldn't believe that my two least favorite institutions had come together this way.

We hadn't walked through the doors of any kind of church since my mother left Lucas. Now we were complete outsiders in a group of about ten people, including my mom, my three siblings, and me. The others were the only Black people I'd ever seen dressed like Amish farmers. The women wore shapeless solid-colored dresses so big that not a bodily curve was visible. They were forbidden to cut their hair and wore white hair nets as head coverings. They didn't say "Hello," but instead greeted with "Praise the Lord," "Grace be with you," or other spiritual salutations. Meanwhile, we trudged in with Girbaud jeans sagging off of our rears, Timberlands, and oversized white tees. We returned their spiritual greetings with a head nod and other irreverent gestures.

As we mingled with the church folk, my mother tucked her chin into her chest. She was worried about what we might say or do, fearful of being judged. When the preacher's wife asked questions about our background, my mother said as little as possible and hung on to her Bible for dear life.

This small congregation used the school cafeteria because it was a free place to meet. They were a charismatic group and they treated the preacher like he was a deity. When he walked through the door, women rushed to carry his Bible and briefcase for him. Everything about this setup seemed odd, but my mother went along with it because she'd heard that this preacher could save us.

She was willing to try anything that offered more hope for salvation than our makeshift services at home. "Bedside Baptist Church" is where we attended. In our version, we'd pack into Mom's bed like sardines on Sunday morning, our eyes fastened on the forty-inch television resting on the dresser. I'd wiggle and complain about being uncomfortable until she agreed to let me sit on the floor. Although I promised that this would help me focus better, I drifted off to sleep as soon as I was out of her line of sight.

Sometimes it was Joel Osteen. Sometimes it was Benny Hinn. At one point it was Jimmy Swaggart, but that ended after his public fall from grace.

Swaggart was too boring, Hinn seemed too pretentious, and Osteen reminded me of Mister Rogers. Judging by our lack of moral improvement, none of the televangelists had any impact.

Despite avoiding church since divorcing Lucas, Mom was ready to give live religion another chance because her children were wayward and nothing she did seemed to make a difference. She had met a member of this church on the street, accepted a tract, and heard the woman's pitch about how this version of religion offered salvation and had nothing in common with what we observed on television. Once there, it was easy to see why the congregation was so small: there was no music or instruments, besides a few tambourines and a cappella singing by old ladies, and the preacher's fire-and-brimstone sermons were all about condemnation and eternal damnation.

When the preacher finished, Mom forced me to the makeshift altar. She asked the preacher to save my soul, though what happened looked and felt more like an exorcism. The elders laid hands on me and spoke in tongues as they tried to force me to fall out. Tired of resisting, I eventually just gave them what they wanted and collapsed to the floor so they would stop, but they didn't. They knelt around me and kept laying hands and praying that the Holy Spirit would enter my body and save my soul.

I was pretty sure this was a cult.

We kept going, until one Sunday I'd had enough. My mother made us sit in the front row of folding chairs, the solemnly clad people beside us. Mom wanted us close to the altar because she assumed a correlation between proximity and probability of redemption.

The preacher approached the pulpit, which in this case was a plain wooden lectern. "Dearly beloved. Please stand for the reading of God's Word," he summoned. Everyone rose except me.

"Let us read aloud," he continued, paying me no mind.

Fury engulfed me and I picked up my chair and slammed it down facing away from the minister. I dropped into the chair, folded my arms, and kicked back in a blue plastic seat that wasn't meant for reclining. I braced my Timberlands on the chair in front of me. The preacher gave me a stare, and I offered him my ass to kiss.

I hated God. And I damn sure didn't want to hear from the man who claimed to be his mouthpiece, so I sent a memo straight to God through the one he called his messenger.

That message: an unapologetic *fuck you*.

My actions stunned the members of the congregation. Mom's head sunk in shame. But one of the creepy woman elders lifted Mom's chin and said, "Don't worry, honey. The worst ones are who God chooses to use the most. Watch what I tell you."

CHAPTER FIVE

SEX & DEATH THREATS

Once I lost control of my life, addiction and lust and anger steered my mind and body into chaos. This almost killed me. And on a few occasions, it almost killed someone else.

It had been a typical school day until Nicole walked by and the world stopped. Or at least the boys did. She was dreamy: five foot five with hazel eyes and a body curvilinear. Her melanin was immaculate and sun-kissed. Her skin seemed like it might feel like silk. Ebony curls flowed down her spine, and when she sashayed by, I could hear "Summer Rain" playing in my fourteen-year-old head.

Her presence was commanding. In the DMV, there were certain girls we called "rollers," because we imagined that they moved from one guy to the next without pause. Nicole wasn't one of these. Even if she was, we would have never known. Upperclassmen like her viewed freshman boys as peasants, regardless of athletic prowess. Jocks didn't impress her. Guys with money, however, did.

So Nicole, like the other senior girls we rated eight and above, only dated high school grads with jobs, cars, and street credibility. I revered her at a distance—partly because I stood no chance, but mostly because my girlfriend Bre was snappy. So when I spotted Nicole approaching from afar, I directed my gaze about ten steps in the direction she was heading; this way, it seemed that her rear features so happened to fall within my line of sight. But this did not escape Bre's vigilance. She slapped the back of my neck and roared, "I ain't dumb and you ain't slick." It was true. Bre knew that Nicole was to be envied, although the two had never really met. She sucked her teeth and rolled her eyes as Nicole walked past us. And with good reason: Nicole was the prize that every guy wanted to win, and that every girl wanted to be.

I was a freshman. Bre was a sophomore. We were fourteen and sixteen years old, we were both standout athletes, and we had been dating since the beginning of the school year. We both had had our share of traumas. When we made love, it seemed like our demons did, too. We came together as two damaged souls and set about weaving a web of teenage calamity. The best of our love was lust. And the outcome was a series of escalating disasters.

We were fearless, or plain stupid. Maybe both. Our lust was magnetic, explosive, and we couldn't keep our hands off of each other. Not even in our fourth period Spanish class. Sitting in the back, we fondled each other— smiling innocently when Ms. Ramirez scowled suspiciously in our direction. Each day, we looked forward to our lunch block. But we never went. The bell rang and we roamed the halls, looking for a break in traffic and usually finding it in the history wing.

One time, we came upon the girls' restroom. I loitered outside while Bre went in.

"Count to sixty," she said. "If I don't come out, that means the coast is clear." I did my best to look nonchalant. When the time was up, I scanned the hallway once more. Then I dashed inside to the handicap stall. Like the sex-crazed teens that we were, we started ripping off each other's clothes as soon as we slid the latch. Our thirst was insatiable, fired by the illicit thrill of it all. But at the height of the action, we heard adult voices that put a stop to everything.

I grabbed frantically for my britches, getting hung up on my belt as Bre motioned for me to be still. Our worst nightmare was being caught in the act—and expelled. Bre peered through the door and saw two teachers. They were exchanging teacher woes, and one of the voices I recognized as Mrs. Johnson, my world history instructor. Bre held one finger to her lips and pointed toward the toilet seat. I had no other choice but to climb up so they would not see two pairs of feet. Then, suddenly, a knock on the door. Squatting on the commode, I prayed silently, "Lord, if you get me out of this, I promise I will never do it again." After a few minutes, the teachers left. We were not caught this time. But our continued exploits soon gave lie to my desperate supplication.

Bre and I tested the boundaries of mercy many times after that. The thrill of creeping was yet another addictive high, obscuring all forms of rational thought. We were two sexually deviant daredevils who couldn't stop. Sometimes we didn't even make it to the girls' restroom. Sometimes it happened after school in the middle of a vacant hallway. If any teacher had walked down that hall, our X-rated escapades would be seared into their memory, and the subsequent expulsion would permanently stain our records.

We even pushed the limits at home. One day, Bre and I were in my bedroom doing everything that we weren't supposed to be doing. But before we could finish, I heard Mom's voice bounce off every wall in our two-story house.

"I done told y'all about leaving this door unlocked!" she roared. "Barry? Brandon? Sierra?" she called out. But it was only me and Bre in the house, just a few steps away from being busted.

I could hear Mom's footsteps mounting the stairs. The first door she would open was mine at the top of the stairwell. My heart was racing so fast I could barely think. I didn't know what to do. I couldn't run. I couldn't hide. I couldn't find an excuse for Bre being in my bedroom with the door closed and the air redolent of sin. I looked at Bre, her face contorted with fear, then I looked beside us at the only way of escape. I ran to the window and opened it.

"I'm so sorry, but you gotta jump," I said without remorse. We had to do it. It was either her or me. I chose her.

"Are you crazy?" she responded in disbelief.

I could hear Mom's heavy footsteps getting closer. We had maybe ten seconds left. Mom was so close that I was hissing my words. "Bre, you have to jump. Now!"

She stuck her head out the window to gauge the distance. The clock was running out.

Mom knocked on my door. "Brandon, are you in there?" she called out.

Bre looked down warily at the two-story drop. She had one leg through the window but her torso was still inside the room. "One second, Mom," I said, watching Bre clutch the windowsill as she tried to ease herself out. But there was no time for that. She was moving too slow. She was too scared to let go. So I gave her a little push, and her body went tumbling down, face-planting in a pile of leaves and mud.

She lived. And so did I. Bre did not have any broken bones. And I opened the door, greeting my mother with a blameless smile.

We took risks like this without thinking. Our fix became more important than life itself. Our lust didn't have fatal consequences that time, but the likelihood was increasing.

We had basketball practice after school every day, or at least some iteration of it. If we weren't on the court, we were lifting weights, doing conditioning drills, or watching game films. On rare occasions, Coach gave us a break, meaning we were excused after school for rest and fellowship. One such afternoon, my friends and I waited for our buses near the school's main entrance, where an amalgamation of cliques assembled: the whites, Blacks, and Hispanics. And their subsets: student council, athletes, gang members. The varsity basketball and football players claimed the turf by the vending machines. Each day, people knew exactly where to find us—instigating fights, seducing girls who liked our flirting, and annoying girls who didn't.

Jocks were obnoxious for no reason. Meat-checking is how we enacted masculinity and male bonding. It was a silly game. An example: Rashe would extend his hand to greet Chad, then he'd point to the ceiling and say, "What's that?" When Chad looked up, Rashe would deliver a backhanded blow to the nuts as Chad's six-foot, two-hundred-pound body folded on the ground in fetal position. We'd all cheer and laugh hysterically. But then people would catch on and stop falling for it, so we'd have to be innovative. When Rashe would greet Chad again, he'd say, "Ayo, catch!" and toss a water bottle just high enough in the air to send Chad's arms reaching toward the ceiling, leaving a clear path for a gut-wrenching meat check. This passed for brains and creativity in our world.

One day I was leaning against the wall, dressed in my uniform of Timberlands, jeans, and an oversized white T-shirt. Behind me, a mellifluous voice said, "Hey, Brandon." I noticed that my friends' faces had frozen in disbelief before I could even turn around. I did not recognize the voice, and I was stunned to see where it came from. It was Nicole.

We had never spoken, and she had no reason to know my name. She had never even looked in my direction, except maybe for an eye roll in response to our catcalls. I looked around to make sure that no one else named Brandon was near me. I was starstruck. I could barely form the word *hello*.

"What you doing after school?" she asked. "I'd love to ride the bus with you." For a heartbeat, I considered that I had plans with my friends, who were all heading to my house. Those plans were canceled, effective immediately. I disinvited them all. This was a major development. Riding someone else's bus was a thing in high school—it was our version of the first date over dinner. After Nicole agreed to meet me after school and walked away, my boys rushed me with handshakes and hugs, screaming, "Yoooo!" None of us could believe what was happening.

Nicole and I sat together on the bus, but I kept my distance, still bewildered. This didn't make sense. She had never shown even the tiniest sign of interest in me, no matter how many times our paths had crossed on campus. On the bus, I was usually raucous—standing on the seats, yelling taunts, ignoring the driver's pleas for peace. But now I sat heels planted, knees tight, not knowing what to do with my hands twitching on my lap. I did my best to keep up small talk, but my thoughts scattered, and my gaze toggled between her eyes and her succulent breasts.

I had no idea what Nicole wanted or why she was sitting beside me, but I knew that a monumental decision loomed. If I advanced and she resisted, high school gossip would ridicule me as a loser who aimed too high. But if I hung back, I would forfeit every penniless high school boy's version of currency: bragging rights. The probabilities were as hard to parse as the spin of a roulette wheel.

The bus turned off of Sacramento Drive to our destination. Suddenly, I felt her skin graze my left pinky. My peripheral vision confirmed what was happening while I avoided any rash moves that might break the romantic tension. I moved my hand onto her thigh. I stretched my fingers to interlink with hers. The connection sent an electric current shooting through my body and a rush of blood to the place that my mind had to convince to stay down. We made our way off the bus, our hands hugging as I led the way.

It was around 3 p.m. My mom wouldn't be home from work for three to six hours; I couldn't be more precise because Mom never disclosed her estimated time of arrival. This was her way of keeping us on our toes. We'd call and ask, "Mom, when you gettin' off?" But she'd respond, "You ain't gotta worry 'bout it if you just do what you supposed to do."

I was used to being with older girls, but Nicole had my nerves snarled worse than the headphone cords coiled in my pocket. I escorted her to the couch and dashed upstairs to find my boom box. I emptied a box of CDs on the bed, frantically searching for the one inscribed with marker GET WET MUSIC VOL. 2. It was a chopped and screwed mix I'd curated for occasions like this. I returned and set the mood by closing the blinds. She slipped off her jacket and we sat close. My arm was draped around her shoulder and my hand dangled just enough to gently graze her right breast. I continued our small talk from the bus, until she stopped me. She climbed on my pelvis with her legs bestride. She filled my mouth with her tongue. I sunk my teeth into her neck. Her head leaned back and the music played as our bodies wound in cadence.

I sat still afterward, not knowing what to make of what just happened, or how it happened at all. I thought of the report I'd give my eager friends. Maybe I would Diddy-bop through the halls the next day. Maybe I would gleefully skip to the main office, seize the microphone, and tell the entire school during morning announcements. Talking afterward can be so awkward, but I murmured inconsequential things because I didn't want this amazing encounter to feel like a heartless transaction. Nicole, however, was impatient. She reached for her clothes and dressed in haste. "I have to go," she said.

I walked her to the door and thanked her for coming. I leaned forward to kiss her, but she turned away. "So, when can we do this again?" I asked, to which she responded, "We can't." "Well, maybe we should exchange numbers," I continued. But she answered back, "There's no need."

Geez, *was I that bad?* I asked myself. It took me a minute to regroup, but I finally stammered out a question. "So, what happens from here?"

She looked at me, chuckled softly, and said, "Just tell Bre that we're even now."

I must have looked like someone hit me with a cattle prod.

"Ask Bre about Trey," she said, and then the screen door slammed behind her and she walked off into the distance.

As soon as I got to school the next day, I headed for Bre's locker, our usual rendezvous. My friends were panting for salacious good news, but I shoved past them: seeing nothing, hearing nothing. I marched a flaming, furious path straight toward Bre. And there she stood, gazing adoringly toward me. I was defused by her innocence, her benevolence, her beauty—but only for a moment.

"Hey, baby," she said, opening her arms and inviting me in.

"Bre," I snarled, "who the fuck is Trey?"

She froze, seeing tears of anger and vengeance welling in my eyes. "Brandon—"

But I interrupted. "Tell me the truth." I banged the locker with my fist. A thunderclap reverberated through the hall. People stared. Bre stared. I stared as we all stood still.

After school, I sat alone in my room, marinating in my sense of betrayal—Bre, Nicole, Trey. Somebody had to pay. My dark and vengeful mood was interrupted by footsteps in the hallway. It was Peanut, my sister's dope-dealing boyfriend. He opened the door and asked where Sierra was, but instead of saying anything, I shrugged my shoulders and looked away.

"The fuck wrong with you, lil nigga?" he asked. Embarrassed, I didn't want to say. I figured that a cheating man is expected, but a cheating girlfriend is an abomination to male pride. Eventually, I gave in and told him. In response, Peanut surveyed the hallway to confirm we were alone, then he came into my room and shut the door.

"So what you gon' do?" he asked.

I fought back tears to avoid looking weak. I tried to act like I didn't care, and called Bre foul names, saying that I had broken up with her. But this wasn't the answer Peanut was looking for. He reached into his back pocket and withdrew a weapon: a deadly six-inch Smith & Wesson switchblade. He flipped it open to reveal the blade's acute tip and jagged edges. He took a few steps closer, his demeanor militant and unyielding.

"I ain't talkin 'bout her," he said, "I'm talkin 'bout him."

Earlier that day, I had demanded that Bre tell me where Trey lived. He was a sergeant and lived on base in military housing next door to her family. I gave Peanut the intel, and he told me that there was only one option: I had to handle my business like a man.

Before I knew it, we were in Peanut's two-door Pontiac and headed for Trey's house. Peanut had the bucket seat on his side reclined so far that it grazed the back seat, which was littered with cigarette butts, scarred with burn holes, and scattered with dozens of empty beer and Hennessy bottles that spilled onto the floorboard. Peanut sat off-center, clutching the steering wheel with one hand and fisting a Corona in the other. As if drinking and driving was not bad enough, he made an art of drinking *while* driving. Then he reached for the joint neatly tucked behind his right ear like a pencil. He fired it up. Smoke filled the car like steam in a sauna. I sat beside him, his angry apprentice, with my adrenaline surging and his knife clenched tightly in my sweaty hand. He called me "lil nigga" a few more times.

We parked at the corner, close enough to spy Trey and three friends drinking beer on his porch. Trey wore cargo pants, combat boots, and a wifebeater, like he had just gotten off duty. Peanut delivered his version of a halftime speech: "Handle your business, nigga," he said. "Don't be a lil bitch." I repeated his words like a mantra, my eyes locked like lasers on my unwary enemy. I popped the door lock, flipped open the switchblade, and inhaled deeply. I looked at Trey one last time. I looked at Peanut. I nodded with certainty and said, "Drive the fuck up." I was ready to kill him.

We pulled up directly in front of the porch where Trey sat with his friends. Their laughing waned when they spotted our car slowing to a stop in front of his house. Peanut glared at them from the driver's window. He said nothing. He clutched the wheel with one hand and the gear stick with the other, prepared to speed off for our getaway after the job was done. He gave me a look that said *You know what to do.*

I opened the door and stepped out slowly. I walked around the hood of the car and planted on the pavement at the foot of Trey's porch. From the look in his eyes, I could tell that he knew exactly who I was and why I was there. My eyes were full of vengeance. I looked like a madman, spouting expletives and brandishing a combat knife. That's when he lifted his shirt just enough for me to see the gun holstered on his waist. I'd brought a knife to a gunfight, but I did not care. I knew what Peanut was packing behind me. I stood there, clutching the knife, rage shooting through my body like a bolt of lightning.

"You fucked with the wrong one!" I yelled as I started to charge toward him. But I was stopped by Bre, who came dashing out of her house next door, screaming, "Brandon, stop!" She ran to wrestle the knife out of my hand. She wanted to save me from making a grave mistake, so much that she had already called the police when she'd spotted me from her window.

"Get the fuck out of the way!" I shouted at Bre.

I was ready to complete the mission. Nothing would change my mind. Especially when Trey looked at me and laughed like I was some little *bitch ass nigga* with a toy. His gun did not scare me. Nothing scared me, until Bre yelled, "The cops are coming!" and I froze in my tracks. Peanut yelled from the window, "Get back in the car, nigga, let's go!" I dove back into the passenger's seat and Peanut slammed the gas. Somebody was supposed to die that day. And if Bre had not betrayed me by calling the cops, the death might have been my own.

CHAPTER SIX

FOULING OUT

When Mom was called to duty in 2007, we didn't realize that her deployment would abruptly end our life together as a family. She was not being sent away for a few days or weeks this time. President George W. Bush had ordered her battalion to join the war in Iraq. She had six months to prepare for deployment, and we did not know when—or if—she would return.

"So what does this mean for us?" I asked, distraught at the prospect of being separated from my friends, my teammates, and, most of all, my siblings. It was among life's deepest sorrows. Especially as I was about to enter my senior year. I could think of no siblings who were more closely knit than us. We had survived so much together, and through it all, Sierra was our protector. Now our childhood was breaking apart and ending. Sierra moved in with her baby's father. Barry had just graduated high school and moved to New York with his dad. My options were few, and Ben's even fewer.

There was no way that my paternal grandparents would accept me and my wayward ways. Plus, Ben and I were a bundle. Whoever took me in would have to take him, too. Ben's paternal family was nowhere to be found.

So my mother sent the two of us to live in South Carolina with my godparents, whom I called Aunt Carolyn and Uncle Eddie.

Not only was I grief-stricken because my family was scattered, but I also lost longstanding friendships with my teammates and the momentum we'd created. We had spent the past four years playing together, traveling the country, and winning championships. Now that I was a rising senior, I was one step away from becoming an NCAA Division I athlete. My years of running the streets were over. The same friends that had once introduced me to the drug game had forced me to quit drugs by cutting off my supply. They really believed that I could make it with basketball, so they stopped feeding my drug habits and started supporting my future. Instead of spending Friday nights on the street corners, they were now in the front row of the gymnasium—still high and smelling like weed—yelling, "Fuck them niggas up!" A familiar phrase but a new context, and it was music to my ears.

Even when they smoked in my presence, they would not allow me even one courtesy puff. "Ayo, let me hit that," I said when the rotation came my direction. But they skipped me every time. "Touch that shit if you want to," Que said, clenching his fist. "I'll beat yo muthafuckin' ass."

They would not allow me to ruin my own life. Together, they decided that if I wasn't going to protect my future, they would.

"Listen, lil nigga," Que said. "We not gon' let you fuck up your future. You gon' be better than us."

I believed them, because they believed in me. No matter how much I resisted, they held me accountable and supported me. I eventually became clean. With a clear focus, my basketball performance rose to another level.

I was a rising senior. After investing years in this school, this city, and this basketball program, the triumph that should have been mine was stolen by my exile from the DMV. But maybe, just maybe, what seemed like a theft was a gift in disguise.

I was saddened that my run with Marquel was officially over. For four years, since we first squared off at the rec center, we had been an unstoppable force. I played point guard and he played shooting guard and we flew up and down the court at speeds that no one could match. But I was heading to a new state, a new school, a new team. My days of being his Pippen were over. For my senior year in high school, I would finally be number one.

Greenville High School was a magnet school admired for academic quality and envied for athletic prowess, but they rejected me immediately. Looking at my disciplinary history and my low GPA, the administrators no doubt profiled me as exactly the student they hoped never to enroll. My aunt's address was zoned for Woodmont High School, which—I was horrified to learn—had one of the worst basketball records in the entire upstate region. The school was notorious for losing at the time. The school is in Piedmont, where we lived, a small town whose business district had been hollowed out by Greenville's sprawl. There was one grocery store, one fast-food restaurant, and one high school. All other needs were fulfilled in the larger city. Many Black kids came from families with little resources, and white kids wore hunting gear and cowboy boots and drove monster trucks with huge wheels. The spectrum was broad and utterly foreign to me.

Woodmont basketball was abominable. The local news made a spectacle of my arrival. I was regarded as the miracle that the school desperately needed. My new coach's enthusiasm said the same. I was in my first period class during the first week of school when he appeared at the door and politely asked the teacher if I could step outside.

"You're the transfer from Virginia," he said. "I'm Coach Morris. I've heard a lot about you from your former coach."

Once preseason practice started, I seized the spotlight that had belonged to two other seniors, Ronell the point guard and Twan the shooting guard. They had been the starting varsity duo since their freshman year. They were the Woodmont version of Marquel and me, but without our winning record. Ronell had been the high-scoring starting point guard since his freshman year, a notable achievement. We were all issued reversible white-and-blue jerseys, and Coach used these to separate us into teams for scrimmaging. The starting lineup always wore white. Ronell flipped his jersey to the white side as usual. I flipped my jersey to the blue side, but Coach said,

"Brandon, you take white." I obeyed his directive. "Ronell," Coach yelled, "you take blue." The whistle sounded for practice to begin.

The season started and we won one, then two, then three games in a row. Three consecutive wins is not typically breaking news, but it was for Woodmont. On December 26, 2007, a headline of the *Greenville News* read: "Fleming Tries to Keep Focus" as "Wildcats Improve to 3–0 in Western AAA Region Play." Reporter David Hood wrote, "Fleming was an artist at work. That he is able to run and fly around, almost lighter than air at times, is amazing considering the heavy heart that he has to carry around as he attempts to familiarize himself with a new school, new community and new teammates."

My face appeared on grocery-store newsstands, and my growing reputation became a topic of conversation. Aunt Carolyn drove me to the local barber shop and we took a seat to wait. The shop was full and rowdy as the men bantered about local sports, talking mostly about the usual regional giants like Southside and Greenville and J. L. Mann.

"I tell you what," a gentleman said, "y'all better watch out for Woodmont this year. Y'all heard about that new transfer?"

Not everyone knew my name, but many knew me as "the Woodmont transfer." I sat anonymous in my durag and street clothes, listening to the men debate. Aunt Carolyn could not contain her pride and yelled, "This is him!" as I covered my face in embarrassment. But inside, I smiled. It was the kind of embarrassing maternal gesture that I had coveted for years.

I struggled to fit in with the guys. Many of them resented me. If not for stealing the spotlight in basketball, for stealing the spotlight with girls. I was new, the opposite of what these girls were used to. I had a New York accent, northern swag, and a clean slate. In a sea of high school jocks that they scorned as jerks, they thought I was a good guy. And I used this to my advantage.

It started one Saturday at the school dance. The winter social could not have been timelier. We had just beaten Southside the night before. Southside was the bully of the region, the high school version of the Detroit Pistons during the "Bad Boys" era. They were big, strong, and hood. In past years, this would have been projected as a blowout and the stands would have been empty. But the gymnasium was filled to capacity with standing room only. People wanted to witness this reformed Woodmont team first-hand. And we won.

My teammates and I arrived at the dance fashionably late. Our grand entrance felt like a homecoming. Our victory over Southside elicited cheers that sounded like we had won a state championship. As we made our way toward the main floor, someone starting chanting, "V-A, V-A," and the crowd joined in chorus. "VA" was the nickname they had given me. I stopped and looked around the room, breathing in the claps and chants and cheers. The approving nods from the guys and the adoring smiles from the girls made me feel, for the first time, like the new school was home. I was ready to party.

My teammates and I lined up against the wall, each of us with one leg kicked up like we were posing for a boy-band album cover. Despite the joy of victory, the floor was empty. It was that awkward moment when no one wants to be the first to dance, so everyone stands around talking until the DJ plays a song that no one can resist.

Line dancing is less of a risk than pairing off, so when the DJ played "Cha-Cha Slide" and "Cupid Shuffle," people got on their feet and starting moving.

A few songs in, self-consciousness fell away when the DJ spun the iconic "Walk It Out" and "Crank That (Soulja Boy)" as everybody *Yooouuu*'d from the windows to the wall.

Then the air got thick. Heels were kicked off, skirts were hiked up, and the party escalated from family reunion to Freaknik. The DJ knew it was time to play the twerking song that would send the party through the roof: "Pop, Lock & Drop It" by Huey.

As soon as the prelude started, everybody yelled, "Ahhh, shit!" The wall cleared and everyone rushed to the dance floor. Through the fog, the effervescent floodlights silhouetted a curvaceous form advancing in my direction.

"She coming for you, dog!" my teammate said while shaking me by the shoulders. I played it cool, but I was breathless. It was Soraya, one of the most desirable girls in school. The prelude was rising and the beat was about to drop. Without an introduction, she grabbed my arm and pulled me onto the floor. There was only one problem: *real niggas* don't dance.

We arrived at the middle of the dance floor and the party was suddenly no longer fun for me. The glamorous "Woodmont transfer" was about to be exposed as a fraud. As soon as the beat dropped and Huey said, "Toot that thang up, mommy, make it roll," Soraya had both hands on her knees and started throwing and thrusting her hips back. She was a girl of shapely proportions—what the Commodores once called a "brick house." In other words, she had a lot back there to handle. I fought to keep my feet planted as she twerked lightly and I tried to guide my hips to follow hers, but her moves were too sophisticated.

Then the climax came: the chorus. The moment that every high school *ghetto girl* lived for. Everyone knew what was getting ready to happen. Once the song said, "Pop, lock and drop it" on loop, Soraya popped her hip to the left, locked her hip to the right, and dropped her booty to the floor and bounced back up with her hips rolling like a tide. The force sent me stumbling backward like a slow-motion sequence from *The Matrix*, and then I crashed to the floor. It felt like the DJ had stopped the music and everyone stared in silence. My teammates gave me a hand up, laughing and saying, "Damn, bro, she put that ass on you, didn't she!"

I did not want to show my face the next day of school. What was supposed to be a moment of celebration had turned out to be a moment of humiliation. I skulked the hallways trying to avoid eye contact with anyone. Without looking, I felt sure that everyone I passed pointed and mocked me.

I sat by myself during lunch, hoping to avoid any rehashing of that dreadful night. As I ate my bland cafeteria food and sipped my juice carton in silence, a girl's voice disturbed my self-imposed exile.

"Hi," she said. I turned to let the girl know that I wanted to be alone. But I was suddenly stunned and mute. It was Soraya.

"Do you mind if I sit here?" she asked, having already dropped into a seat. We talked about the other night. I confessed that I did not know how to dance. She laughed and assured me that it was okay. She saw it as a gateway to flirt with me.

"You must be a virgin," she said as she looked at me and smiled in pity. I sat appalled, thinking, *Virgin? Did she just call me a fuckin' virgin? Does she know who I am? I'm a real ass nigga!*

Then she continued, "It's okay. Virgins need love, too," as she placed one hand on my thigh. Then I thought, *Wait a minute . . .*

And I responded, "Yes, actually, I am."

She talked about salacious things that I claimed to know nothing about. Things that she wanted to teach me. And a few days later, I let her be my instructor and I was her student. I could not believe that it actually worked.

Soon after, I was at a lunch table with a group of girls. A conversation about sex came up. They talked of things they had done. They talked of things they wanted to do. I decided to see if an unlikely gambit would work twice.

"Yeah, I don't know about any of that," I said. "I'm a virgin."

"A virgin?" they exclaimed. One girl said it was cute, another said it was adorable, and another said, "So I would be your first?" We laughed it off, but I sensed a hint of sincerity in her joke. Weeks later, she took my virginity, too.

This reverse-psychology approach worked until senior prom. I was Bill Bellamy in the *How to Be a Player* scene when he finessed his way through a party full of his secret lovers. Except I did not make it out with a face as clean as his. When a posse of deceived and disgruntled girls compared notes and arrived at the truth, Soraya, the most infuriated of all, volunteered to act on behalf of the group. When prom night ended, she left me with a black eye, a busted lip, and a kick in the nuts.

I was on my way to becoming an NCAA Division I athlete. We continued winning and reporters wrote about colleges that were scouting me, including Furman and Liberty Universities.

My days as a troublemaker were over, in most ways. Coach made it clear that legal infractions and school suspensions would threaten my recruitment. And so could low grades. But my academic apathy continued. I did not need to be a good student. My grades were padded by teachers who thought they were doing me a favor by keeping me on the court. I was in IB classes and had no idea how they'd gotten on my schedule. I didn't even know what IB meant. If I turned in homework, it was because a girlfriend did it for me. In classes, I napped. And I still passed with good grades, though I slept through the final exams.

I had one open block before my last period class. I left school during that block and often did not make it back for the final class, which threatened my game-day eligibility. Eligibility rules said that we had to be present for more than half the school day in order to play in games. Coach intervened by taking what had been my open block and filling it with a student assistantship for a teacher named Mr. Mills.

On my first day of what was supposedly work, Coach personally escorted me to Mills's social studies class. "Thank you for taking him," Coach said. "I need to keep him out of trouble." I petulantly pressed past Mills without meeting his eyes or shaking his hand. I was too grown to be babysat, and I hated losing my one free period. Every day I flopped on the beanbag in the back of the classroom and lounged, occasionally removing my headphones to flirt with the girls in the back row. I was more of a student distraction than a teacher assistant. Mills gave me a score key and stacks of quizzes that went ungraded.

Then my MP3 player died and my only option was listening to Mills's lesson on leadership and life habits. He talked about social skills and finance management and taxes. I cringed at his enumeration of all the taxes awaiting me in adulthood. I did not know that there were more taxes beyond the few cents extra the corner store added to the cost of an Arizona iced tea and a bag of chips.

Something about Mills made me actually want to pay attention to his words. For starters, he didn't look like the square-ass male teachers in wash-weary polos, oversized khakis, and all-white New Balances. Mills was a Black man. He was fashionable, personable, powerful even. He walked with swag and wore tailored suits and patterned bow ties, and his baritone voice was as commanding as his towering stature. Students leaned into his every word. I had never seen a teacher hold the attention of teens without spewing threats of failing grades and after-school detentions. He used fancy words that everyone nodded at but surely did not understand. A student raised his hand and said, "Ayo, Mills, what dat mean?" and Mills chuckled in delight. Mills was the type of teacher whose charisma was so infectious that students accepted tardies to their next class just to share one more laugh with him after the bell rang. Everybody loved him. Even I was impressed. But he was a teacher. Therefore, he was my enemy.

Mills asked to speak with me after class one day. I expected him to confront me about the quizzes I hadn't scored, or my disruptive back-row commentary, or the loud music leaking from my headphones. Instead, he just wanted to talk, but not about school or basketball. He didn't ask the standard question, "So, what do you want to do in life?" He wanted to get to know me. The real me that no one else had ever really asked about.

It was odd having a teacher probe into my personal life. He asked about my family and I opened up about the pain of being separated from my siblings and waiting around for that monthly phone call from my mother telling me that she was still alive. He asked about my father and I confessed that we weren't on speaking terms. I was uncomfortable with this level of vulnerability, but there was something about Mills that made me feel safe. Though we had just met, he looked at me like he knew me, like I was his son. I had talked to other Black men, of course, but never like this. He seemed to be the only one who did not want something from me. My friends back home wanted me to get out of the streets and do something with my life. My father wanted me to bring honor to his family name. My coaches wanted me to become their next success story. My teachers wanted to pass me on to the next unlucky instructor. Mills wanted to know who was hiding behind the grimace and durag and sagging jeans.

"Aight, enough about me," I said. "I got a question for you."

Over an hour had passed and it was almost time for me to head to basketball practice. But I could not go until I asked him the question burning inside me.

"Go ahead. What you got?" he invited.

"Yo, straight up . . . how do you talk like that?" I asked.

Mills burst out laughing and asked, "Talk like what?"

I sucked my teeth and said, "Man, you know what I mean. Like, you be using all them fancy words and shit." I firmed my tone so he knew that I was serious, and I continued, "How do you talk like that? I'm tryna peep game."

"Well," Mills said, "I read—"

I interrupted. "So you telling me if I read a couple books, I can talk like that, too?"

Mills was so tickled that he nearly fell from his chair. "It's not that simple, son," he said, trying to contain his amusement.

I looked at him with a blank face, because I was serious. I needed answers. Girls paid attention to him in a way they did not pay attention to other teachers, and I knew it had something to do with those fancy words.

"You laughing, but I'm serious," I said. "You be sounding all poetic and shit. I'm tryna talk like that, too. You know . . . for the ladies."

He toned down the chuckling and gave me a straight answer, whether I deserved one or not. "I used to be an English major in college," he said. "My vocabulary is a result of my studies." I made a mental note and thanked him as I rushed to grab my things and head to practice.

Recruitment letters were coming in from colleges throughout the South. I was sitting in class when Coach's face appeared in the door's window.

"Must be for you, Brandon," my civics teacher said. "Make it quick."

I went into the hall and Coach handed me letters from Lander University, Furman University, and Liberty University, each inviting me to their recruitment camp. It was late in the basketball season and I needed to nail down firm offers and make a choice. The clock was ticking.

Years of playing with explosive force was taking a toll on my knees. I'd developed patellar tendonitis, also known as jumper's knee. From middle school, I'd trained to jump higher than everyone on the court to compensate for my lack of height. I was only five foot seven at the time but I could leap above six-footers to dunk the ball. During practice, teammates would always say, "Yo, Brandon, do that windmill!" and I'd charge toward the basket at full speed and power up as the momentum sent me rising and I slammed so hard that the rim would rattle. Now my knees were wearing down and those high-flying days were numbered.

In the semifinals of the state championship tournament we faced Daniel High School, a team we had beaten during the regular season. The face-off was in the huge gym at J. L. Mann High School, and the stands were packed with fans who had come to see two of the top point guards in the conference battle until the end. The tournament was single elimination. My focus was keen, knowing that if we won, we would head to the championship. But if we lost, my high school glory days were over.

From the tip-off to the fourth quarter, the game was neck and neck. About three minutes remained on the clock. As I brought the ball up the court, Coach noticed that I was limping. He looked at me and tapped his knee, asking if I was all right. I waved him off and called our "Carolina" play. I wanted the iso. I glanced at the shot clock and stalled because we were up two points. My teammates cleared the path so I could face my defender one-on-one. I hit my opponent with a combination of crossovers as I charged to the basket and leaped toward the rim, but I came crashing down on the floor, holding my knee and holding back a scream. Before Coach could dash onto the floor, I jumped up and started running back on defense. On the sideline, I saw Coach grab our second-string point guard and push him toward the scoring table. I thought, *No, no, don't do it. You can't take me out. Not now.*

Austin came running onto the floor and said, "I got you, bro."

I limped to the bench and yelled, "Coach, what are you doing? You can't take me out right now!"

He sat me down and said, "Listen to me, son. You have a college career waiting on you, and I am not about to let you blow that knee in this game." But I didn't care about that. I wasn't thinking about the future. I was thinking about now. We had a championship game to reach. I had a team to lead and a legacy to leave. From my seat, I begged a few more times for Coach to let me back in. He ignored my pleas. My high school career was in the hands of my teammates and we were now down by two. Everyone on the bench and in the stands stood in anticipation. Only seconds remained. Austin pulled up for the three-point shot to put us up by one. He missed. We lost. And my high school career was over.

I could not forgive Coach or my body for failing me that day. But I had to shift my focus toward my college decision. It came down to Furman and Liberty. Furman's recruitment camp was a few weeks out, which gave the inflammation in my knee time to calm down.

I had not seen or spoken to Coach Stevens in nearly four years. I was eager to reunite with the man who ignited my desire to play in the NCAA. I could not wait for him to see how I had evolved from a rising freshman into a high-flying senior. I was eager to show him that I had kept my promise to consider Furman.

It was my first time playing in a college arena. I glanced around wide-eyed and in awe of the locker room alone. It was glamorous and the walls were plastered with the team logo and graphics and action shots from games. The lockers glowed with lighting and they shamed our high school's rusted, hickory-colored cubbies. These were personalized with each player's name and jersey number. I let my fingers glide slowly across the inscription on a placard, imagining that it said FLEMING #15.

We gathered in the center of the arena to begin the session, nearly fifty recruits from schools across the country. Some players' eyes were locked on to the coaches giving us orders for the day. Some of us exchanged cursory glares. It was every man for himself. We were rivals converging on a battlefield—each man fighting to be seen, fighting to be respected, fighting to have a scholarship bestowed upon him.

One of the assistant coaches gave us a pep talk about each of us being chosen for a reason. Then he said, "Now please welcome our coach of the Furman men's basketball team." We clapped and I smirked, knowing that my earlier encounter with the coaching staff gave me an advantage over the other guys. I knew he would remember me and put me at the top of his list. Then my clapping slowed and slackened because the man who took center court looked nothing like Coach Stevens.

"Good morning," he said. "And welcome to Furman University men's basketball."

He asked us to bring it in and we all extended our hands. He said a few final words and we broke for the baseline. I nudged one of the coaches on my way.

"Hey, Coach," I said. "Is Coach Stevens here today?"

He responded, "Coach Stevens has transitioned. Now hit the baseline."

My mouth dropped and my adrenaline rush subsided. I had no special advantage over the other recruits. It dawned on me that I had not even checked the name on the letter that came to me from the Furman basketball office. I'd assumed that it was Coach Stevens summoning me to make good on my promise from freshman year. I tried to shake it off and ran to the baseline to begin warm-ups.

When scrimmaging began, the intensity accelerated fast as we clashed like bloodthirsty brutes. There were no referees, only coaches with folded arms and wide stances, looking for the fittest to survive. Whistles hung from their mouths, but they were seldom used. The game reminded me of the time my varsity coach called no fouls during practice to see how close we'd come to taking each other's heads off. The court started to feel like a blacktop, and I could not be stopped.

Suddenly, my moment to shine presented itself. I was on a left-wing fast break, charging toward the goal from half-court. I saw a clear path, the rim, and a nearly seven-foot defender parallel on the other side, determined not to let me score. He saw himself pinning my shot on the glass. I saw him becoming the victim on my next slam-dunk poster. We met at the basket, leaped at the same time, and converged in midair. He stretched both of his hands high to the sky as I cocked the ball back out of his reach. It felt like we were soaring in slow motion, then his body started to descend as I continued to levitate. On his way down, his arms clipped my legs. In midair, my body flipped upside down until my eyes were staring at the hardwood. I dove and crashed face-first. I hit the court with violent force, splitting my eye at the brow and busting my bottom lip in half. I lay, concussed, in a puddle of my own blood. With my head ringing, I could hear the distant voice of my brother and my cousins in New York yelling for me to get my *bitch ass* up. But this time, I couldn't. The coaches rushed toward me yelling, "Call an ambulance!"

I woke up in a hospital bed with one eye nearly sealed shut and wires protruding from my swollen lip. It took about ten stitches to sew it back together. I turned my head to the right and saw my uncle sitting beside me, waiting for me to regain consciousness.

"You all right, buddy?" he asked.

"I'm fine," I responded. "Did I at least make the shot?"

He laughed and said, "No, but that was one heck of a dunk you tried."

I lay back and rested my head. I was so numb that I could not feel any pain. The nurse came in to let us know that we were almost cleared to go.

"Can I still play?" I asked the nurse. She was taken aback, considering the circumstance, that I would ask to play with a busted face.

"No, son," my uncle interjected. "You need to rest up."

But I did not want to hear that. I was at a pivotal moment in my career and I could not let an injury block my way forward. I had to get back out there. I grew up a streetballer and I had been through worse. I'd been thrown to the asphalt. I'd played with blood streaming down my face, feeling no pain because that is what *real niggas* do.

The next morning, I got to the Furman gym where training was already underway. Whistles were blowing and drills were running when I pushed through the doors at the top of the arena. I was dressed to play and descended the stadium stairs. My right eye was half-shut and wires protruded from my lip like whiskers, but my face was stone with determination. I was halfway down the stands when the coach looked up and saw me. He blew the whistle for everyone to stop. No one expected to see me again, and by the time I reached courtside, the coaching staff and the recruits were clapping to welcome me back. Coach examined my face and said, "Are you sure that you can play?" I looked at him and said, "I don't have another choice." He smiled and patted me on the back of the head. Then he said, "Hit the baseline."

In the end, I did not choose Furman. It was also likely that Furman would not have chosen me, due to my transcript. My overall high school GPA was low and I scored in the lower percentile of the SAT. My best chance for playing Division I basketball was to find a school with more forgiving academic requirements. I chose Liberty.

I'd first heard about Liberty's basketball program from my high school coach, who had been a player there decades before. He pitched me to Coach Dunton and the coaching staff, and we'd courted each other for a few years. I'd visited the campus to meet the coaching staff and team and enjoyed the five-star treatment. Given this, I was puzzled when I was invited to a recruitment camp but there was no official offer. I soon discovered that Coach Dunton had moved on and a new coach was on his way from another university with a fleet of his own high school recruits. Among them was Seth Curry, younger brother of Steph Curry, the future NBA Hall of Famer. We were both guards, which dramatically reduced my chances for a scholarship. Staff members who'd previously worked for Coach Dunton, however, kept advocating for me. And that's why I got a chance to compete for a position at recruitment camp.

I arrived at camp determined to prove myself. I was not intimidated. I had already committed to Liberty for the fall semester, confident that I would earn my position on the team. My performance at camp would ascertain a scholarship. This was my plan.

Training camp started in early August a few weeks before classes. I signed up for courses only if they were compatible with the basketball team's practice schedule, never doubting that I would be on the team. My aunt drove me four hours from Greenville to Lynchburg, Virginia, for the week-long camp. I was ready. And I carried a chip on my shoulder knowing that this coach did not want me as much as the former coach did.

I planned to challenge Seth the first chance I got. But guarding him was a lot more difficult than it looked. He could shoot from just a few steps beyond half-court. And if you decided to play him close, he could blow by you with one jab step or hesitation.

Then the time came to show them what I could do. I had just plucked the ball from my opponent and was charging toward the goal on a fast break. No one was in my path. It was just me and the goal, a perfect opportunity to showcase my high-flying ability. All eyes were centered on me as

I exploded toward the basket. But as I gathered my feet and powered up to take flight, I felt an excruciating tear in my left knee and went crashing to the floor. It was supposed to be a slam dunk. But it turned out to be the end of my career.

"You can try again next year," one of the coaches said. I limped out of the gym to be carried back home. I was damaged goods. And with no scholarship offer, I was expendable. My aunt tried to comfort me, but I was a stone wall. I stared out the window in silence as we made the four-hour drive back home. My future was derailed and I had reached a dead end. Doctors said surgery was not necessary and my knee would heal on its own. But time proved otherwise: my tendon eventually ripped so severely that my kneecap was dislodged, requiring emergency surgery. After ten years of thriving on the court, it was all over. I lost my passion. I lost my purpose. I lost my identity. I had nothing left but school.

That I was in college was a miracle itself. But I was eighteen years old and had stepped into a world I knew nothing about. I had not learned a thing since middle school, or before. I had never read an entire book. I did not know how to write essays. I knew nothing about thesis statements or citing sources. My SAT scores were so low that I was put into remedial, 100-level English and math courses. Even those were hard for me.

Here's the irony: I was a thuggish young man attending the largest ultra-conservative evangelical Christian university in the world. I was clearly an outsider stuck in what felt like a religious dystopia. Worse than the academic requirements were the social ones, also known as "The Liberty Way." At most colleges, the list of offenses that will get you kicked out is relatively short: don't plagiarize, don't harm people, don't harm yourself—more or less. But not at Liberty. Here, the code of conduct banned everything from alcohol to tobacco and premarital sex—both on campus and off. So if I happened to be a twenty-one-year-old senior and school leadership discovered that I enjoyed a cigarette, beer, or sex with my girlfriend ten miles away from campus, I would still face reprimands, fines, and the possibility of expulsion. Girls and boys could not visit each other's dorms. Grown-ass students were not allowed to use profanity, watch R-rated movies, or even play M-rated video games. Curfew required us to be in our dorms by 10 p.m. If we wanted to leave for the night, we had to sign out and tell our resident assistant exactly where we were going and provide a contact to confirm. If that was not enough to ensure that we stayed on the straight and narrow, chapel attendance was mandatory every other day. I wondered to myself whether doing all this would get GOOD CHRISTIAN stamped on our diplomas when we graduated.

The one positive thing that happened to me that semester was no positive thing at all. I was introduced to politics, which was good. The circumstances, however, were not. Years of sleeping in government class left me clueless about what it meant to be a citizen. I knew only four things about politics: a white man's presidential term was ending, a Black man was running, I ain't know shit about him, but I planned to vote for that *nigga*.

Even those of us who cared nothing about Barack Obama wanted him to win. I did not know what policies he stood for. I did not know his voting record in the Illinois Senate. I knew he was a Democrat, but all I knew about Democrats was that they seemed less racist than Republicans. Many of us approached Election Day with such hope, eager to tell our descendants that we watched America elect its first Black president. I only regret that we were at Liberty University when it happened, because the atmosphere was full of tension.

On November 4, 2008, we gathered in Vines Center to watch the election results stream on the Jumbotron. Many of us did not feel safe. Some even feared for their lives as the campus erupted in civil unrest.

Barack Obama's election struck deep chords everywhere in the United States, of course, but it resonated with us in a particular way. In a 2007 article in *The Nation* magazine, a reporter writes about Jerry Falwell Sr., Liberty University's founder, crusading against civil rights and publicly denouncing the *Brown v. Board of Education* decision that outlawed segregation in public schools. The article quotes Falwell preaching to his congregation and declaring from the pulpit, "The facilities should be separate.

When God has drawn a line of distinction, we should not attempt to cross that line." That line, of course, was the color line. "The true Negro," he continued, "does not want integration. . . . He realizes that his potential is far better among his own race."

It is also said that the Baptist minister wanted Black people nowhere near his new segregation academy in 1967. Although this might seem an inherently un-Christian stance, Falwell used scripture to bolster his prejudices. Falwell founded the Moral Majority, a prominent American right-wing political organization devoted to upholding Christian values in government while skipping the part about all of us being born equal as children of God. Many racist Christians who share this belief trace their defense of segregation to the tenth chapter of Genesis. The sons of Noah, in their view, were the progenitors of distinct ancestries. They believe that Europeans are the descendants of Japheth, who are God's chosen people, and that Africans are descendants of Ham, whose lineage was cursed by Noah and given black skin as punishment.

In fairness, it is also said that Falwell eventually disavowed these racist beliefs. But it's hard to imagine that any institution with those origins could ever truly purge itself of a prejudice that is cultural, codified, and systemic. While reformation is possible with new management, new policies, new practices, it seemed that the seeds of racism were dormant in the soil of that institution. And in due time at Liberty, those seeds began to sprout like weeds through a manicured ground cover of superficial tolerance. Those weeds pushed their way into view on election night.

Black students held Obama signs. White peers snatched and ripped them to shreds.

Black students cheered with joy. White students protested with rage.

Black students taunted whites. White students slung slurs in response.

Black McCain supporters hid. White Obama supporters hid, too.

A white guy reportedly prowled the campus with a chain saw, yelling, "Run, nigger, run!"

A friend said she and a girlfriend were followed through town by white men chanting, "Niggers get lynched in Lynchburg."

Black students were beaten.

White students were assaulted.

Black. White. That night, that's all we were.

The night felt like *The Purge*. It was a public display of moral abandonment—at the largest evangelical Christian university in the entire world. One of my former professors describes the election result as having "divided our campus in the same way the O.J. Simpson verdict once divided our nation."

The air was thick the next day. It was as quiet as a ghost town. Some students wore all black to symbolize the death of America. Chalk inscriptions on the sidewalks read, "Obama's America . . . we're NOT gonna take it!" People called Obama the Antichrist. Classrooms and cafeterias were so somber that it felt like someone had died. Most classes continued. But some classes were canceled by professors who were stricken with Republican grief. I heard about one math teacher who tried to press past her tears but dismissed class after a few minutes because the weight of Obama's win was simply too devastating to bear. The color divide was wider than the Red Sea, and it would take a miracle of biblical proportion to part.

I was displaced at a predominantly white institution. Growing up, all I knew was Black people, basketball, and *real nigga shit*. I did not know anything about the academics they were teaching or the politics I was experiencing at this school. All I knew was that my heart hurt. We were not even allowed to hang Obama posters on the walls, yet the hallways were adorned with Republican propaganda. I could not understand why they hated this man so much. Was he that evil? Were his policies that threatening? Or was he just Black?

It all confirmed what I had already known: college was no place for me. At the end of it all, I said, *Fuck this lame-ass school shit.* Especially since I could no longer play ball. I accepted the withdrawals and Fs on my transcript. I packed my belongings and went back to Greenville. I was relieved at the thought that I would never have to suffer through school again.

"I love you," Aunt Carolyn said, "but if you ain't in school, you can't stay here." I understood. Plus, the house was crowded with her own grown children and little grandchildren. There was certainly no room for me. So I found other couches to sleep on. I migrated from house to house until my friends' parents tossed me out the front door like Jazz in *The Fresh Prince of Bel-Air*. I was on my own, adapting to life as a college dropout and struggling to make a living. Pyramid schemes made me a fraud. A call-center job lasted only a few weeks. Then the temp agency placed me on an assembly line at the vitamin factory where my life became an endless cycle of monotony and despair.

I lost hope. I needed help. I was losing my mind and using unhealthy ways to cope. I turned back to drugs after being clean for nearly two years. I was lower than I had ever been. It felt like my face was mashed against the asphalt. I prayed the mantras of my cousins and brother and told myself to get my *bitch ass* up. But I couldn't.

When I dropped out of college, I had lost my golden ticket, the only path to a better life. When I walked off the vitamin factory job, I could see no future at all for myself. I stared down into a dark abyss of depression, and instead of reaching for a steadying hand, I reached for the pills that promised relief. I was ready to die.

When I woke up in the hospital, I could not tell my mom what I had done. I was too ashamed. Aunt Carolyn broke the news to her, and when she called, I did not want to answer. I wanted to avoid the break in her voice and the silence after she asked, "Are you okay?" I said yes. But I was not.

I wanted to hide from her preachy platitudes about going to church and getting right with God. He could not fix her. So how could he fix me?

I dreaded the soft and coddling voice she would use because she thought her usual no-nonsense tone would fracture my fragile spirit. "I'm not crazy," I told her—the same way I told the nurse during the in-patient psychiatric assessment.

I did not want my mom's compassion. I did not want her religion. I just wanted to die, because dying seemed so much easier than living.

"Come back home," she said. She felt so sorry for me that she was willing to break her rule against housing her grown-ass children. Mom was back in the DMV, adjusting to life as a veteran and struggling to manage Ben. For years, he'd paid attention and absorbed all the *real nigga shit* that my cousins taught me. He was a *real nigga* of his own, and my mother was defeated by the continuation of a family cycle.

"I can't, Mom," I said. "There's not even enough room for me there with you and Ben." I could not let my mother take care of me. The pinch of pride that I had left would not allow it. She had retired from the army, she didn't have a job, and she was taking care of herself and Ben in a tiny two-bedroom apartment. There was no honor in living on my mother's couch. I would sponge off friends again before doing that.

I told her that I was fine, but she knew otherwise. Her failures and my own were tangled together like a nest of snakes. For years, she had beaten herself up, wrestling with her past decisions and the lasting consequences for her children. A part of me resented her. Why couldn't she have done better for me? Why couldn't she have done better for us? I looked at former basketball teammates who were now thriving in college because their parents had given them stable homes and family dinners and expectations of good grades and allowance and an inheritance and a good fucking credit score. *Look at me now*, I thought, *because Mom didn't give us any of that shit*. It seemed like all I had inherited was trauma from the toxic people that she'd put around me. She knew this, too. And though she could not change the past, she made a sacrifice that would change the trajectory of my future.

"I want you to go back to school," Mom said.

"Mom, you know I can't go back to school," I replied, annoyed at the suggestion.

I did not just drop out; my transcript was decorated with Fs and Ws. This meant no financial aid for me. No one in my family could afford tuition. And even if they could, my track record did not make me a promising investment. Going back to school would take a miracle. A miracle that suddenly appeared.

"I want you to use my GI Bill," Mom said.

"Your what?" I asked.

She explained that the GI Bill enables veterans to receive a free education after discharge or retirement. Like my mother, many veterans struggle to find jobs—and this benefit makes it possible for them to earn a degree and start a new life after the military. Alternatively, they can choose to transfer these benefits to their children. I could not believe what Mom was saying. She was willing to give up her second chance so that I might have one.

"No, Mom, I can't do that," I said, knowing that Mom had no path after retirement. She had no passions, limited skills, and needed an education to find work. The GI Bill was her only chance at a better life. It was her golden ticket.

"You are my son," she said. "I need you to take this, please."

Tears welled in my eyes. I did not want to do it. It did not feel right. But I remembered regaining consciousness in that hospital bed, bristling with tubes and wires, gazing at the ceiling half-blinded by tears, making a promise to myself and to God. I knew I'd broken promises to God before: in the high school bathroom stall, encounters with the police, and many times thereafter. But this time I was desperate. I promised God that if I was ever given another opportunity, I would take it. I would run faster than I had ever run before. On that hospital bed, I'd prayed for a miracle. The miracle had happened. She was on the other end of the phone, waiting for me to say yes. After all that we had been through, my mother was my miracle. She became my golden ticket.

CHAPTER SEVEN

RENAISSANCE IN ME

I returned to college with far more ambition than agency. I had a new-found sense of self and a passion to succeed, but the academic knowledge of a middle schooler. I was a convalescent suicide survivor, grappling with mental instability. I did not know where to begin. But I was eager.

Liberty was all I had known. And after slaving on a factory assembly line, reading books, writing essays—abiding by "The Liberty Way" didn't sound so bad. I was simply grateful that they'd taken me back. When I met with my academic advisor, he fingered through my transcript with a look of concern. "You have a semester full of Fs and Ws," he said. I explained that I'd withdrawn from school and dropped out a few years back. He scrolled through my record on the screen. I hardly had a GPA, and my status read "Academic Warning," meaning I could not afford any more failed grades or withdrawals.

This was my second time around and I had to start over as a fresh-man. "We'll have to put you in CLST and 100-level courses," he said. The

College Learning Strategies course was designed for students needing academic intervention.

"Why is that?" I asked.

He answered, "For remediation."

"Remediation?" I yelped, rearing back in disbelief. I felt disrespected. In my high school days, that was a curse word. My teammates and I bullied the nerdy, bookish kids by calling them "remedial." We'd give them wedgies, stuff them in trash cans, trip them in the hallway and yell, "Get your *remedial* ass up!" The joke was on me, apparently. It dawned on me that I had no clue what the word actually meant. I thought *remedial* described someone that was lame or corny or a *bitch ass nigga*. Now I was being called remedial by a Steve Urkel–looking white man, the archetype for the nerds I had once tormented out of ignorance. I could do nothing but shake my head and stare at the floor, amused at how the tables turn.

"What'll be your concentration?" he asked.

"My what?"

He leaned in closer. "Your major . . ."

"Ohhh," I said. "What's that?"

I didn't know anything about concentrations or majors. I knew Concentration was a hand game we played when I was a kid, and I knew *mid-major* and *high major* in terms of NCAA lingo. But that was it. Outside of basketball and street shit, I had no clue what to study or what I wanted to be. I could not recall anyone ever asking what I wanted to be professionally, besides my uncle during his occasional attempts to talk sense into me. But I'd respond, "I just wanna run these streets, Unc," as he sighed in distress. I hadn't thought any further than that until now. But one thing was certain: I never wanted to return to that hellhole vitamin factory or anything remotely like it.

Now this nerdy-looking man was pressuring me to decide what I wanted to study for the next four years. But I did not know. Each of us was increasingly annoyed with the other. He was exasperated by my ignorance. And I was tired of listening to him talk white, saying "Yes" instead of "Yeah" and "Excuse me?" instead of "What?" and ending words with hard *ers*.

He showed me a list of majors. My hands felt clammy because I had no idea what some of the words even meant. Terms such as *biomedical science*, *civil engineering*, and *informatics* were as incomprehensible to me as Chinese characters. I was too embarrassed to ask for more information, and to save face I pretended to think rationally and intently about each option.

"Hmm . . . no, not that one," I muttered. "Oh. Eh. Nah."

I stroked my chin thoughtfully as I moved down the list, but his impatience was rising. I felt rushed by the way he cleared his throat. The clock kept ticking. The words on the page were scattering and spiraling into a cyclone of confusion. I leaned closer, skimmed with a finger, and pronounced each word phonetically to show that I was giving each one due consideration. Finally, I landed on a word I recognized, and—*bingo!*—I knew that I had found it. My anxiety waned. A burden was lifted. My fate was decided. I was satisfied that I had discovered the easiest major of all: English.

I walked out of the office thinking, *I speak English, so this will be a breeze!* Plus, I remembered my conversation with Mills—the one high school teacher I respected—when he said that studying English made him a compelling speaker. I grew excited thinking about how the fancy words he used made all of the girls pay attention. My romance game was about to reach the stratosphere. These college girls weren't ready for some *real nigga shit* couched in poetic language, to be swept off their feet and wooed with the elocution of a reformed ghetto Shakespeare. Those were my intentions, until I entered the classroom and quickly discovered that Shakespeare was no friend of mine.

I wish someone had told me what being an English major actually involved. Mills left out the parts about expository writing and literary criticism and six-hundred-page books. As soon as I entered the classroom, impostor syndrome stepped out from behind the door and whacked me in the face with a cudgel. I felt like a peasant in the presence of Shakespeare and Homer and Hemingway and the literary elite. I kept silent to avoid shame, but anyone could see that I did not look like an English major. I was more out of place than the Black girl who scowled at the use of slang, or the Black guy who wore khaki shorts with open-toed sandals. I looked even more anomalous than the goth girl with black fingernails, black clothes, black boots, and a black cape. Imagine that.

My classmates and I could not have been more different. No matter what style they affected, these were mostly high achievers, mostly white and evangelical and privileged. Many came from places where they had little interaction with Black people. And here I sat, a former drug dealer turned ball player turned dropout, fulfilling every Black stereotype they could have imagined.

I listened to the class conversations thinking, *What the fuck are they talking about? Why does everyone look so weird?* and *This poem makes no fuckin' sense!* I was ready to throw in the towel when my professor assigned one hundred pages of Dante's *Inferno* to be read over the weekend. I thought, *Who the fuck reads a hundred pages in three nights?* As soon as I read "Midway upon the journey of our life, I found myself within a forest dark, for the straightforward pathways had been lost," I said, *Oh hell nah, they got me fucked up!* and slammed the book shut. Then the professor asked in a soft, dramatic voice, "And what does the dark forest symbolize?" My face scrunched up as I thought, *The fuck? It means the forest was fuckin' dark!* As for passing those dreadful quizzes, I had a better chance of borrowing the goth girl's cape and using it as a cloak of invisibility. But I remembered my conversation with my advisor. "One more fail or withdrawal," he said, "and you could be done." So I turned to the only mechanism that might help me survive: cheating.

I was tired of being the dumb Black kid. I knew I wasn't as smart as the rest of them. And so did they. A peek through the door of our English class and you'd spot me like the proverbial black sheep in a flock of snowy ewes, sulking silently in the back corner, rap music leaking from the headphones that defiantly plugged my ears. The cord fell down the side of my T-shirt, grazed the floor at the heel of my Timbs, and looped up into the pocket of my bootcut jeans.

I'd jot down character names and quick facts from SparkNotes on facial tissue. During quizzes, I pretended to blow my nose for a quick glance at my cheat sheet. For papers, I paraphrased peer-reviewed essays I found on JSTOR, hoping to outwit the software that automatically scanned our written submissions for plagiarism. For class discussions, however, I had nothing. Classes were small, which made my silence glaringly obvious. Like that inglorious moment when I fumbled William Faulkner.

"Of the themes you all have identified in 'A Rose for Emily,'" my professor said, "which appear to be most consistent?" Then her gaze fell on me as she said, "I'd love to hear from those of you who haven't shared yet."

There were eight of us, and I was the only one who had not said a word. My seven classmates sat in the front row, jumping in with comments on everything we read, and behind them were five rows of unoccupied desks. I sat alone in the back row, slow to realize that my isolation made my failure to participate even more obvious.

"Brandon?" she prompted.

I glanced up from my iPod. Heads swiveled and all eyes were on me.

"I'm sorry," I said, "can you repeat the question?"

I'd heard clearly but needed extra time to find words to hide the fact that I had not read the short story.

"Faulkner's themes," she answered. "Which do you think were the most consistent throughout the piece?"

This English-major jargon didn't make sense to me and I sat through every class feeling like the others were speaking a foreign language.

"I agree with what she said." I couldn't remember her name, so I pointed at the eerie-looking girl in the front row.

"And what did she say?" the professor probed with suspicion.

I hadn't actually heard what the goth girl said, so I abandoned my initial tactic and took a shot in the dark.

"I think it's about love," I mumbled. "The rose." The way it came out jumbled made my statement sound like a question.

"Perhaps it could be." Her suspicion hardened into certainty. "But how would you justify that, considering the story is about death?"

Fuck, I thought. I squinted my eyes and flipped through the puckered printout, turning pages frantically to create the illusion that I was searching for a rebuttal. Or so I thought. My professor was visibly irritated, sitting on the desk, her crossed leg jiggling, her blue eyes peering over her winged glasses, her skeletal fingers clasped at her pelvis. My professor didn't budge as she patiently awaited an explanation. When I gave none, whispers and chuckles broke the interminable and awkward silence. I became a joke, an object of ridicule, and the affirmation of a Black stereotype.

My face contorted. My head sunk with shame. I had never felt so inferior. The discussion continued, but I was excluded by my own incompetence. I felt low, displaced. I had no voice. And as a result, I was invisible.

I couldn't sit there any longer. I reached for my bag and quietly slipped through the door. By the time I reached my apartment, an email had landed in my inbox. The subject: We Need to Meet ASAP. I had no idea that my life was about to change.

Crossing campus to DeMoss Hall, it felt like I was walking the green mile. A marble fountain guards the giant four-story edifice. Roman columns tower above an Olympian staircase ascending to an imposing entranceway. Once inside, it took me a minute to find the offices for the English and Modern Languages faculty, which were tucked away in a side hallway behind an anonymous double door. I walked the main hall of this building nearly every day, but I had never noticed the faculty offices. Nor had I ever looked at the wall of display cases filled with trophies or read the four words emblazoned above the exhibit: LIBERTY UNIVERSITY DEBATE CENTER. It meant nothing to me.

When Professor Nelson saw me at the open door of her office, she gestured toward a chair that was perhaps the only uncluttered surface in the room. Huge bookcases were crammed with shabby paperbacks and pristine hardbacks, and unsteady stacks of books rose from the floor like a city skyline. Her desk was littered with typewritten pages bleeding red ink, empty coffee mugs rested on stained napkins, and a formal, gold-framed portrait of what must have been her family looked disapprovingly down at the mess.

After I sat and shucked off my backpack, she reached into a laptop bag and extracted a sheaf of double-spaced pages with my name at the top. She slid the sheets toward me and let silence settle for a minute.

"Did you write this?" she asked. Her tone was calm, not accusatory, leaving the door open to candor. I considered my next lie, thumbing through the pages before nudging them back to a neutral position. "Yes, ma'am," I said.

Time froze as various scenarios played in my mind. She might pick up the essay and say, "Brandon, this is superb!" Or maybe she'd turn sarcastic and say, "You sure fooled me; there's no way I could have ever detected that you stole this peer-reviewed essay from JSTOR." But she did neither. Instead, she set the essay aside, as if it was not the most important matter. She looked calmly at me, her elbows resting on the desk and her fingers interlaced. She leaned forward and said, "I want to know more about you."

Minutes passed and it was as though the essay was forgotten. She asked about my family, my aspirations, my struggles. Not as though she was interrogating me, but as though she cared to know. As we talked, my lie lingering unattended between us, I felt my wall of wariness begin to crack. But I didn't recant.

In the course of an hour, we exchanged tears, laughter, and promises. She was vulnerable with me: she told me about having surgery for cancer. I was vulnerable with her: I told her about my history of drugs and violence. She made me feel safe. We laughed at stories about her childhood. I told her stories about my own. We went from chuckling to whooping with laughter, like old friends chatting under ideal circumstances.

I never thought that I could bond with an older white woman. Then our conversation suddenly shifted. There was a natural pause in our exchange as she softly smiled at me like I was her own child. Then came the blindside hit.

"Brandon," she said, "just tell me the truth."

She'd tricked me. Soon as I had let her in. I should have seen this coming. My childhood, my secrets, her stories that she used like bait to draw me in—it was all a ploy to make me defenseless. I felt exposed, like I had been meat-checked by an old white lady. I was furious and glared at her across her trashy desk, my fingernails sinking into my palms as I clenched and unclenched my fists because I did not know what else to do.

"You can tell me," she said, seemingly unaffected by the shift happening before her eyes, my anger falling apart into confusion and pain. Her steady gaze spoke volumes. "I'm not your enemy," she added softly. But I did not believe her. My view of the world was so fractured that everyone was my enemy, out to expose my vulnerability and fraudulence. It made sense to assume that I was stranded in my lonely foxhole, and that no reinforcements or rescue party would ever come.

"Fine," I said angrily. "The truth is I can't read this stuff." Faulkner, Homer, Dante—I didn't understand a word of their books. I admitted to plagiarism. I admitted to cheating on the five-question quizzes. I admitted to being just as dumb as she and my classmates supposed. I admitted that I was one F or W away from flunking out of college for the second time. My voice rose and cracked with stress and hopelessness. And when I wound down—before I could bolt from the room—she rose from her chair. She walked over to me. She wrapped her frail arms around my body and promised me that I was safe. I closed my eyes, and I rested my head on her shoulder as her empathy calmed my spirit.

"I understand if you have to fail me," I said, head sunken.

"I'm not going to fail you," she said, refusing to accept my surrender. "We are going to redo it."

I didn't understand what she meant by "we." In this instance, simply allowing me to redo it would be an act of grace. But when I explained that English was too hard, that I wasn't cut out for it because I was so many miles behind everyone else, she wouldn't allow me to wallow in self-pity. She told me that I was not in it alone. She was willing to get down into the trenches and struggle with me until I figured it out. She went beyond the call of duty for me. Over the next several months, she spent weekends and time outside of her office hours to help teach me how to read and write. But the way she did it was, perhaps, the most impactful. She met me where I was, as a Black man. She talked about two other Black men who'd charted their own journeys to literacy. Their names are Frederick Douglass and Malcolm X. But I brushed aside these well-meaning comparisons, certain that my deficiencies were far worse than any shortcomings these men ever had. But she did not enable my self-pity. I saw everything that I wasn't. But she saw everything that I had the potential to be.

"You have two decisions you can make," she said to me one day. "You can moan about your disadvantages, or you can do something about them. The choice is yours."

Suddenly, it struck me that I had been here before—not as a student, but as an athlete. When I was in middle school, I realized that I was not going to grow tall. I was fast, I was strong, I was skilled, but I was short. Yet as an eighth grader, I was recruited to play on the high school level of the Amateur Athletic Union, a national league for elite travel basketball. I'd send defenders crawling on the floor with swift crossovers, plow through the lane with agility, and spring in the air for a layup—only to have my shot deflected to the rafters by a six-foot-something giant who would stare me down as the crowd cheered. My confidence about my skill was undermined by worries about my height. I concluded that I was out of my league.

But Coach would have none of that. With a piece of gum flapping in the corner of his mouth, he'd step to my face and in his drill sergeant voice say, "We don't complain, son. We compensate." Excuses weren't allowed. And if I, or any of us, ever tried to use them—it didn't matter what point of practice we were in—he'd halt and roar, "You makin' excuses, boy?" Then the whistle would blow as he screamed, "Assume the position!"

Fifteen wheezing bodies would hit the floor and, while doing push-ups, we'd chant in chorus: "Excuses are tools of incompetence, which build monuments of nothingness. And those who specialize in them seldom specialize in anything else."

So I'd stopped making excuses on the court and invested in a pair of strength shoes, training sneakers with a platform in the front that forces your calf muscles to bear the strain of keeping your heels elevated. For an entire year, I spent hours in my garage—mornings, after school, weekends—jumping rope and doing plyometric training. By the time I reached the ninth grade, I could soar above the rim—dunking and jumping higher than most guys who were older and taller than me. It was this discipline—and the intense labor—that allowed me to play much taller than I was.

I realized that Coach and Professor Nelson were sending me the same message. There was probably no academic equivalent of strength shoes, but

I wanted to know more about the two Black men she had mentioned. Of course, I'd heard their names before, thanks to dutiful Black history programming in school every February. Those learning modules were meant to engender respect for Black history, but they actually oversimplified and diminished it. Douglass was famous as an abolitionist and the sainted Black friend of Abraham Lincoln, but I knew nothing of him as a self-taught scholar and rhetorician. And when our textbooks or teachers made any mention of Malcolm X, he was positioned as the violent antithesis to Dr. King—not celebrated as a revolutionary and an autodidact.

I purchased the two books. I struggled to read them and it took a long time. My eyes watered, I fell asleep often, and I gave up several times. Not because I was uninterested. I was not conditioned to sit and read for extended periods. I spent more time looking up words than actually reading the books. I read through entire paragraphs and pages, then had to go back and read them again for understanding. It was tough, but there was something new and unusual pushing me through. As I read deeper, I was lost in the best way. And I was found in the same way. The feeling was euphoric, and foreign. Eventually, I finished. And it all made sense. If they could rise above their disadvantages to become scholars, there was no excuse for me.

Douglass was an illiterate slave. Malcolm was a dope-dealing gangster. Douglass had a teacher who barely taught him phonetics, and he took it upon himself to become a voracious and critical reader. Malcolm went to prison, and his journey to literacy began with his decision to copy thousands of words and definitions from the dictionary. They were me. I, too, was enslaved by ignorance. I, too, wanted to be delivered from the prison of my inferiority. I, too, felt the nakedness of being unlearned.

Rage mounted in me as I devoured these books. A certain fire is sparked when you realize that you've been deceived. All my life I'd believed that Black scholars didn't exist. Maybe they existed somewhere in the world, but not in mine. They weren't in my neighborhoods. They weren't on my television. They weren't in the textbooks that teachers wanted me to read. All I saw was Black gangstas and Black drug dealers and Black athletes. So that's what I wanted to be, because that's what I thought Black people did. Representation is the lens through which we aspire. I saw Allen Iverson—with his cornrows and tattoos and urban swag—and I thought I could be him, because he looked like me. Sure, I had heard that only three of every ten thousand high school players ever make it to the NBA. But representation impacted me more than probability. When I saw Iverson, Stephon Marbury, and Vince Carter, I saw myself. And that was all that mattered for a kid who was learning how to dream.

Why is it that basketball was all I ever wanted? It's because passion is born through exposure and affirmation. My mother had put a ball in my hands. She'd showed me what to do with it. Then she'd told me that I was good. But what if someone had put a book in my hands instead of a ball? What if someone had showed me how to read and then told me that I was smart? What if that book had exposed me to something great about my people and my identity that I could be proud of? What if it had showed that I was a part of a rich legacy of greatness? What if it had exposed me to my heritage and native land in a way that did not depict Africa as the quintessence of poverty? What if it had showed me something about my culture that is inspiring, not injurious, and that did not pretend that Black history began with slavery, or that did not relegate Black achievement to a four-hundred-year freedom struggle?

As I kept on reading, I soon realized that history is told by the victor. Told from the perspective of the person who wields the pen like a spoil of war. And the oppressed are left with a narrow study of their own defeat, left out of the story or indoctrinated with the fiction of inferiority. My life would have been completely different had I known these truths. But I knew them now. And I was ready to do the work of undoing my own miseducation.

My newfound passion consumed me like a flame. I was determined to transform myself. And I was willing to pay the price by any means necessary. The first step was my decision to trade my home entertainment equipment for a home library.

On that fateful day, I walked into the apartment as my roommates were playing *NBA 2K* on the PlayStation. I unplugged the cords in the middle of their game.

"Bro, what are you doing?" Stephon yelled, jumping to his feet like I had thrown a punch.

"I'm packing it up," I said. I gathered the PlayStation, the forty-inch television, and every form of entertainment hardware I owned. I took pictures of it all and posted it for sale on Craigslist. I accepted the first bidder. I used the proceeds to buy a cheap desk, an office chair, and some bookshelves. The rest I spent on books, including a set of textbooks covering grammar and reading for grades seven through twelve. I wanted nothing else. I gave up games, sports, and girls (kinda) for over a year. Each day after class and my part-time shift at the campus bookstore, I shut myself in my room. I started with seventh grade and eventually worked my way up to twelfth-grade proficiency. Coach and Professor Nelson had laid down the challenge. And I trained to be a scholar with the same intensity that I'd trained to be an athlete.

I struggled at first. I couldn't keep my eyes from tearing as I tried to understand the literature. But I wouldn't let up. I grew weary and fell asleep, but I woke up and kept pushing. In a notebook, I wrote down the definitions of unfamiliar words. I practiced using them in everyday conversations until they were committed to memory. I kept pushing. I barely wanted to stop to eat. Over time, those big words stopped tasting like spinach. I became a better reader. The paragraphs that I once had to read three times to comprehend I could now understand on the first try. My stamina increased and I could read one, then two, then three chapters without giving up. I felt like a champion. And it hit me that maybe I wasn't dumb after all. Maybe I was always capable of this. Maybe, all along, I was simply disinterested and disenfranchised from a world in which I never saw myself.

One day, I was reading when Walter interrupted my concentration. "Bro, you know those aren't the only Black scholars, right?" Walter was one of my five roommates. We were all recovering dropouts, taking a second run at college while crammed into a two-bedroom apartment where we slept on floor pallets because we could not afford beds. The most any of us paid for rent was $150 a month, yet eviction forced us to move repeatedly.

Walter and I had something in common: back in New Jersey, he had lived the *real nigga* life and then dropped out of college when a knee injury abruptly derailed his football career. He'd moved to Lynchburg to start a new life and enroll at one of the other local colleges. But there was one distinct difference between Walter and me: he had previously attended an HBCU before dropping out. And there, at now defunct Saint Paul's College, students were expected to know about members of the Black intelligentsia who were strangers to me.

"Listen to me, bro," he continued, "Here's who I want you to look up. . . ." His must-read list included W. E. B. Du Bois, Booker T. Washington, Carter G. Woodson, and Alain Locke. I had never heard of these people or the Harlem Renaissance. "They will change your life," he said. And he was right.

I read hungrily, consuming every book I could find written by or about Black intellectuals. One Black scholar led me to another. When Walter returned home from his work shift at Foot Locker, I ambushed him at the door.

"Bro, have you heard of Zora Neale Hurston and James Weldon Johnson?" I thought I was teaching him something. But he sighed, shook his head, and said, "You PWIs." I hadn't known that this was shorthand for schools like Liberty, which were "predominantly white institutions."

Each time I approached Walter with a new discovery, asking if he'd heard about Angela Davis or James Baldwin or Henry Louis Gates Jr., he chuckled in amusement and said, "Of course, bro." Then he would add another name to my scavenger-hunt list of Black scholars.

"Look up Cornel West," Walter said. "He will change your life."

Walter was right for the second time. I found Dr. West's books, *Race Matters* and *Democracy Matters*, and I watched every speech and lecture that I could find on YouTube. He looked like a mad scientist and exuded charisma like I had never seen. I grabbed my pen and pad and became his disciple.

Walter and I had spirited debates that kept us up all night. I learned that Du Bois, Woodson, and West were graduates of Harvard. In haste, I concluded that Ivy League schools must be the apex of academic achievement and the ultimate destination for Black scholars. Walter weaponized Booker T. Washington to argue the contrary. He charged that while those schools have prestige, they do not serve the immediate needs of Black people, beginning with the urgency of teaching the Black man to love himself. I took the opposite position, thinking that studying at an Ivy League would place me in the intellectual ranks of the Black scholars I was growing to admire. I yearned to visit Harvard someday, just to walk the same halls as those legends had.

Walter guided me through the Black literary canon. He helped me understand the Black freedom struggle and the Harlem Renaissance thinkers' brilliant use of art as an instrument of activism and abolitionism. I became passionate about everything Black.

There was a renaissance in me. I was being remade, reborn, reinvented. And it all started to make sense why school had missed me for all of my life. When has anyone ever become passionate about something that wasn't personal? I was conditioned to only see the imperialized forms of Blackness. I watched movies and television shows that commercialized our toxicity and commodified our culture and our traumas in ways that do not improve our social condition. I attended schools that saturated me with stories of white exceptionalism and Black conquest.

Jean-Jacques Rousseau once said that every man is born free, yet everywhere he is in chains. This could not have been truer for Black people in America. At home, at school, at church—I saw the links of chains that we did not create ourselves. And I was ready to free them. Carter G. Woodson exclaimed that teaching a Black man that his skin is cursed and his condition is hopeless is the worst sort of lynching. And as Walter spent hours with me, sharing in the gritty work of digging deep into the mines of my heart and mind and soul to undo my miseducation—it felt like he was doing more than teaching me. He was helping me remove the noose from around my neck.

CHAPTER EIGHT

THE GREAT DEBATER

I wanted to be more than a scholar. I wanted to be an orator. I studied videos of Black orators like Cornel West and said, *I want to do that.* I wanted to electrify large groups of people the way he did. He had a voice that was rich in power and inspiration. He had a voice that I yearned for but had not yet found.

I consumed Black books and I watched Black documentaries and Black movies about Black orators. I watched the biopic about Malcolm X, starring Denzel Washington. When I searched online for similar films, I discovered a bootleg version of a 2007 movie called *The Great Debaters*, set in the wake of the Harlem Renaissance. I clicked the link, sat in my new home office, and was transported.

Denzel Washington plays Mr. Melvin B. Tolson—an avant-garde educator who was influenced by the same Black scholars I'd been reading about. His methods were unorthodox. His style was theatrical. In one of the opening scenes, Denzel enters a classroom of precocious youth. Dressed in his wide-legged suit, he drops his briefcase, plants one foot on a chair, and boosts himself onto a desktop. He surveys the room, and then exclaims:

I am the darker brother.
They send me to eat in the kitchen when company comes.
But I laugh.
And eat well.
And grow strong.
Tomorrow, I will sit at the table when company comes.
Nobody will dare say to me, "Eat in the kitchen" then.
Besides, they'll see how beautiful I am and be ashamed.
I, too, am American.

It felt electrifying. In the film, Tolson is a professor who teaches debate and moonlights as a union leader. The actor Nate Parker plays the supporting role of Henry Lowe, a drunken, sex-crazed teenager. When Lowe nearly stabs a man, Tolson intervenes, looks beyond Lowe's delinquent behavior, and sees within Lowe the captain of the debate team he wants to build.

Watching alone in my room, I wanted to be Tolson. And in Lowe, I saw myself. When Tolson invites elite white institutions to debate his team at tiny Wiley College, he is largely ignored. Intercollegiate debate was highly segregated in the 1930s and Wiley College was too small, too poor, and too Black. But Tolson's team wins almost all the matches he can line up and finally commands the attention of the school they want to face most: Harvard College, the undergraduate division of the university. The historic duel unfolds on the stage of the venerable Sanders Theatre. The place is packed, a national radio audience tunes in, and the Wiley College team wins.

I closed my laptop, stunned, full, and yet empty. I thought, *Damn, if only debate were a real thing.* In those short eighty minutes, I had fallen in love with the charisma and aggression of debate. Injury had ended my life as a basketball star and I had nowhere to channel my competitive drive. But then I thought, *Wait a minute. I've seen* debate *somewhere before.*

I snatched my keys and sped to campus, sprinting to DeMoss Hall— where I had once met with Professor Nelson. Darkness was falling and the cleaning crew was buffing the floors of empty hallways. And there it was. The trophy case glowed with rows of medals, cups, and plaques engraved LIBERTY UNIVERSITY, CHAMPIONS. And on the wall, above the case, were those four providential words: LIBERTY UNIVERSITY DEBATE CENTER.

I earned a position on the debate team, my athletic prowess translated effortlessly into masterful debate, and I became an undefeated champion. That was the story I imagined. In reality, however, that did not happen. Debate was not the sensational gladiatorial contest it appeared to be in *The Great Debaters*. And I was far from Henry Lowe.

I pictured myself on a grand stage, my words stroking the heartstrings of an enraptured throng who would burst into thunderous applause when I finished. Instead, I found myself in a small room with my partner, my two opponents, and one judge, having to argue about the role of nongovernmental organizations in foreign affairs. My sensational dream turned into a nightmare.

I joined the debate team in the early stages of my intellectual metamorphosis, when my wings were still too damp and weak for flight. Most of my reading had focused on Black intellectual history in the United States. I had drawn a color line around my own curiosity. I knew much about the Harlem Renaissance but nothing about Caravaggio. I knew of Frederick Douglass but not of Friedrich Nietzsche. Economic theory, international policy, and comparative government were areas beyond my ken. The only sociopolitical issues that engaged me were ones with obvious connections to me as a Black man, or at least to Black people somewhere. Unfortunately, knowledge of Black history, at the time, counted for nothing in the white-dominated world of college debate where the focus was on socioeconomic policy.

When our team gathered for practice, I knew I was out of my league: my teammates had been recruited because they were top-ranked high school debaters; I was a walk-on who had never been coached and who lacked fundamentals.

Nevertheless, I earned a spot on the novice team and we set out for our season opener at Binghamton University. The novice and varsity teams loaded onto a chartered bus for a seven-hour haul to upstate New York.

As we rolled through the night, I sat in the back of the bus thinking about the even longer journeys I'd made to basketball games and major tournaments. This bus ride was much different. I was traveling with teammates, but not with brothers. There were no freestyle battles, roasting sessions, or coaches yelling at us to stop cursing. There were no cheerleaders in the front to fraternize with. On this trip, my teammates spent the night pecking away at their laptops and exchanging research files.

When we finally arrived, hundreds of college teams gathered for the opening assembly. A quick scan of the auditorium revealed that no one looked like me. There was a smattering of Black students, but even they didn't look, walk, or talk like me. A voice in my head hissed, *What the fuck is your ghetto ass doing here?* The haughty stares of the nerdy kids sizing me up seemed to be asking the same question.

I felt sorry for my partner because he deserved better. After we lost our third consecutive round, Connor was obviously tired of carrying deadweight. Our next stop was a lecture hall where the judge waited with our opponent: two Ivy League debaters with an undefeated record. One of them was a white guy with red hair, glasses, and freckles; the other was a Black guy who wore dress shoes with white ankle socks. A lectern stood between two tables facing the judge, who was armed with his timer and a notepad. We took our seats and opened the files containing our constructive cases. Connor started prepping, and I probably should have, too. But I was so distracted by those white ankle socks that I snapped a picture of them with my BlackBerry phone and sent it to friends, captioned "LOL."

"Are both teams ready?" the judge asked as I pressed send.

He tossed the coin, we called for tails, and the coin landed in our favor.

"Will Liberty University take the affirmative or negative?" the judge asked.

In intercollegiate debate, teams come prepared with arguments for both sides. We had lost the first three rounds with our negative case, so we chose the affirmative in hopes of a better outcome.

Before taking the podium for the first speech, Connor pulled me aside to make sure I knew our strategy.

"I'll deliver the first speech and you do the second," he said. Then he added, "And try not to screw up this time."

Connor had a right to be angry. After all, he did the research, wrote the cases, and practically gave all of the speeches. I was like the kid in the group project who barely participates but smiles and nods during the presentation, hoping to get an A for showing up.

The judge motioned for the debate to begin. "We'll start with the first affirmative constructive."

Michael settled his laptop on the lectern. "Opponents, ready?" He received a nod from the other team. "Judge, ready?" The stone-faced arbiter followed suit. "Teammate, ready?" I gave a signal with my pen in hand.

Then he began. "We affirm resolved: The United States should substantially increase its democracy assistance for Egypt by providing aid for democratic elections."

The ride back to Lynchburg, Virginia, was long and solemn. Connor and I didn't talk to our teammates on the bus, and we certainly didn't talk to each other. I had the entire back row to myself with several empty rows between us, because he didn't want to be anywhere near me. Other pairs celebrated their success, examining the medals they'd received for speaker points and polishing their trophies for earning ranks. Connor and I were the only two who didn't break through prelims. We had lost every single round and were not even close.

I sat with my head against the window, watching the night pass and wishing I could disappear into it. No one would forgive me for that final round. Everyone chokes or stumbles at one time or another, but I'd fumbled over words—or worse, had no words at all—round after round. The constructive speeches were written in advance—by Connor, of course—and all I had to do was stick to the script. I'd channeled my inner Henry Lowe and read the speech with all the passion I could muster. But when my opponent stood to cross-examine me, I'd frozen harder than a polar ice cap. I was not prepared to defend an argument I did not write or engage on a subject I did not understand. My opponent shot me a question that I couldn't answer.

Then he struck me with claim to logical fallacy. And after he'd bullied me into a fetal position, he finished me off with his closing statement: "Judge, it is apparent that my opponent lacks a fundamental understanding of his own case, and for this reason, they cannot win this debate." All Connor could do was watch, like a trainer whose fighter is bleeding on the ropes.

After the duel, I couldn't shake off their smirks when we shook hands. As they'd left the room, exchanging laughs and high fives, I thought I overheard one say to the other, "That was easy."

Those were fighting words, and the repressed gangsta had started to rise up in me. I wasn't a good debater, but there was no way in hell that I would be disrespected by a book-toting white boy and a Black kid who wore dress shoes with white ankle socks. The version of me that had been tamed by years of counseling and a return to college abruptly gave way to the *real nigga* who still lived deep down inside. The Ivy League debaters suddenly seemed like shit-talking streetballers from the block, and I knew how to handle that.

For the first time in years, I could feel myself losing control. I felt pressure building and steam coming off me. I tried to convince myself that I was a reformed and changed man. But the debaters' laughter had triggered a primal anger and they looked no different from Trey and his friends, laughing at me when I was fourteen after he'd had sex with my girlfriend. The Ivy League boys were in my crosshairs, and I'd tossed chairs aside as I charged toward them.

On the tip of my tongue was "Aye! Yo bitch ass got something to say to me?" I was ready for a street brawl. But before I could reach them, Connor had grabbed a handful of my suit jacket and yanked me from behind.

"Dude, what are you doing?" he'd said, clearly shaken.

The judge had still been at his table, observing my outburst and looking on with what seemed like disgust. He said nothing. He passed me a look of disapproval, grabbed his folders, and walked out of the room.

Hours into the evening drive, the bus fell silent. The jubilation and clinking of medallions quieted as my tired teammates fell asleep. I sat in self-imposed isolation in the back row, with winter's cold hand bracing my face pressed against the window. Insecurity settled over me like darkness on the passing countryside, and I thought, *Who am I kidding? I ain't nobody's scholar.* All it took was one tournament, a losing record, and a damning display of unsportsmanlike conduct to expose me as an impostor in the world of debate: nothing but a displaced hoodlum who had traded in my hoodie for an ill-fitting suit.

I felt like I was right back at square one—a person whose ambition would not be able to overwhelm incompetence. Months earlier, Professor Nelson had challenged me out of my rut of self-pity by asking what I would do about my own disadvantages. In the wake of defeat, I was pouting like a petulant child. And her charge pricked me like a mother's pinch. Then I heard Coach's voice echo, *We don't complain, son. We compensate.*

I knew what I had to do: I would have to teach myself about international politics. I went to the bookstore to see what books I could find on the subject. I discovered the *For Dummies* series and browsed discreetly, hoping no one would spot me searching for a manual on how to get smart quick. While plucking titles from the politics section, I stumbled upon a book about the Renaissance period. I immediately got excited because I thought it was another book about Harlem in the 1920s. But it wasn't. Strangely, the book featured old white men draped in colorful robes, sitting on the steps of what I later learned was the fictional School of Athens. The book was dense and looked painful to read.

I sat on the floor and riffled through the pages, searching for the chapter about the Harlem Renaissance. But I couldn't find it. Frustrated, I had almost given up on the book when my eyes landed on a section explaining the concept of a renaissance. It turns out that Harlem was not the only place to experience one. I was shocked to learn that throughout history the world has been changed by thinkers who were philosophically enlightened and brave enough to challenge the conventional social order. For the first time, I realized that what happened in Harlem—the pursuit of freedom, equality, and justice, transfigured through artistic expression—had happened in other places, too. The renaissance in Harlem—and the renaissance in me—happened in other places and people around the world.

My worldview started to expand. I learned that philosophy, the study of wisdom, was the impetus of revolutionary movements in the Eastern and Western world. I read about every renaissance that I could find: the Spring and Autumn period in ancient China; the classical, Socratic era in Athens; the Italian Renaissance in Florence; the Age of Enlightenment in England; the Protestant Reformation of the Catholic Church; the American Revolution; and, of course, the Harlem Renaissance at the dawn of the civil rights movement.

This lightning bolt of revelation illuminated a new landscape beyond Black studies. I now knew that political theory existed, and I immersed myself in Plato and Nietzsche and Rousseau, learning to trace the evolution of political ideology from the classical era to modernity. The deeper I read, the larger my world became.

I realized that my approach to debate was wrong. My approach to education in general was wrong. I had been debating with facts and information that I could regurgitate but did not understand. Like a child trying to walk before he crawls, I was trying to argue before I learned how to question. Philosophy was a tool I could use to dig deep beneath the surface of what was obvious, so I could reach in and extract ideas by the root. I realized that traditional education focuses mainly on the status quo, on the surface of the soil—which allows the seeds of injustice to lie quiescent, until they sprout into weeds of social and political inequality. The aphorism attributed to Socrates started to make sense: weak minds discuss people; average minds discuss events; but strong minds discuss ideas. My mind was getting more than strong. It started to feel like a superpower.

Reading philosophy was an aspiring debater's version of weight training. When I started out as an athlete, I wasn't very strong. So I began with low weight and high repetition to condition my muscles. But over time, I became lean, ripped, and resilient. When I spotted the faint bulge of a small, newly visible vein on my forearm, it inspired me to keep going. My abdomen hardened, creased, and compartmentalized. My chest grew chiseled and cupped at its base. When I looked in the mirror and saw results, my brain flooded with a rush of adrenaline, dopamine, and most of all:

confidence. Over time, my drive increased—and so did the weights, and so did my strength.

As a budding academic, I was training my mind the same way that I used to train my body. When I left the weight room, with my testosterone pumping and muscles swollen, I was convinced that I could take on anyone, even if it wasn't true. Likewise, when I emerged from my bedroom after hours under the tutelage of Plato, Aristotle, and the Enlightenment philosophers, I was ready to question anybody about anything, picking fights and poking holes in arguments. Claude Levi-Strauss once said, "The wise man doesn't give the right answers, he poses the right questions." And this principle became the bedrock of my intellectual constitution. Philosophy taught me how to win debates—because the best debater is the best questioner, and the best questioner is the best thinker. I saw what Plato described in his Theory of Forms, and my consciousness elevated beyond the forms of concepts you can see in the perceptible realm, to the truths that only exist in the imperceptible realm of abstractions.

The plot twist is that not everyone appreciated my new persona. I did not always wear it well. Especially when I picked fights with people, wanting to spar for intellectual sport. You can alienate a lot of people by casting yourself as the Sherlock Holmes of logic. I became the annoying person who takes pride in correcting people when they are wrong. Some of my friends and classmates probably wished I would drink hemlock, join Socrates in the afterlife, and leave them the hell alone.

Religion is the leading industry of Lynchburg and Liberty University is its engine, generating more than one billion dollars of economic activity every year. Liberty is the biggest and best known of eight local colleges and trade schools, and the largest employer in this city of about seventy-five thousand. Search online for "bars in Lynchburg, VA" and you'll only come up with two dozen. Look up churches and you'll find eighty evangelical Protestant congregations and nearly forty mainline Protestant churches. School and church were the two institutions that my upbringing taught me to loathe, yet here I was at Liberty, a church-school chimera.

Liberty University is the spawn of Thomas Road Baptist Church, made famous by Jerry Falwell's televised preaching, and students were encouraged to worship there on Sundays. Some did, but white students in Lynchburg had many other choices. For students from a Black church tradition, however, the pickings were slim. The white evangelical churches seemed very stale to a lot of Black students: there was no hand-clapping and foot-stomping to gospel music, no emotional outbursts and Holy Ghost fits, no preacher whooping and hollering, "Turn to your neighbor!" There were only bright smiles, soft singing, and a preacher who sounded like Joel Osteen.

The options changed when Sean Gilbert came to town. He grew up in Gretna, Virginia, a town with one stoplight, a Dairy Queen, and about one thousand residents. Kids raised there were considered highly successful if they learned a trade or became a postal carrier or a schoolteacher. Only the exceptional ones, like Gilbert, went off to the college thirty minutes up the road.

He was twenty-seven years old when he enrolled at Liberty: old enough to be taken seriously as a leader, yet youthful enough for students to fawn over him. He had a narrow face and light brown eyes. He was clean-cut with a perfectly symmetrical hairline and a manicured beard. He stood six feet tall and always walked like he was important or headed somewhere important, even if he was just walking to class. When Gilbert entered a classroom, toting a Bible and wearing a three-piece suit, it was impossible for the students to stay focused on the professor. He commanded the room. If they didn't already know who he was, they soon found out. Each time a professor said anything that Gilbert perceived as racially insensitive or biblically inconsistent, his hand shot up and when called on he set them straight. He was a thorn in the side for professors, but a hero for Black students—speaking truth to power and saying what they thought but were afraid to voice.

Several years before I arrived at the university, Gilbert set out to fill the need for a more Black, more charismatic form of worship on campus. By the time I was readmitted to Liberty in 2010, his congregation had grown from twenty students meeting in a classroom to an actual church with over two hundred members, blossoming at the foot of Liberty Mountain. Gilbert's church was growing so fast that he had to drop out of college to manage the influx of people drawn to his theatrical style of singing and preaching.

Lynchburg was a social desert. I began attending Gilbert's church because that's what many Black students at Liberty University did. And it's where you could find all of the beautiful Black sistas from campus. We did not have the Greek life or Black Student Unions that flourish on other campuses. For students not interested in organized religion, the church was more of an affinity group than a ministry. And if you grew up in a churchgoing Black family, Gilbert's church was a familiar experience kicked up to another level. At that time, he was only in his early thirties, people found him easy to like, and his preaching was passionate and rousing. His church was rare because it was almost entirely led by college students and millennials—most of them, like me, had been either turned off by religion or raised without it. He specialized in reaching young men like myself and Walter and others who were roughnecks. He kept us by his side. He groomed us. He taught us how to carry ourselves like distinguished gentlemen.

Sitting in the back of the congregation, I watched Gilbert move the crowd in ways that I had never seen. His performance was riveting—a confluence of Martin's savvy syntax, Malcolm's rousing impenitence, and Cornel West's prophetic fire. I wondered how he could stimulate the crowd in so many ways at once. His preaching made people cry, chant, and cheer so loud that it could match the decibel level of a Coachella concert.

I wasn't sure how he worked this magic and I was intrigued. The pews were filled with college students who might have been dragged to church as children, but who actually knew very little, if anything, about religion. Yet at the end of the service, millennials swarmed the altar in droves to receive whatever Pastor Gilbert promised: a prophecy, healing, salvation. Either we were highly impressionable, or Gilbert was irresistible—maybe both. In a socially vacant town, this church was the highlight of every week.

My life took a turn during a one-on-one conversation with Pastor Gilbert. I told him that my heart's desire was to become a powerful orator, keeping quiet about my miserable debate experience. I asked if he could train me to be an orator and a leader like him. He was obviously flattered, he smiled and laughed, and then he said: "Teachers begin as students, and leaders begin as servants." He continued, "You want to lead? Well, here you go." He gave me a bucket and a mop, inviting me to clean the church. I figured he'd missed my point entirely.

My demon stepfather had made me hate preachers, and now I was working for one. This was proof that attending a Christian college in the middle of nowhere precipitates strange and ironic decisions. But I had a purpose: I was going to study a man who embodied at least one aspect of what I hoped to become. After classes and on weekends, I drove Pastor Gilbert to all of his speaking engagements. I sat on the stage with him and occasionally forgot to pour his water because I was caught up analyzing how he used gestures to complement changes of tone and voice. He never told me his strategy, but I could see it: the parallels he'd set up to emphasize a point, the pauses he'd take after each punch line, how his cadence rose to a crescendo, and how his voice softened when heavenly music played and he beckoned listeners toward salvation. It was Rhetoric 101. The more I watched, the more impatient I became to do it myself. I felt like a freshman ball player idling on the varsity bench. In my mind, I was ready. I asked repeatedly if I could give it a try, if I could speak in front of the congregation. But Pastor Gilbert would continually say things like "Keep serving" and "Your time will come."

Impatient, I exhorted an imaginary audience in my bedroom. Having confirmed that my roommates were out, I would pretend that my tiny bedroom was a grand stage. Pacing back and forth, leaping up and down, and pointing at invisible but rapt listeners, I did passionate imitations of orators I admired. The topic didn't matter. I pretended to be a politician leading a huge rally. I recited Shakespearean soliloquies. I impersonated a professor giving a lecture in an auditorium. I just wanted to be in front of people. I wanted to experience the euphoria that comes from using your voice to set a room ablaze. I wanted to see inspiration open people's eyes, see hope fill their hearts, and watch the lightbulb of discovery glow above their heads. I wanted to empower people, to share with them my experience when I found

Socrates and the Renaissance. Pastor Gilbert was wrong. I was ready. I was eager for my turn. And then, it came. Unexpectedly.

My class schedule made it impossible for me to join Gilbert on a speaking trip to Washington, DC, but I was scheduled to meet him at a church in Danville, about an hour outside of Lynchburg. When we spoke, he was only a few hours away. I had plenty of time to grab a bite at Hardee's, then I went over to the office to pick up a freshly pressed suit for him. Suddenly, my cell phone rang.

"Brandon, where are you?" Gilbert asked, his voice sounding tense.

"I'm at the office grabbing your things right now. I'm about to jump on the road to meet you."

He didn't respond immediately, and I knew something was wrong.

"About that," he said, "I don't think I'm gonna make it. It's too much traffic. There's no way that I will get there on time."

I started to tell him not to worry, that I would phone the church and let them know that he needed to cancel due to unforeseen circumstances. But he cut me off.

"No," he said, "we can't cancel. They've planned this conference for months and are expecting nearly five hundred people."

I was confused. Not because he sounded concerned, but because he didn't sound concerned. He sounded calm. Like he had a plan.

My next words came slowly. "Sooo, what do you want to do?" I asked.

He said that there was only one thing to do. This calculation was odd, because I could think of at least five different things that we could, and should, do. So I couldn't imagine what his one viable option was. But whatever he was going to say, intuition told me it would not be good.

"You have to speak in my place," he said, so calmly his words didn't seem real.

"Yeah, right. That's funny," I said, cackling at his joke. But I realized after a couple of seconds that he wasn't laughing with me.

"Brandon, this isn't a joke," he said.

My insides immediately shriveled like a raisin.

"Come again?" I asked, incredulous.

I argued with him for several minutes, suggesting alternatives and grasping for reasons why this was a ridiculous idea. And in the end, I lost my second debate.

"Call me when it's over," he said, and the line went dead before I could offer my final rebuttal.

I broke into a sweat and my heart pounded like it was breaking through my chest. I had a full-on panic attack. I dropped his suit on the floor and grabbed for the chair closest to me. This didn't make any sense. I wasn't a preacher. He had assistant clergy who could easily take his place, just as they had on earlier occasions. He hadn't offered me any tips, advice, or guidance—he had thrown me overboard with no life vest. I didn't know what to do.

"Why would he do this to me?" I asked myself over and over again. My best guess was that both he and God were conspiring against me. I was still recovering from my humiliation at the debate tournament. And now this? If I'd choked with only four other people in the room, how could I speak— not to mention *preach*—before an audience of hundreds?

I looked at the clock and realized that falling apart was not an option. I scooped up my belongings and set off for Danville, driving while desperately conjuring a presentation about the only biblical story I knew by heart. I had rehearsed it many times in my bedroom, and it had been applauded by my imaginary audience. But I wasn't sure that a real audience would be as kind.

Zipping through the countryside, I orated aloud and gave myself pep talks. Passing drivers probably thought I was insane, the way I death-gripped the wheel and yelled at my image in the rearview mirror, jabbing my finger at myself and screaming, "You got this!" There were intervals of total meltdown, too, before the one-hour drive was over. When I reached my destination, the church parking lot had overflowed and cars lined the street and piled on the lawn.

I entered the lobby and was greeted by a friendly staff member.

"Welcome, and thank you for coming! The sanctuary is right this way," she said, beckoning me toward the double doors.

"Hi, um, actually . . . I'm looking for the pastor's study."

"I'm so sorry but the pastor is currently occupied," the greeter said as she again gestured toward the sanctuary. I didn't know how to explain the situation. I kept asking, and she kept explaining that the pastor was busy waiting for the guest speaker.

"Um . . . that's actually what I need to speak with the pastor about. I'm Brandon, Pastor Gilbert's assistant."

She apologized profusely. "Oh, forgive me, I'm so sorry. Please, right this way."

As we walked through the corridor, I contemplated how I would deliver the bad news. The response would not be good, no matter what words I used.

The kind lady knocked on the pastor's office door and introduced me as the guest speaker's aide. The gentleman welcomed me into his office and offered me a drink. He meant water, but I wanted to ask for whiskey to quell my anxiety. I sat on the chaise next to the bookshelf, chugging the glass of water like I was gulping from a fresh spring. Until I nearly choked when he asked the inevitable.

"We are so thrilled to host Pastor Gilbert tonight. How much longer until he arrives?" he asked so excitedly. I was about to crush his expectations. It dawned on me that I should have called to break the news before I actually arrived.

The unabridged truth tumbled out: "Pastor Gilbert can't make it."

The pastor looked like he wanted to understand but could not. He looked like he wanted to say something but was struck dumb. He stared silently at me. Not knowing what else to do, I continued.

"I am so sorry to tell you like this, but he is stuck in DC due to unforeseen circumstances."

Terrified, I delivered the rest of the message. "And he asked me to come here and speak on his behalf."

The pastor was too shocked to be horrified or angry. From the pastor's study, we could hear that the service was well underway. He had no other option but to trust, or at least accept, Gilbert's dicey decision to send an untested college kid to fill the featured slot at the church's biggest annual conference.

The pastor and I stepped onto the pulpit from a backstage passageway. He gestured for me to sit in the speaker's chair. It was so ornate that it looked like a Gothic throne. There was nothing to worry about as far as the congregation knew. Preachers often arrived fashionably late. When they saw me emerge onto the stage, they probably assumed that I was an assistant placing Pastor Gilbert's Bible and water in position.

Pastor Gilbert's face was plastered on the cover of the printed program. How would all these people react when they learned that he wasn't coming? Everywhere he went, swarms of folks traveled miles to hear his preaching. I had never seen an empty seat at a revival where he was featured, and this was no different. There was barely standing room. People crowded against the walls, waiting for the Sean Gilbert experience they yearned for.

When the choir launched into the hymn that was supposed to precede his sermon, my panic rose. People were twisting and turning in the pews, looking desperately for the man of the hour, who was nowhere to be found. The pastor sat rigid and I kept my eyes glued to the floor. I couldn't look. The entire ordeal felt like when a guy brings his side chick to a family cookout instead of the girlfriend everyone knew. It was me: I was the side chick.

The pastor interrupted my reverie. "Do you have a bio?" he asked.

"A bio?" I replied, totally caught off guard. The crowd already looked restless and suspicious, and anything they learned about my past would make things worse.

I imagined him stepping up to the podium with an air of resignation. *I know we were all looking forward to hearing Pastor Gilbert today, but he can't make it. Instead we have a young man with a delinquent past who once dropped out of college. He is not clergy, but don't worry. He has now returned to college, where he is a failed debater and serves as Pastor Gilbert's assistant. Please welcome Brandon Fleming as he gives his first speech ever.*

I lied and told the pastor that I left my bio at home. Lying in the pulpit was the least of my concerns. He now seemed just as apprehensive as I was.

He already questioned Gilbert's decision to send me, and my lack of a prepared introduction undermined his confidence even more, I could tell.

Because I didn't have a written bio for him to read, the pastor decided to skip the introduction and leave me to explain who I was. I wanted to punch the preacher in the face for making me the bearer of bad news. I was convinced that he had joined forces with Gilbert and God to form an unholy trinity determined to take me down.

As the last notes of the choir's pre-sermonic selection faded to quiet, the pastor gently placed the cordless microphone on my lap. I wasn't ready. Beads of sweat dripped from my armpits and down the sides of my torso. I reached for my water, but I had drained the glass in my desperate attempt to relieve a bad case of cotton mouth. Now I had to pee. But it was too late. Because my time had come.

The entire church went silent. The room was so still that I could hear my short, frantic breaths. I could feel my heart throbbing. I gripped the microphone like I was choking it. Beside me were a Bible, binder of notes, hand towel, and the empty glass—all of which I needed to carry to the podium. The pastor offered no assistance. He looked at me as if to say, *You're on your own now.* I made two trips, avoiding eye contact with members of the stoic congregation and pretending that they couldn't see me. I cast a parting grimace at the pastor as if to say, *Thanks for the help, asshole.*

At the podium, I didn't pick up the microphone right away. Slowly, I flipped through my notes and Bible to give Pastor Gilbert a few more seconds to show up and save the day. I sneaked glances toward the rear of the sanctuary, hoping that he would emerge like Superman. Or maybe he would burst through a side door and yell, "Brandon, you've been punk'd!" I would've been perfectly fine with that. Or maybe the Rapture would occur, and everyone would magically ascend to the heavens. If that happened, I wasn't sure that heaven would be my destination. But the alternative would be better than where I stood right now. When I accepted that there would be no redemption, I finally picked up the microphone. And I spoke.

"Umm, good evening," I said after clearing my throat a couple of times. Everybody watched, but no one responded. So I continued.

"Unfortunately, Pastor Gilbert won't be able to make it this evening."

I paused to give the audience a moment to react. But they didn't. I expected groans but their faces were impassive, and their eyes fastened on me as they waited for more.

"My name is Brandon Fleming," I continued.

"I'm, uh . . ." I did not want to say it.

"I'm Pastor Gilbert's assistant. I know how much you were looking forward to hearing him today. Believe it or not, I'm just as disappointed as you." I immediately realized that this was not the best choice of words, but the rhetorical conventions of sermonizing escaped me.

"This wasn't what any of us planned," I said. "But I sincerely hope that I can encourage someone this evening."

I just wanted to get it over with. I forgot to say the commencement prayer. I didn't ask them to stand for the reading of God's word. I announced my title, "You Were Chosen for This," and I launched straight into my speech, beginning with the unfiltered truth.

I had nothing to lose. I had grand ideas about who and what I wanted to become, but I seemed to be getting nowhere. I had just stepped onto a platform where I could be exposed as a fraud, but I just didn't care anymore. I didn't care about the audience. I didn't care about my reputation. I didn't care about my hopes and aspirations. I decided to let go. I stopped caring about failure, because there was nothing failure could do to me that it had not done already. I stood before a huge crowd of people who didn't know me from a can of paint, and for the first time I just decided to go for it. I was scared. But I did it afraid. I closed the binder containing my script.

"I'm just gon' keep it real. I'm not a preacher," I admitted. "To be honest with you, I don't even know why I'm here. But for some reason, God does."

I told them that I was a kid raised in a broken family, and how I'd turned to sex, drugs, and violence to salve the pains of my past. I told them that I was a failed athlete, a college dropout, and a student recovering from years of miseducation, only to find myself wrestling with impostor syndrome and feelings of not belonging anywhere.

Then I told the story of David, beginning with Samuel's mission to the home of Jesse to find the next king of Israel. He gathered up Jesse's sons to discover God's chosen king. He looked at Eliab, the eldest, and said, *I found him.* But God said, *He might have the right physical features, but that's not him.* He looked at Abinadab and said, *Surely, this must be the one.* But God said, *No.* He looked at Shammah and said, *Finally, this is the king.* But God said, *No, it's not him.* Samuel nominated seven of Jesse's sons, but God turned down all of them. Muddled with confusion, Samuel confronted Jesse and said, *I don't understand, God told me that the chosen one is here. Are you sure these are all of your sons?* And Jesse confessed that the youngest son remained, but that Samuel shouldn't waste his time because David was out herding sheep where he belonged. Samuel commanded that the boy be fetched. And when David entered—earnest and pure of heart—emerging from the place where people confined him, God approved and Samuel anointed him as the rightful king.

By this time, I was inflamed by my own passion. This story was personal to me. Suddenly, I heard a voice in the audience yell, "Amen!" and another yell, "That's right!" like they were cheerleaders. I had not felt this in years. The crowd's reaction triggered the same rush of adrenaline that I felt on a fast break, soaring toward the basket. Now I was soaring in a different way. My cadence rose, racing to a crescendo. My energy exploded in a way that I could no longer control. While telling the story, the stage became too small for me. I hopped off the stage onto the floor. Then I jumped onto a wooden pew and activated my inner Henry Lowe as I cried out from the depths of my soul:

> I don't know what you've been through in your life, but I came all the way from Lynchburg, Virginia, to stand here tonight and tell somebody who was told that you're too young or you're too old, that you're not smart or you're not ready, that you're not chosen or you're not qualified—I want you to send a thank-you card to every person who counted you out, because God doesn't call those who are qualified, but He qualifies those whom He calls!

The organ bellowed in C-sharp. The entire room erupted in praise. The preacher jumped up and down behind me. A lady's hat flew from her head as she took off running through the aisles. Men were shouting and high-fiving. People were crying with joy and lifting their hands and leaping with exultation. And I stood atop the pew, celebrating like I was the last gladiator left standing in the center of the Colosseum.

Then the wave broke over me. I stepped down from the pew, shocked by what had occurred. Eyes wide and teary, I couldn't believe what I had done. I wished Pastor Gilbert was there to see it. I wished he could watch me fly. For the first time, I found my voice. For the first time, I sang my song. For the first time, I told my story.

I returned to my seat while the crowd continued rejoicing. I grabbed my belongings and retreated toward the pastor's study. I glanced at my phone to check the time and discovered a text message from Pastor Gilbert. "Great job," it read. "Meet me at the restaurant next door."

I didn't understand. I peeked my head back into the sanctuary, but I did not see him. People were still shouting and crying and cheering but Pastor Gilbert was nowhere to be found. I immediately grabbed my things and rushed out of the church. I hustled to the restaurant wondering, *But how in the world would he know?*

When I entered, there he was. He looked relaxed, sitting in a booth with his legs crossed and his phone in hand. I was torn between wanting to sprint to him with outstretched arms and wanting to drop-kick him in the face for pulling some shit like that.

Instead, I approached him in profound confusion, wanting to demand, "Why would you do that to me? Why would you set me up to fail?" But before I could utter a word, his mouth creased into a smile as he wrapped his arms tightly around me and whispered in my ear, "I knew you could do it." I closed my eyes as he cupped my head and pressed it against his chest. I hadn't felt this since I was a child. It was as if he'd lifted me into the air and called me Superman. And the thought released a torrent of tears that I could no longer hold back.

CHAPTER NINE

A TEACHER BORN

I was never the same after Pastor Gilbert pushed me out of the nest with no warning. Unnerved by failing at debate, I had previously been lying low, scared to try my wings for fear that I would crash again. Before he gave me that fateful shove, I had been watching other students soar and wondering if I could ever do the same.

Driven by the words of Coach and Professor Nelson, I had not wasted time envying classmates who'd entered college much better prepared than me. I had not complained about my disadvantages. I'd studied. I'd learned to watch and think and question and adapt. I'd tended my own sheep, as David did his flock, until Gilbert had come along and saw something in me that I could not see in myself. Having been discovered in this way, I wanted to pay it forward. And that opportunity came much sooner than I ever would have expected.

"I don't know what else to do with him," Mom said on the phone. I knew that broken voice. It was faint and frayed, the agonized sound a mother makes from the shore as her child is carried away by a vicious undertow. She had no hope of saving her son. The sound of her voice carried the same tone as when she was once talking about me, when I was a teenager lost in gangs and drugs and again when I'd tried to kill myself. Now she was despairing over Ben.

"It's like every day he's in trouble," she said. "He's running the streets doing God knows what. And he just failed the ninth grade."

"What?" I exclaimed.

"It gets worse," she continued. "Next year, they're sending him to Bryant."

Those words were like a sniper's bullet tearing through my chest—a bullet I had narrowly escaped thanks to basketball. I nearly dropped my phone. Bryant was the same alternative school where I was once almost cast away. Alternative school was a slow-motion death sentence for many young Black males. It was the one place that I hoped my little brother would never be.

After hearing her litany of complaints about his sins, I said, "Mom, I have an idea." She was eager to hear it, but I knew that she would shoot it down. I continued anyway. "Send him here with me."

"No," she shot back.

"Mom," I said, "we've put you through enough already. You're getting older. You did your part. Just let me help."

It was an outrageous suggestion. But I had to do something. This was my fault, after all. Ben had spent years in the front row of my classroom, where he learned the same *real nigga shit* that my cousins taught me in the Bronx. When Mom was away on duty, we were forbidden to leave Ben home alone. So I'd hauled him to places he should never have been. He saw things no little boy should ever see. Now he was following the path that I had blazed. It was up to me to show him a different way.

"Let me help, Mom," I pleaded. But I understood her resistance. Three of her children had gone astray. Mom blamed herself for this and saw Ben as her final chance to set a child right before he completely derailed. But I knew the truth, which was that she had already lost Ben to the streets. And I was the one who'd set him on that course. So I kept pushing until she agreed to transfer custody to me. Mom signed a power of attorney, she kissed him goodbye, and she shipped him off to join me in Lynchburg, where I was barely even surviving on my own.

Ben joined me in the ramshackle two-bedroom apartment that I shared with five other guys. I somehow believed I could support my brother and me with the $400 I made each month by working part-time at the campus Barnes & Noble. I'd fantasized that working in a bookstore would be a license to read all day, but I was stuck behind a cash register or stocking shelves. I could sneak only a few pages before the manager yelled, "Hey, you're on the clock!" I was only scheduled for ten to fifteen hours a week. Mom sent what she could to help support us, but it was not enough. So I did what I had to do.

I went to the social services building with my hood up and my car parked three blocks away. If I was spotted by a friend, I could pivot toward the James River and hurl myself in to escape humiliation. The walk of shame was familiar. Just about a year earlier, I'd crept into the cash advance store in the same stealthy way. Not much had changed. I was still poor, but it was better to be a poor man in school than a poor man in a vitamin factory. Resolute, I signed in and waited for my name to be called.

"Brandon Fleming!" the clerk yelled. I flinched, thinking, *Damn, lady, why you gotta call my name so loud?* I wanted to crawl under my chair. There were at least a dozen other people in the waiting room and no one was in a good mood. We were all in need but I imagined that we were suspicious of one another's motives. It seemed that judgmental eyes followed me as I tucked my head and approached the counter.

The embarrassment evaporated when I received the flimsy EBT card that felt like an American Express Centurion. "I got the food stamps!" I announced as soon as I returned home. We all cheered and dapped and beat our chests, yelling, "Let's goooo!" like I had just hit the Powerball. We stormed the grocery store and stocked up on cereal, Hamburger Helper, Oodles of Noodles, and packages of hot dogs and ground beef. No more plain noodles for us. We graduated to gourmet noodles with wieners to sauté as we sprinkled premade seasoning packets like Salt Bae. For dessert, we threw bread slices in the toaster, slapped butter on both sides, then dashed them with cinnamon and sugar. We were *livin'*.

But we did not always enjoy Oodles of Noodles, cinnamon toast, or similarly lavish meals. Our hasty splurging depleted my EBT funds. A benefit meant to support my brother and me had quickly turned into a household feeding trough. We often blew the funds in the first half of the month, then survived the last two weeks on grilled cheese, one-dollar McChickens, and five-dollar Hot-N-Ready pizzas.

We could barely make our rent. We could hardly keep the lights on. Interruptions in service made us vulnerable to winter's bite and summer's swelter. Cable was a luxury we could not afford. We entertained ourselves with karaoke, rap battles, and wrestling. When any sort of household disagreement arose, we retrieved the boxing gloves from behind the couch and settled the dispute by sparring. The scuffling took a heavy toll on our living room. The walls were lacerated. Broken lampshades tilted and lightbulbs flickered. Nearly every inch of the original white carpet was stained, and the entire apartment was forlorn. Open the front door and the view featured a defective Philips television on the living room floor and an army-green love seat with a sinkhole in the middle. Girlfriends were disturbed when they saw the place. It looked like the den of Tasmanian devils.

Somehow, our conditions did not discourage us. We sat in a pitch-black living room without electricity or water, using our phones as flashlights. Devouring a struggle meal, Walter and I would look at each other with mouthfuls of leftovers and say simultaneously, "We out here *livin'!*" We'd laugh hysterically, as though our circumstances were ideal. To us, this was the good life. It was far better than where we came from.

My room was a cave of devastation. Stains covered every inch of carpet. I'd scavenged a piece of bed foam, washed it, swaddled a blanket around it, and tucked it in the corner on the floor. I slept scrunched next to my brother, our bodies close and sometimes famished. We didn't have much, but we had each other. I lay next to him full of regret. His ragged snores and nightmare twitches reminded me that he was just a kid, and that none of his family members had been able to provide him with what he needed.

But in that desolate room, there was one sign of hope. A paradoxical and prophetic talisman hung on the wall above our pallet, a pennant associated with a place that seemed completely beyond my reach. It was crimson and it hovered in the dark above my head each night like a dream-catcher. The lettering read: HARVARD.

I'd bought it as a sign of hope and aspiration. It made me feel closer to Du Bois and Locke and Woodson, my Harlem Renaissance heroes. And it's the place where Cornel West both studied and taught. The pennant gave me hope of meeting him someday. But who was I kidding? I was not on a launching pad for such a place. Neither my GPA, my wallet, nor my EBT card would ever get me to Cambridge, Massachusetts. The pennant was ornamental, on some days an inspiration, and on others days an elegy for places that I would never go.

My debut speech at the church, however, was making me reassess my prospects. Maybe I wasn't a failure after all. Other people with untapped gifts probably felt as flightless as I had. And if I could be grounded by insecurity and fear of incompetence, maybe they could also be freed with help from people like Coach, Professor Nelson, Walter, and Pastor Gilbert. Maybe they, too, could discover their purpose and their passions and soar. I thought about the words that had poured out of me: *God doesn't call those who are qualified, but He qualifies those whom He calls*. I realized that the message wasn't only for the congregation, cheering me on. The message was for me. I examined my new wings and understood why it took so long for me to fly. Success was always the goal. But the true gift that was given to me—and the gift that I was realizing I was destined to give to others—was everything that I had learned during my process of reinvention. Maybe I could help others transform, too. Maybe I could help people experience their own renaissance. Maybe I could be for others what I'd once needed.

I finally knew what I was called to be. I rushed to meet with my academic advisor. I barged into his office and said, "I want to change my major." It spilled out of me before I could even take a seat.

"Okay," he said. "What change would you like to make?"

"How do I become a teacher?" I asked. I could hardly contain the excitement and urgency triggered by discovering my purpose. I'd never wanted anything so badly. I wanted this more than I'd wanted to be in the gang. I wanted it more than being the neighborhood drug lord. I wanted it more than being a *real nigga*. Not even basketball could compare. For the first time, everything made sense.

My advisor made the change: English with a minor in secondary education. I did not care that my course load would instantly double. An additional year of practicums, placements, and licensure testing was piled onto my Degree Completion Plan. But I was relentless. I was so eager to become a teacher that I went nonstop: fall semester, spring semester, summer semester, and intensive courses during what would have otherwise been holiday breaks. I was so determined that I finished more than four years of coursework in less than three years.

By my final year, I had completed most of my English courses and all that remained were a few secondary education requirements. I completed my first teaching practicum at Amherst High School. I completed my second teaching practicum at Liberty Christian Academy. All that stood between me and my own official classroom was a semester of student teaching—a four-week internship where I'd teach a full semester of English at a local high school. I was ready. I was eager to change the world one student at a time. Until, once again, failure swooped in like a wrecking ball to shatter my dreams.

I could not begin student teaching until I passed the Praxis, a subject-specific test required to teach high school English. There were two major problems. My first year and a half of college, the second time around, was spent being drubbed by dead poets. I was sucker-punched by Shakespeare, drop-kicked by Dickinson, and clotheslined by Chaucer. I'd cheated to keep upright until I could stand on my own feet. And by the time I could do that, I cared only about the wonders of the Harlem Renaissance, where I'd remained until I became obsessed with philosophers both ancient and modern. This eccentric course of study left me ill-prepared for an exam that assessed my knowledge of the mainstream world literary canon, which is mostly white, male, and Western.

I failed the test. I found myself in a familiar place, one that I thought I had escaped forever. I offered my wishes to the universe like magic dust held in the palms of my hands. But a hailstorm of disappointment came crashing down. I took the test a second time, and I failed. But I did not give up. I went back and took the test a third time. And I failed.

Three years of college were spent. I was in too deep to go back and change my major. My financial aid was about to expire. I could see only two options: pass the Praxis and complete my degree or become a two-time dropout. The test was expensive, and each attempt sent my bank account closer to the red. And if I kept failing the test, I would run out of financial aid before I could graduate. That would force me to withdraw, and I would not let that happen.

My entire future hinged on passing the Praxis, but I couldn't afford to register for it again. Pastor Gilbert stepped in and footed the bill for me. He held my hands and prayed with me. Afterward, he said, "You got this." I was afraid God kept tally on all my false promises. But a calm came over me because I knew God listened to Gilbert. I studied harder than I had ever studied for anything. I was ready to make him proud. I was ready to pass the test, get my degree, and change the world of education like Joe Clark from *Lean on Me*. I walked into the testing center with my head held high for a fourth and final time. I wore a big, confident grin because Gilbert had asked God to go with me. I took the test. And I failed again.

Options exhausted, I turned to my academic advisor in desperation. "You can walk," he said, "but your degree won't be conferred until you pass the Praxis and complete your student teaching." This was devastating. I would be stuck in purgatory, a graduate who could not enter my profession. I'd have to keep working for minimum wage.

"Or . . ." he continued, "since you're almost done with your English credits, you could drop the secondary education minor and graduate with a bachelor of arts in English." It felt like he'd lodged a javelin in my heart. I had completed all those education courses for nothing. This was the worst good news I had ever received. I could graduate, which was enough to make the angels sing. But I could not become a teacher.

I had no clue what else to do with an English degree. I was devastated. I had found my purpose. I had never been so sure of anything. But now it seemed like the universe had dangled this prize in front of me and just as my fingers were closing around it, the prize was yanked away.

A familiar feeling of dejection tugged at me. I could hear my name being called from the depths of a depressive abyss that I'd once tumbled into. But I would not allow it. Not this time. I heard the mantras that had pulled me out of self-pity and set me on the path toward learning. Coach's voice rang in my ear: *We don't complain, son. We compensate.* And Professor Nelson's charge: *What will you do about your own disadvantages?*

If I had learned nothing else on my journey, I had learned how to blaze alternative paths. I had learned that trailblazers don't wait for opportunities; we create them. So I decided to seize fate's pen and write my own narrative. No license or piece of paper would determine whom I was called to be. Since the Virginia Department of Education denied me an official classroom, I decided that I would create my own.

Some of the teenagers who attended Gilbert's church came from broken homes and were dragged there by single mothers struggling to manage rebellious kids while keeping everyone fed and housed. These women hoped church would be a panacea for all their problems. I could relate, not only because these women reminded me of my own mother, but also because I was now Ben's guardian. Ben had made friends easily, but he and these other kids were always up to some kind of trouble.

One Sunday after church service, the teens gathered to ravage the refreshments in the foyer. Meanwhile, the parents bemoaned the complexities of child-rearing. I leaned in like a complete tenderfoot. As an inexperienced guardian, I needed all the tips I could get. Being a surrogate parent was odd because I felt like a grown-up in one sense, but in another, I was only a twenty-two-year-old college kid with five roommates and hardly enough money to keep a quarter tank of gas in the car, food on the table, and the bathroom stocked with toilet tissue. And it was awkward having parent talk with women who were my mother's age.

"I don't know what else to do," Tasha said. She sighed and looked away. Her daughter Shontae had just been suspended from school. It pained me to see her look so hopeless.

"I hear you, girl," Monique said. "Same with Cordell." Cordell had brought home another report card full of Fs. He was on the verge of failing the tenth grade. Ryan, just like Ben, had been held back a grade. He was already eighteen and repeating his senior year. As more parents chimed in, it was clear that these kids were headed toward alternative school or dropping out. My struggles as a single brother were no different, so I fit right in.

I wanted to give them hope. I searched for reassuring words that I could not find. We were all stuck in a dark tunnel, and none of us saw light dancing at the end. We were at an impasse between our desires for the kids and their desires for themselves.

"They'll come around," I said. I promised them that the maternal suffering pays off. I assured them that if I could be transformed, as wayward as I was, the same could happen for their kids.

"I hear you," Tasha said. "But how? And when?"

I had no answer. They were skeptical about a promise so disconnected from their day-to-day reality.

The conversation moved on but I couldn't. Tasha's questions pricked me like a thorn. I looked at the mothers chatting like everything was okay, but it wasn't. I looked at the kids hanging out like they were okay, but they weren't. None of us were okay. We were all laughing to avoid crying, two more generations of people living in a perpetual present because none of us were taught to plan for the future. Frustrated, I wondered, *Why don't any of us have answers?* When I looked at those kids—who were bold and bursting with untapped promise—I saw myself. They were me. That's when I realized that I could be the answer. My purpose was to be for them what I'd needed when I was their age.

"I tell you what," I said to the group of mothers. "Let me spend some time with them this weekend."

I had no plan. But there were no objections, no questions except, "You gon' pay for food?" Without hesitation, they agreed. "Anything to keep him out these streets," Andrea said.

I invited Ben's friends to hang out at our apartment. I was eager to engage them, but my attempts at mentorship immediately fell flat. They shrugged off advice about good grades and college and professional goals, because they could not conceive of life beyond dating and sports and fashion and video games. The times I interrupted their conversations with words of wisdom, their eyes rolled and I could hear Ben murmur under his breath, "Here he go again."

Redirecting my brother was much, much harder than I had expected. I warned him of dangerous behaviors, only for him to aver, "But you did it." He was right. I begged him to learn from my terrible mistakes, but I didn't talk honestly with Ben about our past. It was easier to bury pain than to acknowledge the things he'd watched me do. I had traded in my durag and Timberland boots for Gilbert's hand-me-down blazers and hard bottoms from Goodwill. Ben did not recognize this renaissance version of me. At first, he didn't believe that this person was real: this suit-wearing, book-toting brother who willingly attended church on Sundays. I did not blame him. At times, I hardly recognized this person myself.

I was determined to get through to Ben and his friends. I thought carefully about what I'd needed when I was their age, in a similar family situation, alienated from school. It was not a lecture or a wrist slap. I needed someone to meet me where I was. So I changed my approach and stopped lecturing them.

I soon learned that there is a difference between being uninterested and being disengaged. We often accuse young people of being uninterested in matters we consider important, but seldom do adults claim responsibility for our failure to engage them at their level. When I was younger, I struggled to identify with teachers because they expected us to come to them. They rarely came to us. They did not understand culturally responsive education. But my coaches did. Granted, it did not always work. But they tried. Sometimes they offered outdated and outlandish advice on how to get girls; sometimes they uttered hilarious malapropisms when attempting to use our slang or quote our music. What mattered was their understanding that language can be the great divider or the ultimate unifier. Their attempts to speak our language said, I see *who* you are, I see *where* you are, and I'm willing to meet you *there*. They were like travelers who learn some basic phrases before going abroad, instead of expecting everyone in the world to speak English. They didn't need to master the music, the slang, or the culture. The coaches just needed to demonstrate their interest in and their appreciation of our culture, even if it was different from their own.

I had what these kids needed. I knew it. I had knowledge that I was certain could transform them into scholars. But as Theodore Roosevelt said, "People don't care how much you know until they know how much you care." So when they hung out at my apartment, I stopped lecturing and I started listening. I pressed pause on the advice playlist and focused on learning their language.

I let our interactions be guided by their interests. If they wanted to talk about dating, that's where we went. If they wanted to play games, that's what we did. If they wanted to talk silly teen gibberish for hours, that was cool. Because I had to learn how to love them before I could learn how to teach them. I had to prioritize their humanity over my academic agenda. And when they saw that, I earned their trust.

The six of us kept meeting but my apartment was just too cramped. When my roommates were home, there might be ten to twelve of us sprawled across the floor. One Saturday, I suggested that we take our hangouts to the church. Going to the church was not their preference, but I secretly wanted to try something. Their parents were eager to drop them off.

"God bless you," Tasha said. "One less child for me today!" She had five kids and could use the relief. Andrea thanked me profusely for babysitting her two teens. Monique kicked Cordell out of the car and yelled, "Keep him as long as you want!" as she sped away.

I was left with disgruntled teens who did not share their parents' enthusiasm. They moped through the door, visibly inconvenienced on a weekend morning. They hated being dragged to church on Sundays. The only thing worse was being dragged to the church on a Saturday, too.

The church was in an old warehouse. On one side was a makeshift sanctuary with a wooden stage. On the other side was an empty garage that was either extremely hot or extremely cold, depending on the season. I collected a few white folding chairs and created a circle. I found a small whiteboard in the closet and propped it against the wall. I stood back and beheld it with pride. I had created my first classroom—although truthfully it looked more like an AA meeting.

The kids scoffed and hissed their distaste for our new setting. They sat contemptuously with their arms folded. Shontae smacked her gum and slouched in her seat. Cordell leaned forward with his elbows resting on his knees and his chin cupped between his hands. TJ was looking at the ceiling and twisting his locks. Ben and Angel were preoccupied with their phones. Everyone looked miserable, like Sunday school or the world's most boring history class was about to get under way.

In contrast, I was happy to be there and itching to get started. "There's something that I want to talk to you about," I said, reaching for the whiteboard. "Have y'all ever heard of the Harlem Renaissance?"

There was silence and blank stares.

"Okay, great," I said. "Let me tell you all about it." I unleashed the most passionate lesson that I knew. I told stories about Reconstruction and the Harlem Renaissance and how we are part of a rich tradition of Black ingenuity. I couldn't even stay in my seat. I bounded from one side of the circle to the other, like the ring of folding chairs was a grand stage. I had just reached one of my favorite parts of the story when, all of a sudden, Cordell yawned. This was no discreet yawn. This was a full-body, arms-stretched, legs-trembling, wide-mouthed yawn. I stopped talking. I thought, *Did this lil nigga just do a full-body yawn?* I was damn near performing backflips off the walls, teaching my ass off, and he had the nerve to yawn like he was just waking up for morning coffee. The disrespect. But I wasn't going to allow him to spoil it for the rest of the group, so I stormed ahead.

The story was picking up and my momentum soared. I became so excited that I impersonated my various heroes. I jumped onto a chair like Denzel Washington in *The Great Debaters*. When I reached the climax of my story, I looked around the circle to gauge their excitement—and two of them were nodding off. I thought, *You gotta be fuckin' kidding me*. I was enacting history like I was auditioning for the Broadway cast of *Hamilton*, and my performance was putting them to sleep.

I was crushed. Like school, like English, like debate, teaching was the complete opposite of what I had imagined. I thought, *Maybe the Praxis exam was right about me. Maybe I'm not qualified to do this. Maybe I misheard my calling.*

I did not understand. I expected my first classroom to crackle with electricity and *Aha!* moments. The students would smile from ear to ear as I introduced them to scholars who looked like them. I would command the room like Mr. Tolson in *The Great Debaters*. They would chant and cheer me on like the people who'd heard my first public speech a few months earlier. But none of that happened.

After the students went home, I was so confused. I thought I had the answer, the remedy for disengaged youth. Discovering the Harlem Renaissance and Black scholars changed my life, so why wasn't this working for them? There must be something that I was not doing right. *How could they not care about something so valuable?*

My thoughts turned to philosophy and rhetoric. I thought about Aristotle's modes of persuasion: ethos, pathos, and logos. I remembered reading that humans are more emotional than logical: not everyone thinks critically, but everyone feels intensely. For teachers and speakers and leaders, this means that we mobilize people by understanding that the heart is the gateway to the mind. That's why Maya Angelou said that you might not remember what people say or do, but you will never forget how they made you feel.

I had grabbed teaching by the wrong end, instinctively approaching it like the teachers who had made students numb to learning. I put the subject before the student. Instead of only asking myself, *What do I want them to know?* I started asking myself, *What do I want them to feel?*

Armed with this insight, I was ready to have another go. I begged the parents to give me another Saturday with their kids and they happily obliged. The kids were even more sullen the second time around.

This time, I introduced debate. I wanted them to feel empowered, included, and alive. Nothing does this better than using your voice. People become passionate about things that are personal. The most personal thing you can ever own is your perspective and your voice. Your opinions belong to no one else but you. If I could find something that they cared about, marry that with what I wanted them to care about, and activate their voices—passion would fill the room.

I tried everything during our second Saturday at the church. Nothing worked.

There were no yawns or chin drops, but there was no passion either. I wanted them to love this stuff and be just as jacked about it as I was. But they didn't perk up until I said, "All right, let's take a break" and they huddled around their phones to watch YouTube videos. My efforts to make learning as thrilling as sports and music videos were failing, so I gave up. I abandoned my lesson plan and said, "We're done for the day. Let's just go across the street and grab something to eat at Hardee's."

Nothing excited them more than the twenty-foot field trip across the street. As I watched them strangle and devour cheeseburgers, I listened. I stopped talking and tuned my ear toward the things that mattered most to them. As the girls fawned over their crushes, the boys mocked them. They began arguing about who was in love and who was not, and when banter escalated to insults, I swooped in.

"Okay, okay," I said. "Hold on a second. Let's talk about this, but one at a time." I asked the boys, "Why is it that you think it's not possible for Shontae to love this guy?"

I had my own opinion, having listened to the conversations. But my perspective did not matter. I only guided with questions and moved out of the way as they explored.

Cordell stood so quickly that his seat nearly flew back as he exclaimed, "She just met the guy!"

"So what!" Shontae countered, rising to meet him at eye level.

"Calm down," I interrupted before verbal punches were thrown.

They both sat down. I told them that we could continue the conversation, but we would have a few ground rules.

"Here's what we're going to do," I said. "Cordell, you give Shontae a minute to make her point. Shontae, you give Cordell a minute to make his point. The only rule is that you cannot interrupt each other." They laid out their cases.

After each of them presented their arguments, I said, "Now, I want you to cross-examine each other." Shontae's face contorted at the jargon. "Huh?" she said.

"Basically, each of you takes a turn interrogating the other."

"Ooh, I go first!" Shontae declared.

I laughed and said, "Okay, Shontae. Just remember, the rule is you can only pose questions." Then I added, "And you have to actually let him answer."

Shontae opened fire on Cordell with a mouthful of polemical questions. But Cordell stood firm, responding cleverly and with conviction, not allowing his opponent to break him. Before I knew it, they were delving deeper and deeper into the topic with each question. Their understanding began to crystallize. Their voices rose with ferocity. Their bodies could no longer be confined to their seats. It became so intense that Ben and Ryan and Angel charged in from the sidelines. The boys and the girls clashed with each other like it was the third round of a grand cross-examination. The other patrons grimaced and frowned, but I did not care. The kids were consumed by a new flame as I sat back and beheld the magic unfolding before my eyes. It was beautiful. They were debating. I was teaching. They were learning. It was the passion I had been longing for. We were having our first real class—at Hardee's.

The points on both sides were not entirely logical, but this was okay. We were off to a beautiful start.

"All right," I said, "your thoughts and feelings are all valid. Now let's break it down conceptually."

We dealt with the nature of love: what it is, how it comes to be, and when it can occur. Instead of lecturing, I became a facilitator, posing questions and allowing their curiosity to steer us. I asked questions like "Is love at first sight possible?" and "What is the true definition of love?" to keep the conversation on course. I sat back and watched their inquisitive natures take over.

The conversation reached a point where I could easily introduce an academic concept. I was nervous because I did not want to suck the energy out of the room with lofty language, but I could not miss this teachable moment. I took a deep breath and went for it.

"Love is complicated," I said. "In fact, it's so complex that the Greeks broke it down into four separate words: *eros, phileo, storge,* and *agape.*"

I examined their faces to see if they were still with me. They looked as if I had forced them to bite into a lemon. I knew I needed to act quickly to avoid losing them. Instead of reverting to lecture mode, I brought them back into the conversation with more questions.

"Okay, think of it this way. What are the different ways that you can love a person?"

"You can love a boy," Shontae said as she scowled in Cordell's direction.

"Correct," I said. "What else?"

Ben replied, "You can love a sibling."

"Yes," I said. "Keep going."

They continued with more examples of loving a friend, loving a parent, loving a spouse, and I asked them to break down the distinctions. I realized that this was the key to engagement. I gave them a problem to solve. When kids solve problems, learning becomes experiential; it ceases being one-dimensional and unfolds into a matrix of discovery. For this to happen, a teacher must facilitate an experience, not just transmit information. So many teachers say, *Here's the content, take this test*—and that's it. But Einstein once described education as what remains when schooling is over. Teachers succeed when they incite curiosity and give students an opportunity to create something of their own. Whether students make something tangible in science or something abstract in humanities, it belongs to them. It's theirs to look upon with pride. That is how students come to own their education.

I watched their faces glisten as they collaborated to solve the mystery of love. I stayed out of the way, mesmerized by what was happening. They were immersed in a scholarly exercise and didn't even know it. Because it did not feel like school. I wondered how much deeper they would allow me to take the conversation.

"Want to know something cool?" I gently inserted. "This conversation right here puts you in the ranks of Greek philosophers."

"Philo-what?" Shontae said sarcastically. Her face scrunched like I had just spoken pig Latin. I could not help but laugh.

"A philosopher," I said. "They question ideas about the world to find problems and solve them. Like what you're doing."

"Well, I ain't no philosopher," she responded, "I'm Shontae."

"Or," I said, "you can be Shontae the philosopher." She sucked her teeth and rolled her eyes as we shared a laugh.

"You know what?" Shontae continued. "Now that I think about it, you might be right."

I looked up and smiled, thinking she had finally joined the party that I was throwing.

"I'm the philosopher," she said, "and they the dummies!" She pointed her acrylic fingernails at the boys. They quickly snapped back until I said, "Relax, relax. All of you are philosophers." They did not appear to be turned off by the idea. So I continued.

"Let me explain who they are and how it relates to what you just accomplished."

Later that evening, I sat on my sagging couch and reflected on the miracle at Hardee's. Aristotle was right. I did not have their attention until I had their hearts. Once they latched on to something of personal value, I was able to pull them into a deeper conversation. Carter G. Woodson said that the mere imparting of information is not education; the goal is being able to think and do for oneself. I needed to get better at teaching them how to analyze and think for themselves. Learning is not an interstate highway across a flat plain, it's a meandering journey full of twists and turns and glorious tangents, where curiosity carries the student and teacher to places they've never been. I had never experienced anything else so euphoric as our afternoon at Hardee's.

The bliss of the moment was pierced by a surprise phone call from Tasha, Shontae's mother.

"Hello?" I answered with a touch of wariness.

"Brandon . . ." she began, sounding confrontational. Tasha is from the hood, so her voice has an unabashed trace of ghetto.

"What you do to my child?" she asked. I thought, *Oh shit*. I knew the boys were aggressive during our spontaneous debate, but I did not think anything got out of hand. Maybe I should not have allowed their exchange to be so passionate, but I honestly thought we were doing a good thing. I started explaining but Tasha cut me off.

"She over here talkin' 'bout some man named Plato and his Greek friends and asking me questions like how did I know I loved my ex."

I couldn't hold back the laughter. I was relieved and tickled.

"I ain't never heard this child talk like this!" Tasha said with unusual excitement.

Several Saturdays went by. We met for class in the former garage and continued the discussions that began at Hardee's. But one day I arrived to find that the students had beaten me to our makeshift classroom. I grabbed my whiteboard from the closet and bounced in, ready to say, "Okay, let's begin," but when I looked up, there were about ten kids, not just five. Before I could ask, "Who the hell are y'all?" Ben and Cordell said the newcomers were their friends, some of them from the neighborhood basketball court. Their pants were sagging nearly to their knees and they greeted me with dap and street slang. I loved it. I said, "Welcome home," and we launched into our journey.

The following Saturday, there were nearly fifteen.

Weeks later, there were more than twenty. We upgraded from a circle in the garage to a row of white plastic tables and chairs in the more spacious lobby.

By the next month, about twenty-five inner-city youth were voluntarily showing up for Saturday school. It was a spectacle, a movement. We were experiencing our own renaissance.

At first, they hated it when I called them scholars. I greeted them with "Good morning, scholars" and dismissed class with "See you later, scholars," and they scoffed at the very idea. Shontae, with her unbridled honesty, declared, "I ain't no scholar." I understood; only a few years earlier, I would have said the same thing. "Scholars are lame," Shontae continued. "And I ain't no geek."

Young people love the idea of disrupting the status quo, and the educational system that they had grown to hate was a worthy target. I called them scholars because that's what I saw when I looked into their eyes. I didn't see what their teachers and their principals saw. I wasn't afraid of their attitudes, their street clothes, their explicit language, or their other affectations, because I looked deeper. The uncouth behaviors that others saw—I saw those, too. But I recognized their underlying pain and believed it could be channeled in a different direction.

As the weeks passed, I watched an anger rise within them. The anger of being woke. The anger of discovering the truth. They asked questions that began, "So you mean to tell me . . . ?" and "Wait, but how come . . . ?" They learned what I learned: that we had all been miseducated. Day after day, we wrestled with the hard questions. We cried. We laughed. We did the gritty work of undoing their miseducation. I taught them how to remove the noose from their necks. I taught them about their responsibility to do the same for somebody else.

At this stage, there was only one thing missing. They were starting to talk like scholars. Now I wanted them to feel like scholars, which meant they had to look the part. I knew that style was one of their concerns as popular teens. I realized that meeting them where they were meant marrying my agenda with their interests. So I wanted to redefine the image of a "scholar" into something with swag. After weeks of car washes and bake sales and borrowing money from my girlfriend, I saved up enough funds for a special surprise that I wanted to give them.

One Saturday they arrived to find a box sitting at the foot of each desk.

"You got us gifts?" Shontae said, lunging at a box with her name on it.

"Wait, don't touch it," I said. "Just take your seats. I need to explain something first."

I did that annoying thing that my mother used to do on Christmas, where she gave a speech before each gift she presented. Waiting was pure torture and I'd ravage the box the second she was finished. They looked at me with the same impatience as I went around the room to give each student a personal affirmation about what made me most proud of them. They smiled with appreciation, but I could see that they were antsy, so I made it quick.

I opened a bigger box that had been sitting in front of me. I pulled out a batch of fancy plaid ties and held them up, saying, "These are for the girls." Then I showed off custom-made, hand-sewn, polka-dot bow ties for the boys. Finally, I pulled out a crisp navy blazer with a custom embroidered emblem that read SCHOLARS PROGRAM. The girls gasped and shrieked with excitement and the boys yelled, "Yoooo!" as they ripped into their individual boxes like it was Christmas morning. The girls threw on the blazers and the boys wrapped the ties around their necks.

"Wait, what does this mean?" Shontae said, examining the emblem on her chest.

"We're legit now," I explained. "These are your outfits for class. Just like athletes have uniforms, so do debaters." I explained that they were scholars now, that we were starting a new renaissance, and that we were giving scholarship a new look.

"I feel smart already," Cordell said, stretching out his arms and stroking the new blazer like a royal robe.

"You are smart," I said to him. "These clothes are just a declaration of that."

They were never the same after that day. They walked differently, with a certain scholarly swag. Even the way they sat in their seats, erect and attentive, was different. Now they felt too fresh to slouch and squirm. When I greeted them as scholars, they smiled like they believed it. Being smart looked so fashionable that they even wore their outfits to school. Most kids hate uniforms, but we did what Black people do best and sprinkled some seasoning on their ensemble. Their dress shirts and blazers were the perfect color contrast of red, navy, and white. The boys complemented their dotted bow ties with flamboyant socks that peeked out above their shoes. They walked down the hallway in packs, like they were strutting for a GQ magazine cover shoot.

They were the only Black kids wearing dressy tailored blazers to school. The unique style earned them a badge of popularity. They looked like a movement, like they belonged to something bigger than themselves. Lynchburg began to buzz with word about "that new program for Black kids." More kids showed up, and I was eager to teach them all. We had no enrollment system at first, so it was come one, come all, until we ran out of space.

Local news media even caught wind of the movement. But my first interview with a reporter was unpleasant. She attended one of our Saturday classes to interview a few students and me. I was a nervous wreck. I had not been interviewed since high school basketball. The cameraman gave the on-air reporter a signal that we were live. I clenched my armpits because sweat was seeping through my suit jacket. She asked me a few questions about the program and its inception. Then she asked me a question that almost made me lose it on camera.

"These are at-risk kids that you are serving," she said. "So what made you decide to call this a scholars program?"

I hesitated for a moment as I stared at her. But I kept my composure. I firmly responded, "Because that's what I see in them."

I did not care what other people felt about them, the ones who marked my kids with "at-risk" and other labels. I did not need everybody to believe in what we were doing. I had enough faith for us all. I could not explain the magic that was happening in that room each Saturday. But it was working.

Meanwhile, I was still a full-time English major at Liberty. I enjoyed my American Lit class, and Flannery O'Connor was one of my favorite authors. But one day in particular, I had a hard time focusing as we analyzed "A Good Man Is Hard to Find." It was an ordinary day on the first floor of DeMoss Hall, but for students in the local high schools, this was report card day.

In my Saturday classroom, I did not badger them about grades and test scores. I wanted them to find pure joy in learning. But I worried in private, because I had learned that the kids had about a 1.2 GPA as a group for the previous quarter. I wanted us to have a good time at our Saturday school, but I wanted more than that. I wanted them to grow. I wanted that joy and excitement and intellectual progress to shine forth from the church lobby and illuminate their everyday classrooms. I made surprise visits to their schools. Sometimes they'd spot me peeking through the door window, confirming that they were sitting in the front row like I'd told them. Other times I showed up with McDonald's, which was caviar compared to their school lunch. I wanted them to know that my commitment to them was not limited to Saturday mornings. I desperately wanted them to show the world what I already knew about them. That's why I sat in my English class thinking about their report cards, not about a traveling salesman and an artificial leg.

English was my first class of the day and met at 7:45 a.m. I knew high school report cards were distributed during first period, which fell somewhere between 8:00 and 9:30 a.m. Waiting to hear from them was more suspenseful than the wait when I first got tested for STDs. My entire life felt like it hinged on this one moment.

I was sitting on my hands, trying to keep still, when, suddenly, my phone vibrated. I grabbed for it so frantically that it nearly slipped to the floor. It was Ben. I jumped up so quickly that the screeching of my desk and chair caused everyone to stare.

"Sorry, it's an emergency," I said to the professor as I excused myself.

I burst through the door and answered the phone as soon as I was in the hallway.

"Hello?" I said. "Hello?" I repeated. My heart was pounding so hard I could barely breathe. Suddenly, Ben's response from the other end told me everything I needed to know.

"Let's goooo!" he yelled from the other end like he had just scored the game-winning shot. He did not have to say another word. I already knew what his elation meant. Tears began to fill my eyes. We hung up and he sent me screenshots of his grades. My phone started pinging incessantly. First was Shontae. Then Ryan. Then Cordell. Then Angel. Then TJ. More than twenty text messages with screenshots of report cards flooded my phone.

I was overwhelmed and slid to the floor with my back against the wall. I put my hands over my face to conceal my sobbing. They did it. Together, they went from a 1.2 GPA to an astounding 3.5 for the group. Almost every one of them made A/B Honor Roll for the first time in their lives.

What started as five kids, a circle of plastic chairs, and a college student with a whiteboard became a movement that took the city of Lynchburg by storm. News reporters came in droves. Teachers and administrators were confounded. They all asked the same question: *How did you transform these kids so quickly?* My answer was simple: I met them where they were. I helped them find their voices. Just as someone once did for me.

CHAPTER TEN

A LEADER BORN

Although we still lived in a decaying apartment and feeding myself and my brother was a struggle, I worked without pay at the Anne Spencer House & Garden Museum. This Lynchburg landmark was once the home of a full-fledged member of the Harlem Renaissance, a much-admired poet whose artistic friends from New York often visited this very house.

Volunteer work was one thing; getting academic credit for studying Anne Spencer was a bonus. In my final year of college, I discovered that there was such a thing as an independent study course. So I proposed to study and write about her work, the chair of the English department approved my request, and we developed a syllabus.

Every time I set foot on the black-and-white-checkered walkway to the front door of her Queen Anne–style house, I felt like I was stepping onto holy ground. Inside, I was greeted by the spirits of Langston Hughes, W. E. B. Du Bois, James Weldon Johnson, Zora Neale Hurston, Marian Anderson, George Washington Carver, and the many Black Renaissance leaders she hosted as they traveled through the Jim Crow South. In these same rooms, Anne Spencer and other leaders launched the local chapter of the NAACP.

The vibrant, brightly decorated interior of the house has not been changed since Anne Spencer died in 1975. It is a shrine to Anne and her loving husband, Edward, who designed and built the house in 1903 and added to it for decades. When visitors came, I led tours as part of my volunteer internship. When I was alone, I transcribed original documents written by the famed poet and curated archives, work that benefited both the museum and my own independent research.

It was sometimes hard to focus in this setting. On occasion, I went upstairs and studied *The Cocktail Party*, a mural that artist Dolly Allen Mason had painted on Anne and Edward's bedroom wall. When I held an original letter Du Bois wrote to Anne, the paper now the color of weak tea, my mind traveled to the 1920s. Luminaries of the Harlem Renaissance gathered in the same parlor where I combed through documents. If I could join them, I would not say a word. I would listen and take notes as Alain Locke reclined on the floral chesterfield, one leg crossed, cigar in hand, expounding on *The New Negro*; as Du Bois sat across the room in the cherry wingback chair, self-satisfied and amused, stroking his chin after explaining the concept of *double consciousness*; and as Langston Hughes slicked back his wavy hair and sermonized the weary blues. Maybe we'd all sip a little moonshine. Maybe Zora would tease us with early notes from *Their Eyes Were Watching God*. Maybe inebriation would set in and we'd laugh hysterically when James Weldon Johnson separated us into sopranos, altos, and tenors and scolded us for being off-key when we attempted to harmonize on "Lift Every Voice and Sing." Then Ella Fitzgerald would yell, "Play that record!" and we'd frolic around the room to "It Don't Mean a Thing." Maybe I'd introduce them to the Nae Nae or "Crank That (Soulja Boy)" and they'd tell me to sit my simple ass down. I imagined hearing three knocks at the door and Anne yelling, "Who is it?" From the other side we'd hear a loud, "Hi-de-hi-de-hi-de-ho!" as we laughed and shouted, "Let Cab on in here!" I could see it. I could feel it. So I spent hours basking in the spirit of the Harlem Renaissance.

I climbed the same staircase that Countee Cullen and Thurgood Marshall mounted to the same room where Martin Luther King Jr. slept when he spoke in Lynchburg in the 1960s. Behind the house, I sat in Anne's writing cottage in her legendary sun garden. I tended the pond where water spewed from the mouth of a cast-iron sculpture made by Ebo artisans. Du Bois gave it to Anne after spending time in Ghana. I never wanted to leave this place. Several times a week I stepped into this time machine and journeyed to the Jazz Age that shaped me.

The museum was a gem nestled in the center of Lynchburg, but it was barely seen, touched, or talked about. Apparently, the Harlem Renaissance was dead as far as people in Lynchburg were concerned. Yet it was powerful and magical to me, and its resurrection became my mission. Sitting in Anne's inner parlor, where my heroes had argued and laughed nearly a century earlier, I thought about what mattered to me and what mattered to the people who had no idea why I cared about these artists and thinkers. How could I bring our interests together? I wanted to do something bigger than a Black History Month program or a class project, something that would reach a whole community.

I knew from personal experience that many people would rather be entertained than educated. So whatever I came up with had to do both. That's when it hit me. *What if I threw a festival to bring the Harlem Renaissance to life?* I thought about all the festivals I had seen over the years: Caribbean festivals, pride festivals, music festivals, and so many others. How hard could it be to plan, fund, and build a festival?

I was excited and ambitious, driven by an impulse that I did not understand. But I still trusted it. I was ready to dive into the deep end, blindfolded and without a life vest, giving no thought to risk. My zeal to educate the people of Lynchburg about the Harlem Renaissance blinded me to rational caution. I did not consider the cost of hosting a citywide festival. I did not consider the challenges of planning and marketing such an event, securing a space, finding and contracting with vendors, and organizing the community. I had no idea where to even begin. But I was determined, and that was all that mattered.

My only partner was Shaun Spencer-Hester, Anne Spencer's only surviving granddaughter and director of the museum. She'd set up the foundation that operates the museum and found nonprofit partners to care for the gardens. She had been instrumental in getting the house listed on the National Register of Historic Places. She'd been doing it alone, and now she was delighted to have join her someone young, energetic, and passionate about her grandmother's place in history.

The morning of Saturday, September 22, 2012, was beautiful. The sun glowed, the wind was calm, and the temperature was in the comfortable sixties. More than a month had passed since I'd had the idea, a million details had been sorted out, and I hadn't really been scared until now. This was the first time I'd organized a public event, and Shaun and I were the only staff.

We had planned what seemed like a great program, but there was no guarantee that people would actually show up. We didn't sell tickets or ask people to RSVP. Like a DJ or a little-known band, I had stapled posters to light poles and slid flyers under the windshield wipers of cars in every public parking lot in the city. The flyer read, "Anne Spencer Museum Presents: Harlem Renaissance Festival 2012" and promised an art exhibit, games for kids, open mic, and live entertainment.

We'd gotten permission to close two blocks of historic Pierce Street, from Thirteenth to the ruined tennis court near Fifteenth where Arthur Ashe once trained. Vendors started to arrive around 10 a.m. and soon the area looked like the prelude to a Mardi Gras parade. There were ice-cream trucks, face-painting stations, art for sale, and barbecue tents along the road. The main assembly area was a grassy open lot next to the museum. It featured inflatable bounce houses, a dunking booth, and an elevated plywood stage that we had hammered together for performances. The local fire station brought over a truck to amuse kids. The radio host from Hot 103.9 played music that carried through the whole neighborhood. Everything looked great. Everything was in place. Except for the people. And I thought, *What if nobody shows up?*

I walked past the barbecue tent. There was one man on the grill. His apron draped over his pot belly, he wore basketball shorts with Jesus sandals. Anytime a Black man is on the grill with shorts and Jesus sandals or off-white New Balances, you know it's about to go down. This was the uniform of a southern grill master. He yelled over the music, "All right now!" which meant both hello and goodbye in his southern dialect.

Shaun saw me pacing frantically from vendor to vendor and said, one hand lightly patting my back, "Don't worry, the people will come." Her optimism was comforting, and it proved justified about thirty minutes later. Waves of children, teens, and adults poured from all directions. It looked like the Johnson family reunion. Kids were running around and jumping in the bounce house and playing double Dutch. Teenagers were on the mound hurling baseballs and trying to strike the bull's-eye at the dunking booth. Adults were dancing the Electric Slide with a drink in hand. The DJ played some old-school jams. Grown folks shuffled and two-stepped and yelled across the yard, "You don't know nun' 'bout dat right there!" to the young folks who were not paying them any attention. I looked around at our community. It was perfect. And it got even better when the program began.

Our plan was to re-create the Cotton Club, the Harlem nightspot where many of the greatest Black artists performed. Corderius, my good friend from campus, was the master of ceremonies. He was dressed like a Jazz Age dandy, in a suit with suspenders, wing-tip shoes, and a classic fedora. He clutched the microphone stand with both hands and let out a great big "Good afternoon, everybodyyyy!" The crowd clapped and cheered as he said, "I would like to welcome you to Lynchburg's first-ever Harlem Renaissance Festival!" What we had accomplished became real to me in that moment as hundreds of people cheered and clapped with joy, ready for a good time.

Many of my college friends were gifted singers and they were game to impersonate the brightest stars of the era. Cassie channeled her silvery, angelic voice into "Summertime," Ella Fitzgerald style. Kristal took us to church with "God Bless the Child" by Billie Holiday. Walter transformed himself into the "Hi-de-ho" man himself, the great Cab Calloway.

We danced and sang and grooved like it was the Roaring Twenties in up-town Manhattan. To close the day, we had poetry readings. A friend read "I, Too" by Langston Hughes. We all sang "Lift Every Voice and Sing" by James Weldon Johnson. And I ended with a tribute to Anne Spencer, the American poet who gave rise to the renaissance in Lynchburg.

The Harlem Renaissance Festival became a popular annual event in Lynchburg. I coordinated it for a couple of years. My first attempt at com-munity organizing was a success and now I felt invincible. Bringing all those people together made me euphoric, but I knew this was just the be-ginning. Raising awareness of the Harlem Renaissance was great, but I had a bigger message to share.

As my senior year was coming to a close, I worked as a teacher assistant in the old education building next to the Hangar, one of Liberty's old student centers. One afternoon, Dr. DeWitt, an education professor I'd had before dropping out of the teacher training track, peeked her head in as I was en-tering grades.

"You're not coming?" she asked, one foot across the threshold.

"Coming where?"

"Wait, you haven't heard?" she seemed astonished.

"Heard what?" I was confused.

She told me there was a guest speaker today, some famous guy that ev-eryone was hot to hear. "You have to come," she said. "You can finish that later."

I told her that I would try. Papers were stacked everywhere and I needed to enter more grades before I clocked out for the day.

"I promise you won't regret it," she said, closing the door.

I wasn't convinced because the university's most heavily promoted guest speakers were typically white, male, evangelical, and monotonous. I figured there was no way they would invite a fiery orator like Cornel West or Dick Gregory or Michelle Obama, so I was uninterested.

I kept pecking the keyboard with my index fingers, carefully entering each grade. The noise level rose and I saw that the hallway was now crowded with people, scrunched tightly together and all carrying copies of the same book. They were headed in the direction of the Hangar, and I could sense the buzz. I had never seen such commotion about a guest speaker.

Ultimately, I couldn't resist. I walked over and slipped through the door into a huge banquet hall. Students and faculty were already settled around the big round tables, empty of food or drink for this daytime event. The speaker was already up. As I suspected, he was another white man, most likely conservative, just like the rest of them. But everyone was transfixed. My professor saw me and motioned me toward her table, which was unfortunately near the front. I hunched over and tiptoed toward her, squeezing between rows of round tables.

I sat down and started listening to the man and was immediately enthralled. He moved like a thespian: he was vivacious and theatric and pirouetted around the abandoned lectern. No one could take their eyes off of him. It was the most ingenious display of oratory that I had ever seen. He was an artist, a showman. He used voices that made people laugh. He told stories that made people cry. And when it seemed like it could not possibly get better, he used a chair as a stepping-stone and launched himself onto one of the round tables. Everyone gasped, shocked that he would stand on the white tablecloth. They gasped because they had never seen such a thing. I gasped because I thought only Denzel Washington and I did that. I looked down at the program lying on my table to find out who this man was. I needed to know his name because he had already joined my list of heroes.

His name was Ron Clark.

Wisdom was pouring from him and I started jabbing away with my thumbs, taking notes on my phone. He told about being raised in a small town in rural North Carolina, then moving to Harlem to teach in a neighborhood where people like him did not belong. The kids he taught achieved what had seemed unimaginable. He was named the Disney American Teacher of the Year. He was on *The Oprah Winfrey Show*, twice. He wrote a book, and a movie was made about him. The man was everything I wanted to be. No wonder there was a stampede in the hallway and no wonder everyone had his book, eager to get it signed. No one even looked at their phones. Except me, because I was thumbing as fast as I could, trying to take down everything he said. Then, all of a sudden, he stopped talking.

He took a beat, then said, "Come on up here and join me since you're texting during my talk." I kept typing furiously, wondering what fool would be texting during such a stellar presentation. I closed my notes and glanced up from my phone thinking, *I wish whoever he is talking to would get the hell up so the speech can continue.* I looked around for the culprit, but everyone's eyes were centered on me. I was so confused. I looked at them like, *The hell y'all staring at?* I looked at Ron Clark with his hands on his hips. "Yes, you," he said, his eyes fixed on me.

"Oh no, sir," I responded, "I wasn't texting, I was taking notes on my phone. I'm so sorry."

"It's okay," he said. "Come on up here anyways and help me."

As I rose from my seat, everyone clapped like I was a lucky winner. What I felt was embarrassment, not luck. I walked up and he reached out to shake hands. I shook his hand and then he announced, "See, people. This is an example of a weak handshake." I thought, *This man brought me up here to embarrass me, I oughta whoop his ass.* But I smiled and laughed with everyone else.

He showed us how he teaches his students the importance of handshakes and first impressions. "You don't look down at the hand," he said. "You reach while maintaining eye contact." I did as he instructed. "Yes, just like that," he affirmed. "Excellent job."

I did not feel embarrassed anymore. I felt empowered. No one had ever taught me so-called soft skills. I was eager to learn more from him. He patted me on the back and said, "Thank you, buddy." I said, "Thank you, sir." He reached out his hand. I extended mine without breaking eye contact. Before I walked away, he said, "See me at the book-signing table after this."

"Yes, sir," I said and returned to my seat.

The line stretched from one end of the building to the other. After a few minutes, I realized that if I didn't leave then, I'd be late for my next class. The line was agonizingly slow because Ron Clark's fans didn't just want their book signed, they wanted their own moment with the education icon. I looked at the time again and decided that I would just go up and wave at him before I left. I skipped to the front of the line and said, "Thanks again, Mr. Clark. I have to head to class."

"Wait," he said, beckoning me to the table.

I was worried he would expect me to buy a book. They were about $20 and I could not afford it. Twenty dollars could feed my brother and me for an entire week or more. He inscribed a book for me and handed it over for free. We took a picture and shook hands again. I got it right for a second time.

On the cross-campus bus, I was on fire. After hearing Ron Clark speak, I knew that I was destined to do more than teach debate on Saturday mornings. Clark had showed me what was possible. I wanted to revolutionize education as much as he did, sharing my discoveries as he had done. I was so excited about changing the world that I could hardly concentrate as I sat in the back of my English class. My other class meetings were the same. I couldn't tune in to my professors or classmates, although I read the books and passed the quizzes and wrote the essays. I daydreamed about how Ron Clark had gotten to the point of traveling everywhere, using his voice to empower teachers with strategies for making education work better for more children. I wanted to do that. I wanted to bring people together in the same way. But there was a big difference between Ron and me. Ron spoke at these places by invitation. Me, on the other hand, no one had ever heard of me. But I supposed Ron had started out as an unknown classroom teacher as well, and then blazed his own path to reach huge audiences. So I figured that I could do the same. After all, I was discovering myself as a trailblazer. And I remembered that we do not wait for opportunities, we create them.

I was passionate about reforming education and I had ideas to share. I thought, *Instead of waiting for a platform, how about I build my own?* The way to do this, I thought, was to hold an academic conference on education reform right there in Lynchburg. I had pulled off the Harlem Renaissance

Festival, so nothing seemed too big. I envisioned what the conference might look like and began thinking about everything involved. Where would it be held? Who would attend? How would I convince them to come? How would I pay for it?

Though my scholars program had grown rapidly and gained some regional notice, many people were skeptical about its sustainability. I would not get far with seasoned educators by saying, "Hi, I'm a former dropout and a four-time Praxis failure with no teaching license or experience, would you like me to train you on best practices?" I believed in the curriculum and process I had developed, but I could not be the main attraction for the conference I dreamed about. In fact, I couldn't make it about me at all. It needed to feature authorities, people whose names would make educators say, *I have to be there, I have to hear this person.* And I knew exactly who that person would be.

I searched online for Ron Clark's contact information. I called his school in Atlanta, Georgia. A woman named Mrs. Mosley answered the phone at the Ron Clark Academy. She had the kind of energy that reached through the phone and lifted you up, no matter where you were.

I told her that I wanted to book Ron Clark for my upcoming conference. She let me know, in the gentlest way possible, that an agent handles his bookings and gave me his contact information. I knew nothing about agents or speakers bureaus. I called and the agent asked me a sequence of questions that I couldn't answer.

"What's the date? Do you have a location? Is there a venue?" he asked. I had no answers.

He finally asked, "Well, do you have a budget?" I asked him what he meant by this and he told me Ron's customary fee. I nearly dropped my phone. Naively, I asked, "He can't do it for free?" In response, the agent took time to explain the speaking business to me. I understood. It made sense. But I would not take no for an answer.

I wrote a letter to Ron Clark and sent it to the school. I introduced myself as the young man he'd met at Liberty. I told him about my work and the revolution that I was trying to create. I asked him to help me by speaking at my conference even though I couldn't afford to pay. I never heard back, and I assumed my long-shot letter was buried at the bottom of a giant pile of fan mail.

I went back to the drawing board. *Who can I invite that people will want to listen to? And who will do this for free?* Local leaders in education and politics seemed possible: the mayor, the superintendent, and well-known professors and principals. I reached out to them with an ambitious pitch: I promised the biggest education conference the city had ever seen, a fancy banquet with live jazz and hundreds of participants from throughout the region. I knew I had to make it sound like a thing before it actually became a thing. Everything was pie in the sky at that point, but hearing Ron Clark speak had emboldened me. I was not afraid.

I got no response from the most prominent names on my list. I was an unknown but ambitious college student with no experience planning conferences. So I formed a speaking panel with six people who had made me audacious enough to dream up this event, and they all agreed to speak. I soon discovered that students could reserve event space on campus for free. I picked a date, booked the banquet hall in the Hancock building, and created a flyer. At the copy shop, I printed, laminated, and cut 150 tickets to be sold.

I had what seemed like the ideal marketing strategy. I had drafted ten of my friends to be on an advisory board for the organization. If we each sold fifteen tickets, then we were sure to have a full house. I distributed the tickets to my board members. A month later, I called a meeting to collect the funds. Four weeks had passed and only fifteen tickets had been sold. All by me.

I panicked. We were one week away from the event. I was angry, heartbroken, and had no idea what to do. I went to Pastor Gilbert and vented about how much I hated being the one in charge. I hated delegating and depending on others to deliver. I hated not being able to do everything myself. He let me vent. Then he said, "The mark of a great leader is not what he can achieve on his own; it's what he can achieve through other people." It made sense, but I was not in the mood for his philosophizing. I had to find another way. I collected the 135 unsold tickets from my board members.

Lynchburg has about twenty public schools, and their websites listed email addresses for administration, faculty, and staff. I contacted all the principals, told them about the event, and asked them to share the information with their faculty. Some never replied, and the ones who did said they could only promote events sanctioned by the superintendent. He had declined my invitation to speak at the conference, so I didn't bother to ask for his help now. I took matters into my own hands.

I spent my English classes surreptitiously scouring the web for the emails of every Lynchburg teacher, copy-and-pasting them into a spreadsheet one by one. When I got home that night, I sent a personal note to hundreds of them offering a discounted ticket. I was ready to give tickets away just to fill the room, but the catering invoice would be coming in a few days.

The emails worked: nearly a hundred teachers bought tickets, and the education department at Liberty purchased the rest and gave them to teachers in training. I collected just enough money to pay for the decorations and the catering. We were officially set for Lynchburg's inaugural education symposium.

The event was a hit. There was not an empty seat in the banquet hall, and we ate an elegant dinner with live jazz in the background. The panelists went first, and then it was finally my time. The master of ceremonies introduced me as the founder of the program. I felt like I was sitting on the bench at courtside, waiting for the announcer to say my name so I could lope through the tunnel of cheerleaders, emerging from the dramatic fog and flashing strobe lights. I knew what that spike of adrenaline felt like. But this time it was different. I was about to take the stage at my own event, and for a moment I was speechless. I rested my trembling hands on the sides of the podium and looked out over a gathering of people I respected, people I wanted passionately to reach. The music faded. Everyone sat still, eyes fixed on me.

This was my second time speaking to a large crowd and it was nothing like the first. Months before, I'd stood on a stage that I had not created and was not really invited to. But this time, I stood on a stage that I had built on my own, against the odds. As I looked around the room, details leaped out and I gave thanks. I was grateful for the linen and centerpieces on each table. I was grateful for the jazz performed by the same friends who'd starred at the Harlem Renaissance Festival. I was grateful for the people in the audience, who'd paid for tickets and shown up. And I was grateful for the panelists, who'd believed in me. Pastor Gilbert was there. Two of my beloved college professors were there. And a man who'd driven all the way from South Carolina, who looked at me with pride and tears as I took the stage: Mr. Mills, the high school teacher who never counted me out.

I did not have a script. I spoke from the heart. My first words were "I'm not supposed to be here." I sang my song, I told my story: how I'd almost died, and how I was learning to live. I told how each of the panelists was a teacher who had shaped and changed me when I needed molding and changing. I said that I was committed to inspiring other young people as they had inspired and motivated me. There was hardly a dry eye in the room. Afterward, I remained at the foot of the stage to shake hands and take pictures. People shared kind words with me like "Keep fighting the fight" and "This is only the beginning." But no one's words struck me like Kelly-Ann's.

Kelly-Ann and I were high school friends back in the DMV. She was studying at the University of Virginia to become a teacher, and she'd driven down from Charlottesville for the conference. I always knew she would be successful, though she could not say the same about me. She could hardly believe her eyes when she saw a social media post about the education conference. She double-checked to see if the Brandon Fleming displayed on her screen was the same dope-dealing jock that she once knew. She had tolerated a lot of childish antics from me in our high school home economics class. She hung around until the well-wishers had moved on, and when a path cleared, she pounced on me and threw her arms around my neck, saying, "I can't believe it!"

"I can't believe it either, Kell," I said as we shared an emotional moment.

We visited for a bit more but it was getting dark and Charlottesville was more than an hour's drive away. Just before she left, Kelly-Ann said, "You've got something special here, Brandon. You should consider taking it on the road. Start with UVA, I'll help you." I was so exhausted that I brushed off the suggestion without much thought.

Back at my apartment, I collapsed on my bed, still dressed in my suit. I slapped my face a few times to reassure myself that the conference hadn't been just a dream. It wasn't. It was real. Reassured, I slept deeply and woke up the next day feeling so alive and ready for the next big thing. That's when Kelly-Ann's words came back to me.

I called her and she told me again how glad she was to see that I had turned my life around. We caught up on lost time. I told her all about the scholars program. She told me about UVA and about pledging Alpha Kappa Alpha. We talked about her plans to teach after she graduated. I hid the fact that I would not be able to do the same. Then I couldn't hold my question any longer.

"Were you serious last night?" I asked.

"Serious about what?"

"About bringing the symposium to UVA. You really think we could do it?

"Absolutely," she said. "Just say the word and I will help you." There's no feeling like when a Black woman tells you that you can achieve something. I believed what she said she saw in me. So we went for it. I launched the Symposium Tour and we took the event to several college campuses on the East Coast. Starting with the University of Virginia.

My students sometimes traveled with me when I was invited to speak about education at nearby conferences. I was living my dream as a budding orator. But I still did not have a teaching license or a job lined up, and graduation was coming. I applied to public schools, but the answer was always the same: "Sorry, we cannot hire unlicensed teachers." I applied to just about every private school in Central Virginia, but none of them would take me. I looked at my scholars program and my events and thought, *What was all of this for if no one thinks I'm good enough to teach at their school?* I had no idea what to do. No administrator thought my successes outweighed my lack of credentials, except for one principal who'd attended my symposium.

"I can't hire you as a teacher," she said. "It's public school policy." I had heard this a million times already. The news did not surprise me.

"However," she continued. "I have an office position that I can give you."

I had no other choice. I could either work in her school's front office or keep making minimum wage.

"And I worked something out," she said. "Ms. Prewitt has an open fourth period. You can use her classroom to teach an elective on leadership." I thought, *Leadership? What the hell is this, a daily pep talk?* I wanted to do some *real ass* teaching. I wanted to teach English and philosophy and rhetoric like I taught my scholars on Saturdays. But her offer was the only one I had, so I accepted.

I spent most of the day in the main office. As visitors entered the building, I was the guy who swiped their ID cards and said, "Look at the camera, please." I handed them a stick-on name tag, smiled, and said, "Have a good day." But on the inside, I was saying, *Fuck my life.* When I wasn't signing people in, I was tracking truancy. I didn't need a college degree for any of this, not even for my so-called leadership class. That's why I decided to change it.

That one hour in the classroom became my salvation five days a week. It was the only thing I looked forward to other than Saturday school with my scholars. Several of them were enrolled at the high school where I now worked. They were excited to see me every day, but I was embarrassed. I traveled with them to events where I inspired hundreds of people, only to crash-land on Monday at a clerk's desk. That fourth period class gave me something to be proud of. It gave me purpose in what felt like an unending purgatory.

I was eager to teach on the first day. I had just turned twenty-three years old. If I'd worn polos and khakis like most of the male teachers, I would've looked like a student with no fashion sense. But I did not want to dress, talk, or walk like any of those stuffy teachers. So I dressed to suit myself. The school gave me a cart to shuttle my laptop and belongings to

Ms. Prewitt's classroom. It wasn't the classroom I dreamed of, or one that I created, but it was better than the front office where I looked like a doleful kid trapped behind a lemonade stand.

I was enchanted the first time I walked into the classroom. There were real desks and real chairs, not like the white plastic ones we used on Saturdays. Instead of a small whiteboard balanced on my lap, I now had a wall-sized Smart Board. It felt like I had finally arrived. I set up my workstation and watched the clock advance. In a few minutes, the bell would ring and my students would tumble in. I could not wait to meet them and see the room fill with eager learners. I could not stand still. It was as though the drummers were beating and the rowdy crowd was poised for tip-off, with the cheerleaders chanting, "Jump ball, get it, get it!" Finally, the bell sounded and the entire class burst into the room with excitement. The entire class was one student. One whole student. Exactly one person had signed up for my elective class on leadership and she sat in the front row with a big smile. It was Shontae.

"What we learning today, Flemmy?" she asked, just as eager as she could be. I was crushed, but the otherwise empty classroom did not matter to her. Shontae hadn't been the same since I made her give a speech at the UVA symposium that Kelly-Ann had helped arrange. The day before the event, I'd said, "Shontae, you're giving the opening speech tomorrow." She immediately said, "Who?" as she sardonically glanced around the room. "No, sir," she said, "not Shontae." She was adamant that she was not ready to speak in front of an audience that size when she had never even spoken publicly before. But I knew she could do it. I knew she could channel that *ghetto girl* persona into Black girl magic. Every Saturday when she walked in popping gum and patting her electric-blue braids, I saw it in her. I saw a tender heart, a brilliant mind, and a courageous voice. A voice that only needed a nudge to show itself to the world. When we arrived at UVA, she'd begged, "Please, Mr. Fleming. Please don't make me do this" with nervous tears. But I'd wiped away the tears and locked eyes with her. "You're getting ready to fly," I'd said.

That day had turned Shontae into a fierce ball of fire. Whenever I told the kids that another symposium was scheduled, she was quick to ask, "Flemmy, can I speak at the next one, too?" And I usually said, "Of course." No platform was too big. No classroom was too small. She had found her voice, and she carried it with her like a loaded pistol.

I was saddened by the empty classroom and angry that the principal hadn't warned me. But Shontae's energy lifted me. If I was enough for her, then she was enough for me. So I taught my heart out like the classroom was an arena filled with thousands.

When I returned to the main office, I asked for a word with the principal. Electives can be a hard sell, she told me, then suggested I make a pitch as part of morning announcements. I had thirty seconds to say something that would make students want to drop their current fourth period class for mine. I was nervous about the pitch. I was even more nervous about the letdown if it failed and kids walked by my empty room, pointing and saying, "There's the clown who told us to sign up for his leadership club." Apparently, whatever I said worked, because the next day's attendance was over capacity.

Teachers were not happy about kids dropping their classes for mine. Parents emailed to complain about their teenager dropping an honors class to take an elective with a rookie teacher who was not really a teacher. I had not enchanted or bullied kids to sign up, and they knew nothing about me as a teacher. But they were drawn to me as a person. I did not look, sound, or act like a traditional teacher. Every day, I wore suits and bow ties and flamboyant socks. When the fourth period bell rang, I grabbed my squeaky black cart with my laptop and portable speakers, queued up the trendiest hip-hop songs, and turned the volume up. I bopped down the hallway, twisting and turning and dancing with my cart as students gaped like, *What is this crazy man doing?* They laughed, but I kept at it. Pretty soon, the kids started tossing compliments like "Loving the socks, Mr. Fleming!" Before long, random students joined in and we danced through the halls together like a Second Line.

Eventually, some of the roughest kids in school picked up on my style. They came to school with scavenged bow ties, unearthed in a drawer or borrowed, and stopped by the main office to show me before they went to class. They'd peek around the corner at me, grinning from ear to ear and pointing at their ties with excitement. Most of these were clip-ons, but it was a good start. This grew into a campus trend that we called Wall Street Wednesdays, where hundreds of kids wore their most dapper dress clothes and a pair of flamboyant socks. A renaissance was under way.

We were reforming the culture of the school. Style was important to young people, and it enabled me to connect with students who might otherwise have kept their distance. They looked at me and saw a piece of themselves, reinforcing my belief that nothing fosters education like human connectivity. When they saw our interests converge through style and music, the cultural connection drew us closer together. It's the absence of art and culture that makes school feel like school—and sometimes like prison. When the Renaissance was born in Florence, Italy, there's a reason that artists were in the vanguard. Art is what fills the outlines of life with color. The way we dress is art. The way we talk is art. The way we teach is art. But monotony comes to suck the marrow out of school. It drains learning of personality and locks us into a grayscale version of existence. I could not live like that. During school hours, I wore properly accessorized suits. But the way I dressed for football games made an even more immediate connection with the kids.

Our school was playing its most hated rival, and tension was high in the fourth quarter. The stadium was packed from the top of the bleachers to the fence bordering the field. The Friday-night lights bounced off the gridiron as the players collided and the cheerleaders chanted. But our team was suffering a miserable defeat and our fans could not be rallied. On the opposite side of the field, rival students danced and taunted, waving their middle fingers like school banners.

Some kids came to watch the game, some came to socialize, and some came for the brawls that often followed any competition with this school.

Whether the event was on a field or a court didn't matter: a phalanx of se-
curity guards and armed police officers were assembled to keep the lid on.

Most of the faculty and staff wore school logo apparel. Selections at the
school store were stale, and I never wanted to do what the stuffy teachers did. So I wore my street clothes: Timberlands, straight leg jeans, and
an American Eagle hoodie draped over my head. My look earned their
respect. Most of them wanted nothing to do with teachers, but I did not
have a teacher's vibe. I was their ally. That's not necessarily what the school
wanted me to be. When Black men are hired in schools, they are often
tapped to be the authoritarian stereotype of school enforcer. The guy who
would have held the paddle a generation earlier. My approach was different:
I understood that we must love our students before we can teach them.

I left a few minutes early to beat the parking lot crunch, and as I headed
for the exit gate I heard, "Yooo, what's good, Mr. Fleming!" It was Montrez
and his friends, kids who couldn't get into my class because it was at capacity. But fourth period was their lunch block, so they would pick up their
food and sit in the back of my classroom anyway. When administration saw
too many kids doing this, they decided to put an end to it.

"I see you with the fresh Timbs on," he said. He reached out his hand to
give me dap. We locked hands and brought it in for a hug and a fist-pat on
the back. His crew chimed in with compliments to my outfit. I smiled and
said, "You already know I come with it" as we all laughed and showed love.

I looked into their hazy red eyes and knew they were high. The skunky
smell when we hugged confirmed it. Before walking away, I wrapped my
arms around them again. "I love y'all boys," I said. They responded, "Aye,
we luh you, too, Mr. Fleming." I told the boys to keep their heads up and to
stay safe. I feared that trouble might follow them. But I had no idea that it
was looking for me instead.

When I arrived at my car, I reached for my keys in the usual pocket.
They weren't there. I patted my body and looked around to see if I had
dropped them. Then I realized that I had left my keys and wallet in the
bleachers. I pivoted and hurried back through the gate when an officer
yelled, "Hey! Stop!" I figured he was talking to one of the kids, so I kept

trucking toward the bleachers. Suddenly, a hand grabbed my arm and spun me around.

"Yo, what you grabbing me for?" I asked.

"Because I said stop," he barked. "The game is almost over, we are not allowing any more students in."

"I'm not a student," I said. "I'm a staff member." The officer looked me up and down and accused me of lying.

"Give me a second and I'll show you," I said as I turned, heading for the bleachers to retrieve my school ID. I took three steps and then two hands grabbed me and slammed me against the nearby fence. "I told you not to move!" he said, mushing the side of my face against the wire.

"Get off me," I said. "I'm on the staff, I'm trying to show you." I tried to turn my body to see if I could find another staff member to corroborate. But the officer perceived it as resistance. He released my hands that he held behind my back. He latched on to both of my arms. He slammed me to the ground and pressed his knee into my back.

"What the hell are you doing?" I yelled. "I'm a teacher!"

"Shut up!" he yelled back. "Stop resisting."

"I'm not resisting," I said in a rage. "I'm trying to show you—"

"I said shut up!" He jammed his knee harder into my spine.

The commotion drew a crowd. I could not see what was happening, but I heard Montrez and his friends running toward us yelling, "Ayo, get off of Mr. Fleming!"

"Montrez!" I yelled. "Stay back! Please, stay back!"

More of my students rushed to the scene yelling, "Get off of Mr. Fleming!" But the officer did not let up.

Finally, a white female teacher rushed up and said, "Get off of him right now. He is one of our staff members."

His weight lifted off me. I lay there for a second. I was not hurt; I was ashamed. I had no reason to be, but I was. There were times in my life when I might have deserved to be braced against a fence or thrown to the ground with my hands pinned behind my back. But I wasn't that person anymore. Then I realized that it did not matter. None of it mattered: not the Harlem

Renaissance Festival, not the education symposiums, not the scholars program or any fact about my work. All that mattered was that I was a Black
man in a hoodie. That was what he saw.

I had a following among the students, but I could not say the same about
the school's administrators. Some of this was my fault: this was my first
real job, and I had not yet matured into an understanding of workplace
diplomacy. Not only did I openly disagree with senior faculty and admin-
strators when I thought they were wrong, but I also was not really teaching
the "leadership" class they had asked me to teach. They told me to use my
own curriculum; I asked myself, *What does every leader need to know?* and
the answer was simple: every leader needs to know about debate and the
Harlem Renaissance.

In addition to my fourth period class, the principal asked me to lead an
after-school program for boys who were at risk of failing. This, unfortunately, involved a curriculum that I considered to be ineffective. This was no
different from the boring shit these kids had already been told, and I hated
it. So I pulled out my scholars program curriculum and started teaching
them debate instead.

We started a revolution in that school. I had to stop kids who were not
registered in my class from skipping their fourth period to sit in mine. I was
one of the youngest staff members, and other teachers weren't necessarily
happy about my popularity. I was called into the office to respond to base-
less rumors and lies. I was accused of upsetting seasoned teachers who felt
like I was out of my lane. Word spread that I was not even licensed to teach.
My age, my experience, and my credentials were called into question. In
the halls, I felt like a moving target. I felt peaceful and at home only in my
classroom—one hour out of the entire day.

Everything came crashing down midway through spring semester. I was
summoned to the principal's office, which was no surprise. It was contract
renewal season and we plodded through a standard performance review. We
talked about the highs and the lows and all of the boundaries that I pushed.
The whole time, I thought about how tiresome it was when people acted like

I was some radical kid with no clue as to what I was doing. Every suggestion I made was greeted with wide-eyed incredulity. True, I didn't have a license or decades of teaching experience. But I had results. Most of the teachers and administrators at the school had never walked in the shoes of the students they were struggling to reach. I had. I was once those kids, and I knew how to reach them. If I could reinvent myself as an academic, I could teach others to do the same. I turned my own journey into a curriculum for building scholars. But my clout with the kids did not translate into respect from the faculty and administrators. She broke the news to me at the end.

"Thank you for your hard work," she said, "but we won't be renewing your contract next year." The words sliced me like a box cutter. What was I going to do? I had tried all of the other schools in Lynchburg, both public and private, and none would hire me. How was I going to find work? How was I going to pay rent? How was I going to feed my brother?

I went back to my daily routine after the meeting, but everything was different. I couldn't summon a smile when kids dropped by the main office. I stopped leaping onto tables and chairs during class, knowing that it would all end soon. Students asked, "Aye, Mr. Fleming, you straight?" I said yes. But I wasn't. I did not know how to tell them the truth. They asked about the next school year. They wanted a part two to the course and they had fresh ideas for maintaining our cultural revolution in the school. The light in their eyes was so bright and their energy lifted me. But only for a moment. We had come so far from the first day of school, when Shontae and I were alone in the classroom. Now we dressed up and danced through the halls on Wall Street Wednesdays. They wanted the movement to continue, and I reassured them that it could. What I did not say was that they'd be on the ramparts without me.

One day I was sitting in the office as usual, checking in visitors, counting down the minutes until my fourth period class. The school year would be over in a month. The phone rang and the secretary picked up. I overheard her answer some questions, then she said, "Yes, sir. I will transfer you to her right away." She pressed mute on the phone and shrieked so loud that everyone in earshot snapped to attention.

"Oh my God!" she said. "I can't believe it!"

"What is it?" we all asked.

She was nearly hyperventilating. She started fanning herself and said, "It's Ron Clark!"

She ran into the principal's office, bursting through the door and yelling, "Ron Clark is on the phone!" Everyone had been waiting for his call. The principal had contacted his agent to book him for the school's next professional development conference. The secretary returned to her desk and transferred the call. Everyone in the front office stopped what they were doing and nearly put their ears to the door, waiting for confirmation that Ron Clark was really coming to our school.

Something wasn't right. I had tried to book Ron Clark before. He would not have called himself to confirm. It would have been his agent. He had to be calling for some other reason. I kept minding my business at my desk, away from the commotion. I pretended not to care, but I was certainly curious. The principal emerged from her office when I wasn't looking, and when there was no gossip, I figured she had gotten bad news or no news at all.

The minute I arrived the next morning, the secretary said, "Pssst" and wiggled a finger to summon me. When I reached her, she beckoned me closer with a secretive air. I leaned in.

"Ron Clark called yesterday," she said.

I was here when that happened, I reminded her. We all figured he was responding to the principal's speaking invitation, right?

"No," she said. "That's not what he called for."

She looked at me and smiled like she was handing me a secret gift. "He did not call for us. He called for you." I was so stunned that I froze in place and could not speak. All I could think was, *Wait, what? How? Why?*

It was the letter. The one I assumed was buried under a mountain of fan mail. It turned out that he'd actually read it but he was already booked for the day of my conference. The letter put me on his radar and he started following my work, especially the growth of the scholars program in Lynchburg. He called the school to inquire about me. He wanted me to move to Atlanta and teach at his world-renowned academy. I was so overwhelmed that I locked myself in the bathroom for a few moments. I wanted to be alone to process this. I clutched the sink as tears fell from my face like water breaking through a dam. This was going to change my life forever. I looked up at my blurry likeness in the mirror. I looked deep into my own fuzzy eyes and thought, *He came for me. Just like Samuel came for David.*

CHAPTER ELEVEN

DREAMS COME TRUE

Two years before the 2010 opening of the Wizarding World of Harry Potter in Orlando, Ron Clark and Kim Bearden dreamed up a real-life Hogwarts for middle school students in Atlanta. The Ron Clark Academy is more than a child's dream come true. It is a teacher's dream, too. Thousands have applied to join the faculty. And tens of thousands of pilgrims, most on a quest to improve their own teaching, have traveled far to visit what looks like a medieval castle dropped down in the middle of the hood.

The turrets, iron gates, and dragons looming over the main entrance took my breath away. I had only been here once before, when Mr. Clark first invited me to join the faculty, and now I was going on a trip with all my new colleagues. I stood outside the lobby doors, suitcase in hand. Most of the others were inside, everyone with luggage, waiting for stragglers. We were heading to our summer planning retreat at Myrtle Beach, South Carolina, where we'd plan the coming year.

"Come on in!" Mrs. Mosley said, holding open the door. She'd answered the phone when I'd called the school over a year ago, eager to have Mr. Clark speak at the first educational symposium I planned as an undergraduate. Who would ever have thought I'd be standing here as one of his teachers?

RCA teachers are more than teachers, they are authorities, award winners, and icons. The academy is an international magnet for teachers from the United States and around the world, who come to learn how to be better at their profession. Some school districts load all their teachers onto buses and planes and send them to RCA to participate in seminars and observe in classrooms, learning new ways of engaging students in learning. On social media, some RCA teachers are followed and fawned over like rock stars. Because they are. And here I was, a first-year teacher, with a skimpy résumé and no curriculum vitae. Yet I would soon be expected to teach thousands of seasoned educators how to do their jobs.

Many of my Black colleagues were HBCU grads. During our van ride to Myrtle Beach, they were comparing the advantages of a culturally centered education versus an Ivy League experience. This reminded me of the spirited conversations that Walter and I used to have, back in our grimy apartment, about Du Bois's views of the education of Black folks. I saw it as a chance to jump in just as Camille was expressing her fierce loyalty to Spelman. I made the mistake of playing devil's advocate. I learned one of life's greatest lessons that day: you don't fuck with a Black woman's HBCU, or her sorority. Especially if you have the audacity to compare it with predominantly white institutions. Her face hardened and she glared at me. All I could think was *Ah shit, I done fucked up.* She came back at me with a verbal flamethrower and I retreated fast.

Obviously, I had flunked first impressions. So I shut up while the others talked. An hour or more passed before Camille swiveled in her seat to face me.

"How old are you again?" Camille asked. I hesitated because I couldn't tell if she was really interested or just coming back to finish me off.

"I'm twenty-three," I said.

"Wow," she responded. Then she faced forward again, leaving me staring at the back of her head. *What the hell is that supposed to mean?* It did not sound like a good "wow," so I added, "But I'll be twenty-four soon," hoping to sound older and wiser.

She turned toward me again and asked, "And you've been teaching for how long?"

"One year," I said.

"Oh wow," she responded again.

Then I added, "Well, two. Kinda."

She kept probing this time. "And where did you teach?" she asked.

I saw where this was going. But I could not stop it. I was spread-eagled on the rails and a freight train was coming.

"Well, it's kinda complicated," I said. "I taught, but I wasn't an official teacher."

Camille's face contorted. I explained that I had created my own classroom in an old warehouse. I told her that I had been teaching kids in the community, which only made me sound like a glorified tutor. I was reluctant to talk about the high school that fired me. I feared this would arouse even further suspicion.

"So you're a first-year teacher?" she asked. It sounded even worse when she said it.

"Well . . . yes . . . technically," I said.

"Wooooow."

Mr. Clark's instinctive decisions are legendary. He is a visionary and a seer. He's grown famous by taking brave and radical risks. Members of his team didn't always understand his choices, but everyone trusted him. This might have been the exception. Most of my colleagues knew nothing about me until moments before I showed up. It was as though Ron Clark went out of town and came back with an illegitimate son.

Camille continued her interrogation and asked if I had ever done student teaching. Already skeptical because I hardly had one year of experience, she'd be horrified to discover that I also lacked a license. "It's a long story," I said, hoping for mercy.

"It's okay," she said. "We have time." And it was true. We had nothing but time. We were still hours away from our destination and she showed no sign of letting up. So I decided that exposing myself would be better than being exposed.

"No," I said. "I've never done student teaching." I wanted to rip the bandage off fast, so I immediately said, "I couldn't pass the Praxis."

The van fell silent and my embarrassment made the air feel too thick and steamy to breathe. They were like players on a winning varsity team who've just been told that a nameless freshman is now on the starting lineup. In their shoes, I would have felt no different. They were the dream team of education. They knew nothing about me, and my revelations in the van had surely made them wonder what the hell I was doing there. In my paranoia, I felt like a drama was brewing and my new colleagues were sipping it like tea. Maybe things would have been different if they'd seen me in action before Mr. Clark brought me in. But that was not the case.

Ron Clark had turned away applications from hundreds of qualified teachers. The faculty seemed eager to know why he instead hired an unlicensed, inexperienced twenty-three-year-old recent graduate of a conservative college to join a roster of revolutionaries who had been transforming education for decades. And they had the medals and the scars to prove it. My feet were barely wet. I did not have those years. I did not have those awards. But I, too, had scars that bore witness to my own fight. A fight that I'd survived. A fight that had prepared me for this position. I knew they wanted to know what qualified me. So I spoke my truth, starting from the beginning.

I told them how I'd suffered as a child. How I escaped the streets. How basketball saved my life. Then I told them how I failed.

I told them how I'd dropped out of college. How I tried to give up. How I tried to take my own life. How a miracle sent me back to school. Then I told them how I failed more.

I told them how I'd struggled to read. How I reinvented myself into an academic. How I competed in debate and failed some more. How I used debate to transform at-risk youth. How I started programs and events and movements. Then I told them how I failed again when I thought I was flying.

But Mr. Clark found me. He looked at my raggedy wings and picked me up anyway, because he believed that in this new place I would fly. I told them that my journey was storm-tossed but filled with second chances and reinvention and failing forward. That's what qualified me to be in this van, with them. I told my story. I sang my song. And they sang theirs, too.

The sweet sounds of our songs softened our hearts. We each had our own struggles, our own triumphs, our own paths to this convergence. Our stories connected us in ways that academic credentials could not, and by the end of the van ride we were wrapping our arms around each other. We became family. I became the baby brother who was loved on consistently, occasionally teased for my inability to hold liquor, and assigned early-morning breakfast duty because no one else wanted to do it.

"I'm so proud of you, Black man," Camille said. "People need to hear your story." She was surprised to learn about the Saturday scholars program and the events I had created over the past couple of years. And she was stunned that I had walked away from it. Abandoning my own vision to help build another man's must have seemed strange. But this was my dream: having my own classroom, being a real teacher in a place free from the conventions of regular school. I honestly never thought this dream would come true.

"Fleming," Camille said, "you have a gift." She shifted into big-sister mode, assuring me that my wildest dreams were yet ahead. But I couldn't see that far. I laughed it off, but her face stayed serious. "Listen to me," she said. "This is only the beginning."

On the first day of school, I took a moment to look around and take it all in before the students arrived. I was standing in my own classroom. It was not borrowed; it was all mine. Even the design. An artist was in the process of spray-painting murals that I had chosen to bring my subjects to life. On the front wall was the profile of a young boy gazing at the American flag. The flag blended into MLK's image on the right wall. His arm was outstretched across the Atlanta skyline as he delivered an impassioned speech. On the back wall was Captain America. Beside him was Auguste Rodin's sculpture *The Thinker*. And next to it was a giant US Presidential Seal. On the left wall were all my books, my own canon for academic transformation. Rows of tables faced a stage at the front of the classroom. This is where I would teach.

I spotted a gaggle of little fifth-grade heads peeking into the doorway. Their eyes were anxious and hopeful.

"Come in!" I said. "Move quickly." I gestured for them to hurry. At RCA, students were expected to move about with a sense of urgency.

Isaac and Keanen came in together, neither quite five feet tall. Isaac was confident. He was not afraid to introduce himself, with his thick southern accent and his old soul. Keanen was the opposite. He was fretful and timid and likely to take refuge under his desk when he was especially stressed. Anxiety had already caused the poor kid to throw up in his previous class.

Different as they were, both rushed in and took seats in the front row. A loud thud startled the students when I hopped onto the tabletop. My feet were level with Keanen's eyes. He examined my hard-bottomed shoes and gazed up at me towering over him.

"Good morning, scholars," I said. "My name is Mr. Fleming. I will be your philosophy teacher this year." The students stared back at me in silence. Their empty expressions indicated that they had never heard the word. Isaac was not afraid to break the silence.

"Excuse me, Mr. Fleming," Isaac said, raising his hand. "What is philosophy?"

"Glad you asked," I said, smiling down from my elevated position. "Philosophy is everything. Everything is philosophy. Let me explain."

RCA is known for exposing middle schoolers to material typically reserved for high school. Mr. Clark had said that I could teach whatever I wanted, and when I revealed that I wanted to teach philosophy to fifth graders, he didn't balk. Looking back, I realize I had no idea how hard it would be for ten-year-olds to comprehend Confucianism or Plato's Theory of Forms. Debate had helped me get these ideas across in the past, but I wanted to try something new. Although every RCA teacher had their own unique way of teaching, they all turned academic content into songs. This was a common thread in the school's pedagogy and I desperately wanted to fit in. Besides, this gave me an opportunity to resurrect Killa B from my teenage rapping days. But this time minus the *real nigga shit*.

I created songs for every unit in the semester, setting a high-energy tempo for class. I wrote a song about the Greek philosophers and I dressed up like Socrates with a long gray beard, a white toga, a fake hunchback, and a cane. The students glimpsed me from the door window and I could hear their loud gasps as they waited to be invited in. As soon as they entered, I hopped on the stage and stretched my cane to press the play button on my Smart Board. The "Knuck If You Buck" instrumental blared through the sound system as the kids cheered and danced into the room. We all jumped on top of the tables and started singing the words on the screen:

> *Socrates started from the bottom, came to the top,*
> *Only way we know about him from the students he taught.*
> *He questioned everything,*
> *Call it interrogating.*
> *But the government officials thought it was irritating.*
> *What is wisdom, justice, life, and beauty?*
> *What is love, compassion, morality, and duty?*
> *He knew by questioning you can discover the truth,*
> *So they sentenced him to death for corrupting the youth!*

During the chorus we whipped from side to side chanting, "Greek philosophy! Greek philosophy! Socrates, Aristotle, Plato, let's go! Socrates, Aristotle, Plato, let's go!"

Their enthusiasm was so electric that it reverberated through the building. My colleagues bopped past in the hallway or they barged in and joined the fun.

During my unit on the ancient Eastern era of philosophy, I made songs about Confucius and Sun Tzu and the Chinese dynasties using the "Nae

Nae" song that was currently trending. During my unit on the European Age of Enlightenment, I made songs about John Locke and Thomas Hobbes and Sir Francis Bacon.

When we arrived at the American Revolution, I wrote lyrics explaining the Constitution and the Bill of Rights. I decided to use "Crank That (Soulja Boy)" to teach the branches of government, but I wasn't satisfied with my first draft. I listened to the song over and over during my planning period and finally focused on the part of the chorus where you put your hands up on the handlebars of an imaginary motorcycle and say, "Youuuuu, crank dat Soulja Boy! Youuuuu, crank dat Soulja Boy!" A lightbulb went on when I heard "Youuuu" and thought *US government.* I scrambled for a piece of paper and began jotting down lyrics of the chorus:

> *First is legislative branch,*
> *Then is the judicial branch,*
> *Last is the executive, which is the US president,*
> *Youuu S government, Youuu S government, Youuu S government.*

I looked at the slides I had prepared and decided to scrap them. Instead, I turned each bullet point into a line that matched the beat. I wrote lines and struck through them and balled up pieces of paper. But by the end of the day, I had written a full verse for all three branches of government. It started out:

> *First is legislative branch,*
> *Watch me lean and watch me rock.*
> *They're the branch of government in charge of making all the laws.*
> *Congress has 535 members,*
> *4-3-5 in the House and a hundred in the Senate.*
> *The House of Representatives is based on population,*
> *And the Senate has two from each state representin'.*
> *We debate and we regulate the budget and laws,*

We can override a veto if we find that it is flawed.
There's a limit on the terms till we get someone new.
The Senate serves six years, the House serves two.
Through checks and balances we make sure there's no hypocrisy,
So now you see,
Without a Congress there is no democracy!

The kids loved it. I loved it. The hundreds of visiting teachers who observed my classes loved it. But I went home feeling incomplete. There was something missing. It was fun, but it was not fulfilling. It was sensational, but it did not feel transformative. I was happy, but I was not satisfied: my students could sing about concepts that they could not intelligently debate.

Without question, music belongs in schools. It belongs in the classroom. I would not want to teach in a place that did not share this belief. I fought for it at the previous school that fired me. I used it to lure students in and connect with them in ways that only culture allows. But after drawing them in, I felt responsible for taking them deeper. I felt responsible for showing them how to do more than regurgitate facts to a beat. I saw the consequences of this when I asked questions in class like "Who can name every US president?" and a sea of hands shot skyward. But when I went deeper and asked, "Now who can compare and critique the ideologies of self-described conservatives and liberals in present-day America?" those hands dropped like deadweights.

I was learning the difference between teaching content and skills, facts and utility, what you know versus what you can do. I wanted to equip students with tools they could take with them into college and the workforce, into boardrooms and public forums. "The mere imparting of information is not education," Carter Woodson wrote in *The Mis-Education of the Negro*. And I could not shake the famous words of Socrates, who argued that weak minds discuss people and average minds discuss events, but strong minds discuss ideas. I wanted my students to have strong minds. I wanted them to understand how ideas are created and how they can be challenged. This is how they would change the world. This is how they would liberate and mobilize our people. This is how they would shift the balance of power. And this is what is learned through debate.

I was becoming steadfast in my philosophy of education and regaining my confidence in debate as my strongest game. Meanwhile, videos of my classroom songs were already circulating online. These reached local politicians who invited us to be part of the program at the Atlanta mayor's annual ball. The invitation to this glittery event made me ecstatic, imagining that this would be like the symposia I used to organize, except this time with even more people listening to young Black voices. My first thought was which students would deliver the speeches. Then I realized that these people did not want speeches from us. The students were invited to perform a song and dance.

It was a generous request but it made me profoundly uneasy. Still, I accepted. My class is about politics, so how could I pass up an opportunity to expose my students to a major political event? But I could hardly watch when our turn came on the big night. I stood in the wings, and beyond the footlights I could see smiles and white teeth and hands clapping for the cute little Black kids singing and dancing. And it made my stomach turn, because I knew that my students were more than that. I would have been fine if they were a step team or a chorus. Our class focused on the ideas instrumental to democracy, yet we were not called upon to educate; we were summoned to entertain.

It was a campaign season, so more invitations followed. This time, we were invited to the Democratic Party of Georgia's statewide convention. Once again, we were not asked to speak. We were asked to sing. We were asked to dance. And this occasion gave me even more angst, because this audience would be much whiter than the event honoring our Black mayor. The white people showed nothing but kindness toward the kids and me, but I still hated the spectacle of little Black kids amusing a white crowd like some sort of minstrel show. This is how I saw it, no matter what others thought. One person stopped my student mid-conversation and asked them to demonstrate a dance move. Countless people patted my students on the back and said, "Wow, you're so articulate," as if they did not expect sophistication from Black children. I hated it. From that day forward, I was hell-bent on ripping the seam of that stereotype. If people were going to watch my class, if we were going to have a public platform, I was committed to showcasing Black intelligence.

Soon after that, the students came into my classroom one day and found me sitting in my leather lounge chair in the far corner. They greeted me as they entered, but I ignored them. I pretended to be invisible.

"Why isn't Mr. Fleming responding?" Isaac asked as they settled in.

Keanen pointed to the board and said, "Look!" There was text and the top line said: "One person stand and read the following directions."

Keanen instantly jumped to his feet and started reading aloud. "You must complete the following exercise as a class. It is pass or fail. As a group, you have twenty minutes to solve the problem below."

The problem was an ethical dilemma that together they had to reconcile. But there was one caveat. Before they could solve the actual problem, they had to decide how to approach it:

Option 1: They could choose one person to solve the problem on behalf of the class.

Option 2: Either the girls or the boys could solve the problem.

Option 3: They could nominate five people to represent the class and answer the question.

Option 4: Everyone could have a say and vote.

Keanen continued reading. "When the buzzer goes off, the exercise is over and your conclusion must be presented. Your time begins in five . . . four . . . three . . . two . . . one."

I clicked a remote concealed in my hand. A countdown appeared on the board. Several kids shot up to lead the exercise. Isaac was one of the first to seize control.

"Okay, here's what we're gonna do," he said. "I'll solve the problem for the group."

"No!" Jasmine yelled across the room. "That's not fair."

"Define fair," Isaac rebutted.

The two charged back and forth at each other. Isaac argued that option 1 was the most efficient. Jasmine argued that option 4 was most just.

"We don't have time to be worrying about everyone's feelings," Isaac asserted. "Our grade is on the line." But Jasmine pushed back.

"Exactly," she said. "And only having one person's perspective puts all of our grades at risk."

Keanen jumped in to break up the duel. "All right, all right," he said, hoping to advance the conversation with half the time gone. "How about option three?"

Keanen made his case for the class to vote on the five smartest kids in the class who could solve the problem for everyone.

"No!" Jasmine yelled again. "Then we'll spend most of our time debating who's the smartest instead of solving the actual problem."

Jayla stood up and yelled, "Five minutes left!" and everyone became frantic. It was the most beautiful chaos filled with passion. Students were standing on chairs and shouting from the tops of the desks and some were practically pulling their hair out.

"Okay," Keanen said. "Let's just start solving the problem because we're losing time."

They settled on option 4. Everybody was given a chance to contribute to the discussion and cast a vote. Except the vote never happened. They were struggling to reach a conclusion when the buzzer went off. But the commotion was so loud that no one heard it.

I ambled up to the stage from my corner chair. They were so immersed in the debate that I had to shout to get their attention. "That's enough," I said. "Your time is up." They went silent and quickly took their seats. I glanced around the quiet but uneasy room. They did not realize that the exercise had been a great success. I was so proud, but I pretended to be disappointed.

"So what is your conclusion?" I asked.

The students looked around to see who would break the news. Their faces were so downcast that they appeared to be melting. Some couldn't fight back tears as they contemplated how they'd explain a failing grade to their parents.

After a moment of silence, Isaac bravely rose from his seat. He grimaced like he had just gotten out of a street scuffle. He unleashed a diatribe against his peers.

"We don't have an answer," Isaac finally said, his head hanging low.

"Interesting," I said. "So you mean to tell me that you all had twenty minutes to solve a simple problem and you couldn't do that?"

"It wasn't that simple," Isaac said, triggered by my words.

I was internally overjoyed. Isaac was going exactly where I wanted. I held a straight face and said, "Oh, really? Please explain." All eyes were fixed on Isaac.

"We couldn't get to the actual problem," he said. The choice between the four options was too complex to be decided quickly.

"So we went with option four," he said, "which in my opinion was the worst decision ever."

"And why is that?" I asked. Then it came rushing out of him like a tidal wave.

"There are several problems here," Isaac said. He broke down the nuances of option 4 and why he disagreed. He understood why everyone wanted to have a say and conceded that it seemed most fair. But what seems most fair is not always most efficient, he said, and a leader must be willing to make hard decisions. To close his case, he added that it makes sense for the most qualified people to contribute.

"Many of my peers were given the chance to contribute and still chose not to," he said. "So why waste time trying to include them in the first place?"

Keanen charged in to disagree. "But that still does not take away their right." He drew a distinction between rights and personal responsibility. Keanen argued that because everyone in the classroom will get the same grade, their right to participate is inherent. "Their right belongs to them," he said. "They can choose what to do with it."

Other students jumped in and the argument heated up again. I took a few steps back and let them have at it. They spent the entire class period analyzing and debating the pros and cons of each option, which is exactly what I wanted them to do. I looked at the clock and it was almost time for dismissal. Dozens of arguments were going on at once, and the most fired-up students were standing on tables and hurling words across the room like Molotov cocktails.

"All right!" I yelled to end the commotion. "Look closely, I have something to show you." Everyone was silent and leaning in as I stood next to the board pointing at the prompt.

I smiled at them and said, "You did not fail this assignment." The students looked at each other, saying, "Huh?" "What?" "How?"

"What if I told you that it was never about the ethical dilemma?" I asked. "What if I told you that the exercise was all about those four options?"

No one said a word. Some were processing. Some were squinting at the board trying to see what I saw.

"Think about the arguments that you made," I said. "Think about the bigger picture, and tell me what the four options represent."

They were still scratching their heads. Suddenly, Isaac jumped up with his hands locked together atop his head and yelled, "Oh my God! I think I got it!" He had their undivided attention immediately. "They represent forms of government!" The kids were so mind-blown that they nearly fell out of their chairs in astonishment.

Isaac was right. Option 1 was dictatorship. Option 2 was oligarchy. Option 3 was representative democracy. Option 4 was direct democracy.

I did not have to give them a list of vocabulary words and say, "Go home and memorize this." I did not need them to regurgitate facts on a test. Those kids will remember these concepts for the rest of their lives. Not because they *heard* it. But because they *experienced* it.

I never questioned the power of debate as my main teaching tool, no matter how many times parents objected to how hard I pushed their kids. I believed in what I had and its ability to transform students into scholars. We were wrestling big questions. We explored Jean-Paul Sartre's theories of existentialism. We debated René Descartes's theories of epistemology. There were times when I wondered if I was in over my head. But I was determined to help them get it. About halfway through the year, I felt familiar flames come to life in these kids. The revolutionary changes I had seen in my Saturday scholars were happening here.

By the end of class, their heads looked ready to explode. Mine was, too. "All right, scholars," I would say, "that's enough for the day." Debating can be as physically tiring as it is mentally exhausting. We were all glad when lunch rolled around and the students gathered their belongings and lined up at the door.

"You're dismissed," I'd say. "Enjoy your lunch."

The hallways were loud as they marched quickly to their meals. I'd sit down to enjoy a few moments of silence before joining them. In my leather reading chair, I'd lean back and prop my feet up. One day, my eyes were shut for only a few seconds before I heard a knock at the door.

"Come in!" I yelled, feeling interrupted. Isaac cracked open the door and peeked his little bald head around the edge. "Come on in," I repeated.

"Sorry to bother you, Mr. Fleming," he said, walking toward me.

I responded, "It's okay, buddy. What do you need?"

He was standing next to the chair where my feet were braced.

"We're all philosophers here, right?" he said in a stern voice.

"Yes," I chuckled. "We're all philosophers."

"Well, I have a question for you, then, if you don't mind," he said, stepping a little closer. His voice had grown harder and he was obviously serious.

"Of course," I said. "Go for it."

He clasped both hands behind his back, like a lawyer before a jury. I felt a little uneasy.

"What is nothing?" he asked.

I paused for a moment of clarity. "Excuse me?" I said.

He leaned in and repeated himself. "What is nothing?"

I knew what he was doing. He was testing me. In the same way that I tested their nimbleness during cross-examination. I could not delay. My wheels turned fast and I shot back a response that would keep him from ever having the nads to try me again. I sat upright and squared my shoulders.

"The absence of something," I said. "Nothing is the absence of something."

I sank back in my chair, confident in my answer.

"Wrong," he said.

I leaned forward and said, "What?"

"Wrong," he repeated. "Nothing is the absence of the *knowledge* of something."

Before I could even process his words and retort, he wheeled back and walked slowly away, arms folded across his chest and one hand stroking his hairless chin. As he disappeared through the door, my jaw dropped. *Did this little Negro just check me?* Yes, he did. He checked his teacher. And I was proud.

Keanen was undergoing similar changes. He was no longer a shy kid puking from anxiety and ready to crawl under the desk. He held on to debate like a sword and swung it like a warrior. Even when that was unwise.

I was on the phone with Keanen's mother one day when she said, "Mr. Fleming, you better get 'im. I'ma kill 'im." She had come home from work and found his room a total mess.

"Keanen!" she'd yelled. "Why didn't you clean your room?"

Keanen had decided it was time for target practice with syllogisms. I had taught them how to shift the burden of proof and bait their opponent into a contradiction. Unfortunately, he'd decided to try this on his mother.

"Mom, if you don't mind, I have a question," he'd said calmly. "Does this room belong to me?" She answered yes.

"Do the items in the room belong to me?" She answered yes again.

Then he continued, "So if the room belongs to me, and the items in it belong to me, how do I not have the authority to determine the arrangement of those items?"

I do not know what Mrs. Harris did to Keanen after that. But if I know what I know about Black mothers, some of those items he claimed to have owned might have taken flight across the room.

"Let me tell you something," she'd told him. "You better leave that debate stuff at school with Mr. Fleming."

Mrs. Harris was angry at first, mostly because he had bested her with a valid point. And he had asserted it with audacity. But then she thought about what had just happened and realized that her son exuded a confidence that she had never seen in him before. That's when she realized that he was no longer the same kid who was once timid and soft-spoken. He was a debater now. And his evolution, she told me, made her smile with pride.

Isaac and Keanen became debate ninjas. No one could have a pleasant, casual conversation with the boys because they always wanted to spar or flex their muscles. It even wore me down during lunch. I just wanted to eat, and at times I tried to hide from them. But they'd find me and fire a clip of questions at machine-gun speed. Everything from "Who created God?" to "Is water wet?"

I needed a break, so I offered an alternative. It was logic that they were falling in love with. I had a glass chessboard in my classroom. I took it with us to our next lunch break and taught them how to play. After a week, kids from all over the cafeteria were piled on top of us. I ordered about twenty chess sets so more kids could learn. The lunchroom went from a rowdy cafeteria to a board-game battleground. "It's just like debate," I told them. "You don't outfight. You outwit."

Logan loved sitting by my side to watch. He was a student in my eighth-grade political science class. He was an Italian American kid with dark, shaggy hair. He was bashful and reclusive. Logan was the type of student who did not speak until he knew he had the right answer. Then he would stand up and present his solution, never lifting his eyes from the floor. He was smart, but he did not want to be seen.

Logan watched the game, but he never wanted to play. He just sat there on my hip, pencil and notebook in hand, doing homework as I defeated every student who tried to knock me from my championship pedestal. It never worked. Since learning how to play in college, I had never lost a single game of chess.

I shared pictures on social media of my vanquished opponents, all of them middle schoolers. My posts reached a local chess champion who invited me to pick on someone my own size. I accepted the challenge. One day, she came to school during lunch for a public bout. Dozens of students hovered over us, waiting to see if their seemingly invincible teacher would be dethroned.

"You can't lose, Mr. Fleming," Logan said. I leaned left and whispered in his ear, "Don't worry, buddy. I got this." I kept playing and he went back to his notebook to finish his homework.

The game was tense and still underway when our thirty-minute lunch period ended. We took a picture of the board and resumed the next day. I was under pressure. She had the advantage but I wanted to maintain the illusion of control, so I cracked a smile as I moved my piece. She countered that move in seconds, as though I had fallen into her trap. She smiled back at me and added a chuckle.

She almost had me. But she made another move and exclaimed, "Shit!" She clapped a hand over her mouth, remembering that we were surrounded by kids. Logan grinned at me, like he knew what move I was about to make. I made that move. And I won.

The kids thought I was some sort of chess god. When we broke for lunch, they grabbed the folded chessboards from my closet and set them up in the lunchroom. They usually argued over who would get to play me, but on this particular day no one stepped up. After shutting down my computer and Smart Board, I went to the closet to retrieve my lucky glass set. The one that the kids were not allowed to touch without permission. But it was gone.

I rushed to the cafeteria and scanned the rows of chessboards manned by students on both sides. I turned toward the spot where I usually sat. My lucky glass board was on the table, set up and ready for play. Logan was sitting with it, but not in his usual spot beside me. He was sitting across the board in the opponent's seat, patiently waiting for my arrival, his pencil and notebook nestled at his side.

"I'd like to play you," he said as I sat down. I laughed in surprise, but his expression remained serious. He opened his notebook. Then he moved the first pawn.

"Okay," I said. "Let's make this quick." I entertained his challenge. But it did not go the way I expected.

The game took three days. By the third day, other students abandoned their games to watch me struggle. It did not make sense. My best strategies were suddenly falling short. He anticipated every one of my moves. All of my tactics and tricks, he evaded. Only a few pieces remained on the board, and it looked like a stalemate. Or maybe I was hoping for a stalemate. But he checked his notebook, as he had done several other times during the game. He picked up a piece and gently slid mine off the checkered block. He looked up at me and met my eyes. He did not smile or smirk. He gave me a few seconds to examine the board and see what he had done. When I raised my eyes, he extended his hand across the board to shake mine, and those gut-wrenching words spilled from his mouth: "Checkmate."

I soon discovered that his notebook did not contain homework. It was filled with computations. He spent months by my side, documenting my every move, calculating counterattacks, and waiting like a black mamba to strike. When his victory came, he was calm. He'd expected it. He'd prepared for it. He'd earned it.

Isaac was becoming an intellectual juggernaut. Keanen emerged as one of the biggest and most brilliant voices in the school. Logan had a mind that was pragmatic and prodigious. The three boys were coming into their own. They were becoming so good at debate that I knew they were ready to compete.

I used debate as an instructional tool in class, but I'd never coached a competitive team. All year, I taught my students about case construction and cross-examination and rebuttals in our philosophy and political science classes. Instead of using conventional tests, I evaluated them using

ballots from Lincoln-Douglas debate format. They became passionate debaters and often asked, "When can we compete against other schools?" I
was nervous about it. The last time I'd stepped foot in the competitive debating circuit, I went out worse than Nate Robinson in his boxing debut.
But that was before my renaissance. I was ready to try again—this time as
a coach. We registered for our first tournament, organized by the national
debate league. It was a statewide competition for Georgia middle school
ers and it was only a few weeks away. We practiced each day after school
until the competition. There was one hiccup in our plans: at age twenty-
four, I was considered too young by the school's insurance company to
drive the school van. My colleague Kenneth drove us to our first middle
school competition, and we won. We went to our second competition, and
we won again.

A couple years went by. The kids were growing older, smarter, and
boastful. "We can't be beat, Mr. Fleming," Isaac said. "We too sick wit it,"
Keanen agreed. I told them to calm down because they had competed only
twice and had some growing to do. But that's not what they wanted to hear.
Concerned that going undefeated would make them less teachable, I decided to orchestrate a lesson in humility.

"I tell you what," I said. "Since y'all think you're invincible, the next tournament we enter will be a high school tournament." They looked at each
other and laughed as if there was not a trace of fear in their hearts. "They
gon' get this work, too," Keanen said as they giggled and dapped each other.
"Okay," I said, "we'll see."

I was ready to teach my kids a lesson. But I ran into a problem. I called
the National Speech & Debate Association headquarters and learned that
middle schoolers are not allowed in high school tournaments. The competition was only a couple weeks away and my students had already started to
prepare. We'd put in weeks of practice and I did not want to confess that we
had wasted our time. I called the headquarters again, hoping to get someone
else. But the same representative answered the phone and reinforced the bad
news.

That's when I had an idea. Teams register for tournaments using their school name. They sign up, pay the fee, and show up to the competition. The only way we would get flagged is if the school name indicated that we were not a high school. But our school was Ron Clark Academy, plain and simple. So I went to the national debate league website and clicked on the tournament. I completed the online registration form, entered our payment information, pressed submit, and crossed my fingers. The registration went through. I refreshed the browser and looked up the roster for the high school tournament. I scrolled through the hundreds of school names and there we were, Ron Clark Academy. I clicked on it and the names of all our debaters were listed. Middle school or not, we were off to the statewide varsity tournament.

My students got on my nerves during our ride to Johns Creek, Georgia. When I was an athlete, I always put on headphones, sat still, and meditated before a big game. It was considered bad luck to joke around and be unfocused. It gave the impression of overconfidence and underestimating the opponent. As I drove my Honda with the kids in the back seat, I glanced in the rearview mirror and saw Isaac, Keanen, and Logan tickling each other and playing games on their phones.

"Y'all need to stop playing and review those cases," I said.

"We're good, Mr. Fleming," Isaac responded.

"I was not asking a question," I said. "That was a directive."

They sighed and put away their phones and pulled out their computers to review files of arguments and evidence. I kept watching them in the rearview mirror, thinking to myself, *Just wait. Y'all gon' learn today.*

We finally arrived at Johns Creek High School. Walking toward the entrance, I was flanked by kids who were barely five feet tall. They were munchkins compared to high school debaters nearly twice as big and up to five years their senior. As we entered, everyone stared as if they knew these couldn't be varsity debaters. These environments are not easy to walk into. The situation reminded me of my discomfort as a novice debater at my first tournament at Binghamton University.

We found the pairings posted on the wall. The first round was about to begin. I opened my arms and pulled them into a tight huddle. I looked each one in the eyes and said, "It does not matter what happens today, I am so proud of each of you." I did not want them to take it too hard when we lost. After all, this was meant to be a learning experience. I wanted them to understand that there's always someone willing to outwork you. That is why we must stay humble.

Coaches were not allowed in the competition rooms and were confined to a designated lounge for the entire day. If there were spare minutes between rounds, we could check with our team to see how they were doing. It was midday and I had not heard anything. The reporting on the tabulation site was slow. The kids were not checking their phones. I was anxious because I wanted to know what was going on. I figured they might be taking it hard, and I wanted to at least be there to comfort them. Desperate to fill time, I was planning the coming week's lessons when another coach blurted something that commanded everyone's attention.

"Have y'all seen those Ron Clark Academy kids?" she said. I turned around with a grin. I figured she was bringing the news that I had expected. I was certain they were getting their asses kicked and learning a good lesson. But that was not the case.

"They are whooping everybody!" she said. "Whose kids are those?"

I could not even raise my hand. I was stunned. My first thought was *Wait, what?* My second thought was *Nooooo, that's not what was supposed to happen!*

By the end of that tournament, we had not lost a single round. As a middle school team, we went undefeated at a high school competition. Before we left for the day, a woman approached my kids and said, "I want to meet your teacher." They brought her to me as I was gathering our bags and computers and trophies.

"Hi, Mr. Fleming," she said, stretching forth her hand. She introduced herself as a representative of the Harvard Debate Council at Harvard College. I greeted her and she praised our first-place finish. She went on at length how impressed she was by the students. I was still shaken by it all.

What we had just done was still setting in. I thanked her for her kind remarks and assured her that I would keep in touch. She assured the same.

"There's something I think you would be perfect for," she said.

The woman was as pleasant as she could be. But the kids were tired. I was tired. And we were just ready to go home. I pulled myself together to listen politely.

"What would that be?" I asked. And her next words changed my life forever.

She said to me, "I think you should teach at Harvard."

My mind was trying to process her words, because I could not have heard her correctly. She could not have been talking about *the* Harvard. All I could say was "Wait, what?" with my mouth halfway open. She told me that she would be putting in a recommendation for me to join the Harvard Debate Council summer faculty. "Be on the lookout," she said. "You'll hear from us soon."

The kids slept the entire hour drive back home. I couldn't listen to music. I couldn't call anyone and say, "Oh my God, you'll never guess what just happened." I drove in silence, trying to convince myself that it was all real: the undefeated record, the prospect of teaching at Harvard. I added it to my list of life's ironies. I was at a tournament for which we were not technically qualified, coaching for a school where I was not technically qualified to teach, where I was recruited because I taught debate, a sport I failed at in college. During those college days, I'd dreamed of going places that seemed utterly beyond my reach. And as we rode home that night, my mind traveled back to that grimy college apartment and the crimson HARVARD pennant that once hung over the floor pallet where I slept. It hovered over me every night like a dreamcatcher. I once feared that neither my GPA nor my financial status would ever get me to Cambridge, Massachusetts. Now it seemed I needed neither. Because I was not going there to study. I was going there to teach.

CHAPTER TWELVE

SCHOLARSHIP MEETS CULTURE

For most of the year, the oldest part of Harvard Yard has a kind of Yankee simplicity, crisscrossed by utilitarian footpaths, shaded by large deciduous trees, and without decoration. Only in the summer are the brightly colored chairs delivered, ready for rearrangement by anyone who chooses to use them. The chairs move about the Yard all summer, like grazing animals in shades of periwinkle and lime. On an especially hot and motionless mid-July afternoon, I reclined in one of them, thankful for any puff of breeze that stirred the humid air. Not much is happening academically at that time of year. But flocks of tourists roam the paths in sunglasses and straw hats, eager to locate the statue of John Harvard and snap selfies while petting his lucky foot.

I was scanning the fine old buildings that surround the Yard, taking in architectural details no doubt chiseled by my ancestors. Looking at the paths radiating in all directions, I wondered which were most often trod by

W. E. B. Du Bois, Carter G. Woodson, or Alain Locke. Then my gaze fell to my own feet, indenting the Ivy League grass where I never, ever expected to tread. I was wearing wheat Timberlands. Yes, Timberland boots in late July. At Harvard. Without apology. The Timbs reminded me of where I'd started and the countless missteps I'd made on my journey to that place. Regardless of my zigzag path, the fact was that I was there now. And I figured that the reason had to be much bigger than just me.

Founded in 1892, the Harvard Debate Council is one of the oldest campus organizations at Harvard College. Each summer, hundreds of high school debaters from all around the world converge on campus for the council's annual summer residential program. The days at the debate residency were long for instructors and students. Instructors lectured and the students debated for twelve hours, six days a week, for two weeks. Classes started at 7 a.m. and ended around 9 p.m. We had a two-hour break for lunch and I was spending mine basking in the Yard.

It was the last day of the residency. I would leave for Atlanta the next day. I was running out of time to say what I needed to say, and unexpressed thoughts were gnawing at my conscience like termites. I was about to wrap up my first term as a summer instructor, and I was afraid it would be my last. I was getting ready to screw it all up by being the *angry Black man*.

It was possible that I was in over my head and had no right to question anything. My being there was itself a miracle, a dream come true. The other staff were highly acclaimed debate instructors and professors—some had been teaching and coaching for longer than I'd been alive, and many had been debate champions in their day. At a staff dinner just a few days earlier, I had listened as they deftly swirled cabernet sauvignon in stemmed glasses and swapped stories about their decorated careers. My middle school debaters had won one high school tournament. But if I told that story, they might laugh and metaphorically pinch my cheeks, as if to say, *That's so cute.* What my students had accomplished felt like nothing compared to the instructors' many national championships. Silenced by insecurity, I focused on swirling my wine like everyone else, hoping to blend in and prove to them, and myself, that I belonged. Until I over-swirled and splashed wine on my clothes, leading to my early departure from the dinner.

Now, sitting in the Yard, I typed variations of the same message to the head of the Harvard Debate Council. But I kept deleting it. I decided it was a bad idea and shoved my phone back in my pocket. But groups of white students and Asian students kept strolling past, and I couldn't stop thinking about the Black students who deserved to be here, too. I knew the ones I had trained back in Atlanta, the ones who had whipped all the high school teams, could hold their own at this debate residency. But I also knew that their families could not afford the tuition. Such is the story of American inequality. Too often, Black youth, no matter how gifted or talented, miss out on opportunities because their family's earning power is less than their white classmates'. Lack of access, not lack of ability, often keeps Black people from accomplishing what they could in a more equitable world. This truth beat inside me like a drum that would not be ignored. I reached back into my pocket and wrote a text message to my boss asking if we could meet. I inhaled a breath of courage. And I finally pressed send.

Later that day, I arrived at the administrative office at the Hilles building in the Radcliffe Quadrangle. I was afraid to knock on the door even though they were expecting me. Nervous or not, I gave the door a rap.

My boss welcomed me to a round table where he and two other important administrators were already seated. There was a chair waiting, which in my worst imagining looked perfect for an interrogation or an execution. But I sat down and we exchanged pleasantries before the two men and the woman looked at me expectantly. I had asked for the meeting but did not know where to start. For a minute, I panicked. They had no idea that a reformed dope peddler had infiltrated their Ivy League inner sanctum. The nerve I had to barge in, pumping my fist and yelling, "Black power!" It was as if they had generously opened the door to let me in, then I ran back to the porch and yelled toward Dae Dae 'n' them, "Come on, y'all! There's room for all of our Black asses!"

I snapped out of it and realized that gratitude is always a good starting point. "Thank you so much for taking the time to meet with me," I said. "I cannot express how honored I am to be here."

Teaching at the summer residency had been a revelation: it was my first exposure to international debate competition and I had been delighted to work with hundreds of students from more than twenty-five countries. But the experience had left me intensely frustrated. Because almost none of those students looked like me.

"I don't mean to offend anyone," I continued. "But I think something needs to be done about the lack of African American representation here at the residency."

I continued at length about the need for diversity and the importance of representation as my supervisors listened without interruption or inquiry. I emptied my soul onto the table and then exhaled, having said everything I came to say. I had thrown an unexpected punch and braced myself for their reaction. But there was none. No nodding or smiling, no flash of denial.

The three of them exchanged looks, then turned toward me. Dr. Tripp Rebrovick, Harvard's director of debate and my boss, leaned in. My body tensed because I was sure he would strike back. But his response stunned me. "You're absolutely right," Dr. Rebrovick said.

A weight lifted from my shoulders but slammed back down with his next words.

"We agree with you," he said. "So what would you propose we do?"

Oh shit, I thought. I came with a problem but no solutions. My boss tossed the ball back to me, and now I was in the surreal position of being poised to tell Harvard how to fix something broken. I'll come up with a plan, I told them.

I spent the next several weeks envisioning a program that would recruit Black students in Atlanta, turn them into superior debaters, and bring them to the summer residency on full scholarship. My bosses loved the idea, but parts of my plan struck them as overly ambitious.

The first was my recruitment strategy. Atlanta is a big city with established debate leagues, and my boss asked if I intended to recruit Black students from their ranks. I said no. I planned to seek out Black students from under-resourced schools who had probably never even heard of academic debate. There was a valid concern as to how those students could possibly compete against some of the world's top young debaters—kids who came from elite public and private schools and were battle-hardened competitors.

I assured my boss that the young people I chose would be ready by next summer. I would level the playing field by schooling them in philosophy, political science, rhetoric, and other disciplines rarely available in high school. I was confident that in less than one year, I could train them to be superior. This part I was sure of. But the rest of it, not so much.

In the summer of 2017, I established the Harvard Debate Council Diversity Project, or the Harvard Diversity Project for short. I designed a blueprint for the organization, developed a strategic plan, and presented it to my administrators at Harvard. They accepted my proposal and adopted the Harvard Diversity Project as a campus organization—but under several conditions:

1. I would have to build the organization.
2. I would have to staff the organization.
3. I would have to run the organization.
4. And because campus organizations are independently funded, I would have to raise the money to sustain the organization.

None of this intimidated me, though all of it should have. I had established a debate program in Lynchburg as an undergrad. But it was more like a Saturday club, open to whoever showed up, with almost no overhead. When we needed refreshments—or even blazers—all it took was a car wash and a few friends with checkbooks. But this next venture was a different beast: an official project backed by the Dean of Students Office at Harvard College, a world-famous institution that takes the use of its name very seriously. There was far more at stake than I could even understand. Naivete was my friend; only someone who knew so little could be so bold. They even recommended that I raise the money before publicly launching the initiative. But I was relentless. "Yes, sir," I said in response to Dr. Rebrovick's concerns. "I understand." And I promised to make it happen.

I had no idea what such an endeavor would entail. Suddenly I was the founder of a startup, an executive director, a chief marketing officer, a chief philanthropic officer—and a staff of one—needing to turn students into debaters while raising hundreds of thousands of dollars immediately.

Dr. Rebrovick gave me his trust, along with a small seed grant from the college to begin my capital campaign. I went back home and launched a citywide campaign inviting high school students to apply for a program that would eventually take them to summer school at Harvard University. And the next ten months were the most frightening ride of my life.

On Sunday, January 14, 2018, a group of eager applicants arrived at the Harvard Debate Council's new satellite campus in Atlanta. A local college had donated a wing in their building for our central office and classrooms. Hundreds of high school students from around Metro Atlanta applied, but we invited only twenty-five of them to interview for a spot in the inaugural cohort. They had been told nothing about the interview process. The email was clear about just two points: dress professionally and show up on time. At 11:30 a.m., twenty-five anxious teens entered an art gallery full of adults—my friends, local corporate and community leaders—ready to shake their sweaty hands. The interviews began at that moment, though the kids had no idea. They were so fidgety and high-strung that they mistook the adults for greeters opposed to interviewers.

I walked around the gallery, eavesdropping on conversations, studying their soft skills, analyzing their body language. I was just another greeter, for all they knew. I was clearly the youngest adult in the room, and probably the least likely to be suspected as the director. None of them had even heard my name. All they knew was that there was a new program in Atlanta that could send Black students to Harvard.

An hour passed and the group was herded for entry into a large assembly room with rows of theater-style seating where their families had been waiting.

"What happens from here?" one parent asked another. They knew nothing; they sat in their seats exchanging speculations, and the decibel level rose to commotion. Everyone stopped talking when the doors opened and the candidates filed into the room. One by one, the students filled the empty chairs arranged in a crescent at the foot of the stage. Watching from the rows behind, parents stretched their necks to search their children's faces for signs of hope. They silently implored, "Please, dear God, let my child get in," the parents would tell me later.

The suspense was electric. My friends who had volunteered to staff the event took seats after directing the students to theirs. And although they knew what was to come, the volunteers could also feel the tension and balanced on the edge of their seats. But students and parents were still looking around for the unidentified program director.

From the back-door window, I could see when everyone was seated. I entered and every head turned as I marched down the aisle in a black suit and red bow tie, toting my leather briefcase. "Is that him?" I heard a parent whisper as I passed through the rows. I later learned that I was not what the parents expected. "He's awfully young," some said. *Harvard's assistant debate coach is Black?* others thought. Some were even startled as they noticed my millennial-looking Mohawk fade. Instead of mounting the stage, I grabbed the microphone and jumped on one of the audience chairs.

"My name is Mr. Fleming," I said. "If you are accepted into this program, I will be your teacher." I paused for a moment and, my face impassive, surveyed the room. And then I dropped the bomb: "You might not have realized it, but you have just completed the first part of your interview."

I could have collected their jaws with a dustpan. It seemed to dawn on them that this was not a traditional selection process. Those who had hung back during the meet-and-greet in the gallery, unaware that their ability to work a room was being evaluated, were now filled with remorse. Their faces fell. Then the situation got worse.

"The second part of your interview," I said, "begins now." I hopped down and took a seat. A slide appeared on the large screen at the front of the room, explaining that they had fifteen minutes to openly discuss and resolve an ethical dilemma. A prompt followed, a timer appeared on the screen, and the clock started running. Some students instantly jumped to their feet to begin conferring with their peers. Some students talked. Some students listened. Some students sat there paralyzed by fear.

After fifteen minutes, an alarm signaled that time was up. I remained motionless. The students averted their eyes and I stared at them as if I had just witnessed the world's greatest failure of human intelligence. After a few moments of silence, I stood and paced in front of them while staring deep into their eyes.

"What the hell was that?" I said. I maintained eye contact with each of them, one by one, even when they were afraid to look back. No one answered my question.

"I'm sorry," I scoffed. "Perhaps that sounded rhetorical."

After a few moments of silence and an intense stare-down between me and the candidates, a boy named Jordan stood to break the silence, stumbling over his words.

"Well, we tried to—"

"Take a seat," I interrupted. "I'm not talking to you. I'm talking to those who had the unmitigated nerve to apply to a Harvard debate program but you're too scared to open up your mouth at an interview."

I raised my eyes to check on the parents. Some faces were contorted with panic, wishing they could throw their child a lifeline or snatch them out of the fire. Some looked shocked, even angry, to hear a teacher talk to their children this way.

"Okay," I said. "I see no one wants to answer. I tell you what, I'm going to give you one last chance. You have one final exercise to prove that you're not wasting my time, because I have another group of willing applicants coming in right after you."

One student had already shed a nervous tear. She discreetly dabbed her eyes, then squared her shoulders and listened for all she was worth.

"Pay very close attention to my instructions," I said. "There are bags underneath your chairs containing two items for the final challenge. When I say 'Go,' you will reach under your chair and pull the items out of the bag. There are different colored sweaters and a folder with instructions. You have ten seconds to throw on the sweater, race to the middle, find your group with the same color, and open the folder to begin the exercise."

"Are you ready?" I said. Everyone nodded.

"Three . . .

"Two . . .

"One . . .

"Go!" I yelled. They snatched the bags from under the seats, fumbling in haste. They tussled their arms through the sleeves, tugged the sweaters over their heads, and wrestled them into place. By the time their faces popped up, they were all on their feet and crowded in the middle of the floor. Their eyes whipped back and forth, looking desperately for others in their group. Then they froze in disbelief. The sweaters were all the same color.

All the students now wore crimson pullovers with large white letters across the chest that spelled HARVARD. Parents leaped to their feet, gasps bursting from open mouths, falling on one another for support and obviously thinking, *This can't be so!* The students were startled. Then they remembered that they had one more thing to do, so they reached for the folders, which all said HARVARD on the front.

"Wait, what?" they exclaimed, looking at their peers for a reality check. Then they all focused on me, seeking confirmation that their wildest dreams were coming true. Shrieks filled the room and hands reached high in the air as confetti suddenly rained from above like the tears flowing down their beautiful brown faces. And I yelled, "Congratulations! You're all going to Harvard!"

The following Saturday was their first Harvard debate class. Almost six months had passed since Harvard approved the program, and I had not raised a single cent. One week earlier, I had promised twenty-five students that they were going to Harvard. The dramatic surprise acceptance event was being broadcast on the news and shared across social media.

Meanwhile, a mentor I deeply admired knew the truth. When he saw the headlines, I thought he would be happy for me. But he did not hold back his criticism. He called me insane, a liar, and a fool. I would have been less pained if he had plunged a dagger into my gut and twisted it. "You promised those kids that they were going to Harvard but you have no money," he said. "How will you feel when those poor kids' hearts are broken for being lied to?" he asked. And I had no answer.

"What makes you believe that you can raise hundreds of thousands of dollars in six months?" he asked. Still I had no answer. My head hung low as I thought, *What in the world have I just done?*

I believe in loving first and teaching second. So when the students arrived to class on Saturday, we began with them, not with lessons about logic or politics. I wrapped my arms around each scholar as soon as they walked through the doorway. Mahlon's curious eyes were partly obscured by dreadlocks and his bow tie was sloppily unfastened. He stretched out his arm to shake my hand, but I cuffed it aside and wrapped my arms around him. "Oh," he grunted as I gave him a good squeeze.

Each time we met, I hugged all of my scholars, especially the young men. I told them that they were valued, that they were missed during the week, that they were loved. This was particularly awkward for Mahlon and others who had never been embraced by a male mentor in this way. Mahlon attended one of the worst-ranked high schools in the state, a forlorn place in a forgotten neighborhood on Atlanta's west side. He had mastered the same *real nigga* look that once armored me: the inflated chest, the furrowed brow, the *I don't give a fuck* demeanor. I was aware that Mahlon was the oldest of three, there was no man of the house, and he had been working multiple jobs to help keep the family afloat. When he'd first heard about the new pipeline-to-Harvard program, he was reluctant to apply because he'd need to cut back on working hours and his family needed the money. "Go ahead, baby," his mother had said. "We'll figure it out." Because she knew that this opportunity could help unlock the door for him to finally escape the hood.

On that first Saturday, when the students entered the classroom, they were surprised to see that orderly rows of tables had been replaced by chairs in an open arrangement. "This is what we will call circle time," I said, beckoning them to sit down. "Before we begin learning as scholars, this is our opportunity to connect as brothers and sisters."

Over the months, magic happened in that circle. It's where we danced, where we laughed, where we sometimes cried as we opened up our hearts. It's where the kids learned to trust each other. It's where they learned to trust me. And trust was an essential foundation for the tumultuous and unconventional process they would soon undergo. The Harvard summer debate residency would begin in just six months, and I was going to have to bend them so far that their parents sometimes feared they would break, I'd later learn.

"What is the fundamental question of politics?" I asked while writing the question on the board during our first session. Hands shot up at the desks where the students were now seated.

"We don't raise hands here," I said. "If you have something to say, stand up and say it with a sense of urgency."

Payton was the first to jump up and speak. "I think politics is—"

"Take a seat," I abruptly interjected. "I do not care what you *think*. We win debates by what we *know*."

Payton was fearless. She wore her hair slicked back in a ponytail like she was ready for a fight. Now I had punctured her brazen confidence like a balloon. She was used to being the smartest in the room, even smarter than many of her teachers. She was candid about the fact that no one had ever said words to her like "Think bigger," "You can do better," or "I expect more from you." She was used to being patted on the head by teachers who praised her for being the articulate Black girl. She was used to being celebrated in a system that calls Black kids "gifted and talented" if they happen to stretch their hands higher than the disrespectfully low bar set for them. Falling short was a new and necessary experience for Payton. Understanding the pressures and struggles and challenges waiting to meet them in a pitiless world, I needed all of my scholars to run faster, reach higher, and learn how to fail *forward*. Her face froze in disbelief as she slowly sunk back into her seat.

The rest of the class was suddenly afraid to speak, terrified of suffering the same fate. Finally, Osazi stood up and took a stab at it. He began, "I feel like the fundamental—"

"Take a seat," I snapped. "Next!"

I scanned a roomful of worried faces, and when no one rose to the challenge, I turned back to Osazi and asked, "Did you not hear what I just said to Payton?" He looked up at me with watery eyes. "I don't care about how you *feel* right now. We already talked about your feelings in circle time. I want you to make an argument."

I explained argumentation in academic terms. I looked back at Osazi and saw that his chin had sunk to his chest. I advanced toward his desk.

"Look at me," I said. His eyes met mine. "Don't ever let your opponent see that you're under pressure. Why didn't you get back up?"

He hesitated and then said, "Because you told me to sit down, sir."

"But did I tell you to stay down?" I retorted. He dropped his eyes again.

"Look at me," I repeated. "I don't care *who* or *what* knocks you down. You get back up and try again. You understand me?" He said, "Yes, sir" as he lifted his head with a new sense of resolve.

"And you," I said, making my way to Maya sitting next to him. "You haven't said a word all day. Why?"

Maya glared back at me as if to say, *Look, sir, I ain't the one.* Maya could turn on a dime from soft and pleasant to feisty and defensive, I'd find out. She was quick to clap back when she was attacked. And she was quick to defend others. That was why she'd given me a mean side-eye when I challenged Osazi. I saw her as a leader in the making. It would take a little work to get her to see the same.

"I was just listening," she said, her posture upright.

"And can you win a debate by just listening?" I asked.

"It's part of it," she responded.

"Clever," I said and chuckled. "But notice that I modified 'listening' with the word 'just.' So answer my question: Can you win a debate by just listening?"

"No, sir," she conceded.

"Correct," I said. "So don't ever let another class go by without standing up to speak."

I returned to the front to address the entire class. "In this society, there are existing systems of injustice whose survival relies on your silence. So hear me clearly: silence is not an option here." I reminded them that our task was much bigger than debate. They were preparing to go out into the world and step into spaces where they are not only seen, but they are heard. This was bigger than us. This was bigger than Harvard. This was about teaching them how to use their voices to start movements and disrupt systems and shift the balance of power.

"Training for debate is like preparing for warfare," I continued. "Your mind is your shield. Your words are your weapons." I walked slowly down the middle aisle as their eyes followed me raptly.

"But here," I continued, clenching my hand into a fist, "we do not outfight. We outwit."

Before dismissing class for the day, I gave the scholars one more opportunity. "Would anyone else like to take a stab at the fundamental question of politics?" Jordan unfolded himself from the desk and straightened to his full six-foot height. He was a burly guy, a budding star at lacrosse until he was sidelined by injuries and surgeries. Just as I had done years earlier, he pivoted from athletics toward debate. He almost didn't make the cut. Our program was limited to twenty-five participants. Of all applicants, he ranked twenty-sixth and was wait-listed. Just a few days before the dramatic acceptance ceremony, another student dropped out and Jordan got a last-minute invitation. And here he was, taking on the challenge when no one else would.

"Well," he said. "Before determining the fundamental question of politics, I think—excuse me—I know that we should first define politics conceptually." He paused for a moment, awaiting my response. The tension was high as his peers waited for whatever I would fire back at him. But he was correct.

"Yes, Jordan!" I said. "We must always define before we conclude."

Shocked by my affirmation, the entire class erupted in applause as he slapped hands with the boys beside him. With a smile on my face, I turned toward the whiteboard and wrote a formula:

$$\text{In what ways?} > \text{What is?}$$

"Listen to me closely," I said as the commotion settled. "When we define words, we don't ask, 'What does x mean?' We ask, 'In what ways can x be defined?' Somebody tell me the difference."

Everyone's energy had suddenly shifted, like Jordan's small victory had sparked a fire in the room. Bodies were popping up everywhere.

"By asking, 'What does x mean?' you are thinking one-dimensionally," Maya said, "because you're only looking for one answer."

"Yes, Maya!" I shouted and threw my hands up. She broke into a full-faced smile as the energy in the room continued to rise.

Then Osazi jumped up. "Whereas asking, 'In what ways?' leads you to multiple answers and diverse perspectives."

"Yes, Osazi!" I cheered. "And why is that important?"

Mahlon rose to his feet. "Because when it comes to argumentation," he said, with all eyes fixed on him, "debate is all about weighing definitions and impact."

"Yes, Mahlon!" I chanted.

I abandoned the whiteboard and stepped closer to the scholars with my hands outstretched. I dramatically lowered my voice to crystallize the lesson. "Here's what I need you to understand," I said as the scholars quieted and everyone leaned in. "Debate is all about two people approaching the same idea. But who can *think* the deepest? That is the one who wins." I could not hold back my smile as I saw the childlike wonder glistening in their eyes.

"This," I said, "is how you will become champions this summer."

The countdown was real: I had exactly six months to transform a group of inexperienced teens into superior debaters. And I had six months to raise hundreds of thousands of dollars. Starting in the early morning, I worked full-time as a teacher at the Ron Clark Academy. Beginning in the afternoon and lasting into the night, I worked full-time as an executive director, writing grant proposals and begging banks and corporations and foundations to invest in our cause. Many never replied. The few who did respond said, *I'm sorry, but we are not looking to fund a new venture without a track record of success.*

For months, I hid my travails from my Harvard boss because I didn't want him to worry. But I reached a point of desperation. Eventually, I requested a meeting and asked if the college could cover my salary, enabling me to leave my teaching job at RCA and invest all my energy in the capital campaign for the Diversity Project. To my surprise, he agreed to take the risk. But like our last deal, this one came with conditions. Harvard would pay my salary for three months, then reassess the circumstances in May. If I was at least halfway to my fundraising goal for the fiscal year, they would keep me on the payroll.

I was relieved and terrified. If I quit my job at RCA but failed to reach Harvard's fundraising goal in three months, I would have no source of income during the school year. I was risking my livelihood. But I was also risking a promise to my scholars. There was only one choice, and I had to make it.

I knew saying goodbye to Keanen, Isaac, and my other students would be heartbreaking. I had no idea that it would be one of the hardest days of my life.

It was the last day before spring break began. Keanen and Isaac were now seventh graders. I was packing boxes when they bounded into my classroom, eager to be the first to greet me. Their classmates were filing in behind them.

"Hey, Mr. Fleming!" the boys called out before they noticed my solemn expression and the empty shelves where my philosophy books had been. I was surrounded by partly filled cardboard boxes. "Mr. Fleming, what's going on?"

I had not expected my words to catch in my throat. I didn't move and neither did they, as though a giant pause button had been pushed. The kids stood at their seats, books in hand, staring at me and waiting for an explanation.

"Everyone take a seat," I said. The commotion of chairs scraping the floor broke the awkward silence and gave me time to think. I told them that it would be my last day; I would not be returning after spring break.

When the bell rang, I tried to carry out my boxes with no fanfare. But my departure drew an emotional crowd. Some students grabbed hold of my boxes and we played tug-of-war. Others latched on to my arms and my legs crying, "Please don't go." Others blocked the exit but I plowed ahead, averting my face so they would not see my tears. "Please don't do this," I begged. "It's hard enough already."

The commotion summoned the other teachers to the scene. They held students back as I pushed through the doors toward the parking lot. Keanen and Isaac wrapped their arms around my torso one last time.

"Look at me," I said, lifting their chins. "We will meet again soon, I promise." At that point, when so much was uncertain, it was impossible to explain that I'd created the Harvard pipeline with them in mind. But I knew that in a few years, if everything worked out, we would again make history together.

The capital campaign became my full-time job. Every day I woke up at 5 a.m., put on my business suit and bow tie, stuffed my briefcase with brochures, and headed out. I had made a printout of local companies and organizations with charitable giving programs. I relied on it like a GPS programmed for potential donors. My treasure hunt took me from bank to bank, from business to business, and even from one office to another within the same organization. Cold calls were rarely answered, and only now and then did I make it past the front desk without an appointment. Once, I managed to score a meeting with a foundation that could cover our entire budget with the stroke of a pen. But I never heard back from them.

Although a few of my prospects remembered news stories about Black kids going to Harvard, most had never heard of our program. When I did get inside an executive office or conference room, I did everything except beg on my hands and knees. "I just need someone to believe in this," I'd say, searching the faces of executives whose expressions said they had better things to do.

It was now late April. Another month had gone by with no success. I had written more than one hundred grant proposals and applied to more than one hundred foundations of all sizes, from small family charities to giant national organizations. Crickets or "no thank yous." That's all I had to show.

Then May arrived, the month of my payroll reassessment. The Harvard residency was only about sixty days away and I dutifully chipped away at bureaucratic details related to our participation. On Saturdays, I taught everything I knew to teach. But watching those kids evolve into elite debaters, and watching their faces light up as they counted the days until the big event, tore me up inside. Many times, I walked into class resolved to tell them that we wouldn't be going after all. The longer I waited, the more devastating the blow would be. So I had finally decided that I would break the news to them at our next class. I thought of a million different ways to say, "I know I promised you would go to Harvard, but I couldn't raise the money. I'm so sorry." But the same week that I decided to drop the bomb, a miracle happened.

Every Wednesday, I had dinner with legendary Atlantan Ann Cramer at FolkArt restaurant. She's a tiny white woman who bursts with energy and charisma like a human exclamation mark. She'd retired after years as IBM's director of corporate citizenship and corporate affairs for the Americas. Since stepping aside, she consulted for nonprofit organizations like mine. I had recently been accepted into LEAD Atlanta, a leadership program targeting young professionals on the rise. The program paired us with prominent figures in the community; I was assigned to Mrs. Cramer as a mentee. And she was a godsend. During our weekly meetings, she taught me the basics of starting a new nonprofit, helped me recruit an executive board, and served as its senior advisor. But more importantly, she is like my second mother. She does not take kindly to self-pity.

"I did everything you told me to," I said to her. "But the foundations are all saying the same thing." Now I needed to exit as gracefully as possible and control the damage. But she would not allow me to accept defeat.

"No, no, no, my dear," she said, reaching her hands across the table to grab mine. "There is still one person that I want you to meet, Rodney Bullard from the Chick-fil-A Foundation."

I met with Mr. Bullard shortly after Mrs. Cramer arranged it. I figured it was a waste of time because I had already been turned away by Chick-fil-A corporate. But it turned out that Mr. Bullard was the company's vice president for corporate social responsibility and executive director of the Chick-fil-A Foundation. I was tired of taking punches, but I went out of respect for Mrs. Cramer, whom I felt obliged to obey.

Mr. Bullard is a Black man. He looks like he could have easily played linebacker for the Atlanta Falcons. He's intimidating at first glance, but we shook hands and he invited me to take a seat. "So, tell me what you have here," he said, focusing his attention entirely on me. I got ready to unleash the most passionate sales pitch for the Harvard Diversity Project that anyone had ever heard. But this time, I couldn't. I was tired of impersonating a nonprofit executive. I was tired of marketing and commercialism. So I decided to be myself. I decided to tell my story.

"To be honest, Mr. Bullard," I said softly as I set the brochures aside. "I'm not even supposed to be here. I should be in a factory, in a prison, or dead."

I told him how my life was spared, and how I'd finally discovered why I had been given a second chance. "That is why I'm here," I said. "It's to make sure that those kids have access to everything that I needed when I was their age."

I told him that debate had transformed my life, but that the Diversity Project was about more than debate. It was about using educational equity to build new and enduring pathways for Black youth. I was confident that what I was teaching my scholars would not only make them successful, it would make them academically superior and position them to compete against elite scholars from around the world. And I promised him that they would come out on top. I just needed someone to believe in us.

By the time my cathartic monologue wound down, he was regarding me with a lopsided grin. He uncrossed his legs and leaned closer to the table.

"I believe in you," he said. "Tell me what you need."

Then and there, he committed to a sizable investment in the Diversity Project when it seemed that no one else would. And Chick-fil-A's stamp of approval had an immediate ripple effect. Next came the Coca-Cola Foundation, then the UPS Foundation, then WarnerMedia, then Kaiser Permanente, then Publix Super Markets Charities, and many more. Thirty days before our departure for Cambridge, we had raised enough to cover tuition, travel, and room and board for all twenty-five of our students. It was no longer a question of whether they would go. It was now a question of whether they could rise to the occasion.

July 1, 2018, we crossed the bridge connecting Boston to Cambridge over the Charles River, the Harvard Houses rising above the trees. When we reached the campus, I smiled proudly and said, "Welcome to Harvard University" as though I were handing them a cherished gift. The kids pressed their faces against the bus windows as I named some of the landmarks we passed. I asked the bus driver to turn onto Massachusetts Avenue so they could see Harvard Law School, where Barack Obama once studied. Then we turned into Radcliffe Quadrangle on Linnaean Street to find our dormitory: Currier House.

We had a few hours to kill before opening assembly. After the scholars picked up their Harvard IDs and loaded their luggage into their dorm rooms, we walked across campus to Harvard Yard. The scholars followed behind me in a large cluster. Jordan was carrying a portable speaker that blared Migos and Future and Lil Baby as we danced and strolled through the Ivy League campus. When we reached the Widener Library, Jordan climbed the vast staircase like he was Rocky Balboa. The other scholars followed up the stone steps toward the enormous pillars that march across its front. Halfway up, as if on cue, twenty-five identically dressed Black kids began Milly rockin' and dabbin' and hittin' dem folks. They were impervious to passersby who looked appalled by the spectacle of their Black joy. But I was overwhelmed with pride, because those steps were designed in the early 1900s by Julian F. Abele, a then prominent African American architect. And this moment was their inheritance.

"Come on, Mr. Fleming!" they yelled down at me. I dropped my briefcase and ran to join them on the steps. They huddled around me and cheered as I did my best Milly rock. It was a moment I will never forget. The kids cheering and jumping and bouncing off of each other like we were a college football team preparing to rush the gridiron. Energy surging through my body and making the hairs on my arms stand up. It felt like crowding together with my teammates in the center of the basketball court, chanting, "We readaay! We readaay!" And it was true—without question—my scholars were ready.

The assembly hall held groups of students from China, Russia, a host of European countries, and every corner of the United States. These were not average students and debaters. Members of the Chinese team, for example, were selected by their organization based on a performance assessment. Many of the students came from places where they had little if any interaction with Black people. Their knowledge of Black people came from television, which probably accounted for the crude comments and strange questions that my students heard during the residency:

"Why are Blacks so aggressive?"

"Can I touch your hair?"

"Is your father in your life?"

"You have a better chance getting into a good college than me."

And the times they were referred to as the "affirmative action kids."

This was a culture shock for my students who attended Black schools in Black communities with nothing but Black people. I'd worked hard to teach our kids how to love themselves and how to love each other, because I knew that existing in elite spaces is a challenge. Some assumed that our kids had been given a handout, that they were not equally deserving and qualified. But once classes began, that stigma was blown away by the performance of the Atlanta scholars.

The Harvard debate camp is not for the faint of heart. It reminds me of the elite college camps that I once competed in as a basketball recruit. The days at Harvard are long and arduous. During our stay, twelve hours of intensive learning about international policy would end at 9 p.m., then participants would head for their dorm rooms and buckle down to research and case writing until after midnight, only to rise at 6 a.m. to do it again. Everyone was working on the same topic for the whole two weeks: "Resolved: The United States should accede to the United Nations Convention on the Law of the Sea without reservations." All students attended the same classes, heard the same lectures, read the same materials, and underwent the same skills training. The goal was to craft their own cases—for and against the resolution—for the tournament held during the residency's final two days.

Day one of the culminating tournament was filled with preliminary rounds, and in order to advance a student had to win at least five of their eight rounds. Those who fell short would be out of the competition; those who won five had an even tougher day ahead in the single elimination rounds. The results wouldn't be announced until the morning of the second day.

"Listen to me," I said as we huddled at the beginning of day one. "When I walked into your very first class in Atlanta, what did I say?" Our arms were latched and our heads were nearly touching.

"You said this is bigger than debate," Osazi said.

"That's right," I responded. "And what else?"

Maya lifted her head and added, "You told us to leave if we were not ready to start a movement."

"That's right," I said again. "Look around this circle. It's you. You are the movement. And it's bigger than debate, because it's about your community and showing the world who we are and what we're capable of." I tightened my grip on Jordan and Osazi, who was always by my side.

"You know what we came here to do," I said as I looked them in their eyes. "Let's show the world what it looks like when scholarship meets culture."

I arose early on the final day of the tournament and got to the Hilles assembly hall before anyone else. The suspense had kept me awake all night and I needed time to center myself in the space where it would all happen. I thought about what I'd said back in Atlanta whenever Jordan would get so hyped that he'd jump on a chair, beat his chest, and yell, "We kickin' everybody ass this summer, Mr. Fleming!" I'd always said, "Relax, Jordan. It's not all about winning." Nor is education all about passing the final exam. But here we were, facing a final of sorts, and it was time to see if we would pass what felt like the biggest test of our lives.

The auditorium filled quickly. Everyone was dressed in business attire for the big event. Most of the residential students had taken seats, pulled out their laptops, and started prepping for the first round. Suddenly, I heard music blaring from the back of the auditorium. The doors flung wide as Jordan burst in with his handheld speaker blasting Migos, the rest of our team dancing behind him. Every eye in the room was riveted on them. My heart danced as they paraded in like an HBCU marching band, wearing their navy blazers, polka-dot bow ties, and flamboyant socks. They were Black, proud, and utterly unselfconscious.

We stood together while the judges prepared to name the sixteen students who broke prelims and were advancing to octofinals, the debate version of the NCAA Sweet Sixteen. We crossed our fingers, hoping that at least four of us would make it, giving us four chances to make the championship round. But when the octofinalists were announced, we learned that we did not get four places. We got ten. Ten of the top sixteen students in the Harvard tournament were ours.

After each round, all students reported to the auditorium as results were tabulated. I was a nervous wreck. My scholars huddled as we waited for the results to post. I could not sit. I paced around until I heard someone in the auditorium yell, "Results are up!" We all rushed to the nearest laptop and hovered over it as a student scrolled to reveal the next pairings.

It felt like a devastating blow. Six of our students were eliminated. But four of us advanced. We were four out of eight students in the quarterfinals.

My scholars and the other students who had been eliminated flocked to the rooms where their friends—or rivals—were competing. This time I really could not watch. I went outside to walk off a combination of nerves and caffeine that had my adrenaline racing.

In the next round, two of our students were eliminated. But two of us advanced. We were now two of the four heading to the semifinals.

I stayed to watch this round, because the results would be tabulated and announced immediately after the debate. Jordan was one of the semifinalists, and in this round he took an alarming risk. His opponent presented an argument that he perceived as a counterplan, which is an illegal move. It means that a debater is advocating a solvency that falls outside the boundaries of the resolution. This particular topic required debaters to argue that the United States either *should* or *should not* accede. No other choices were on the table. A counterplan would propose that the United States do something completely different. Here's the risk: if you flag a counterplan and spend the entire debate defending that charge, only to have your opponent prove that it is not in fact a counterplan, then you will inevitably lose. Jordan decided to scrap the argument that he'd used to win his previous rounds and instead attack what he saw as a counterplan. I was horrified. All I could think was *Jordan, what the hell are you doing?*

The debate went off the rails. It went so deep into definition of counterplans that neither debater was talking about the United States or the United Nations or the Law of the Sea. Jordan invoked the National Speech & Debate Association handbook as evidence that his opponent should be disqualified for presenting an illegal counterplan. The whole audience was thrown for a loop. At the end of the round, bedlam ensued as audience members debated with the people around them. The results were agonizingly slow to come because the judges had a debate of their own.

After nearly thirty minutes, the judges announced, "We have a decision." The entire room went mute. "We decided that the case presented by the negative *is* in fact a counterplan. The win goes to the affirmative." I nearly fell from my seat. I gulped in air like someone who had almost suffocated. Jordan was advancing to the championship to represent our team.

At the Harvard debate residency, it's traditional for the two finalists to make remarks before their opening speech for the round. When it was Jordan's turn, he mounted his laptop on the podium, adjusted the microphone stand to his height, and leaned into the mic with a big sigh as he looked into the audience and said, "Wow, what a journey it has been." He gave heartfelt thanks to the faculty and all his classmates at the residency. "And of course," he said, "I gotta give a huge shoutout to my Diversity Project teammates from Atlanta!" They immediately leaped to their feet in the front row and cheered and chanted, "Ayyyeee!" while holding up the A-Town sign with their fingers. Then he said, "There's one more person that I want to thank before I start this round." He paused for a moment as he looked toward the back of the auditorium. When he made eye contact with me, he continued, "Because we would not be here if it were not for him." Tears filled my eyes, but I gazed up to keep them from falling down my face.

I don't remember much else that happened during that round. I heard the voices of Jordan and his opponent, but they were distant. I was looking at them, but I wasn't. My mind was a kaleidoscope of images and moments from the past year.

Struggling with a decision in Harvard Yard the previous summer.

Having that scary conversation with my boss.

Confetti raining down at the surprise acceptance ceremony.

Our very first class.

The skeptics who called me crazy.

The parents who called me a tyrant, thinking I was too hard on their children.

The capital campaign that left me feeling like the Maze Runner.

The board member who petitioned for my removal, suggesting Harvard should hire someone with more experience.

It all played through my mind. The highs. The lows. In that moment, it was all worth it. Because a group of Black kids from Atlanta came to one of the world's most elite institutions and shattered the myth of Black inferiority.

"Congratulations to both teams," the lead judge said after the final arguments concluded, snapping me back to the present. The waiting was nearly unbearable as the five judges huddled to make a decision. Jordan remained on the stage, staring down at his clasped hands resting on the table as if he was too anxious to look at anyone. My scholars were on the edge of their seats, locking arms and holding each other close. I stepped out into the lobby because the tension and suspense were asphyxiating. I tried to convince myself that the outcome was less momentous than it actually was. But no Black team had ever won the public forum debate competition in the history of this residential program.

I looked through the door just in time to see the judges break the huddle. I slipped into my seat in the back of the auditorium. "We have a decision," the spokesman for the panelists said. My heart beat percussively. My scholars clutched their brothers and sisters tighter and dipped their heads as if in prayer. Jordan looked heavenward. I broke out in a cold sweat as the judge rose to his feet.

"The decision is unanimous," he said. "With a perfect 5–0 ballot— congratulations to the negative team."

Jordan's jaw dropped and his eyes widened as thunderous applause filled the room. I was frozen in place as Jordan's twenty-four teammates leaped over chairs, rushed the stage, and piled on him, screaming and shouting and crying, "We did it!" Every student and faculty member and even Jordan's opponent stood and grinned as the historic moment unfolded. The next day, news broke fast in national media. *Headline News, Huffington Post, Black Enterprise,* and many others told the story: twenty-five Black Atlanta teens made history at Harvard.

Osazi was one of three graduating seniors on our team. Our victory in Cambridge gave our scholars a powerful story to tell about starting a revolution, and he wrote about it in his application essay for Harvard. He talked about what it meant for him growing up in poverty with siblings and a single mother who struggled to support her family while grappling with her own mental health wellness. When Osazi had first come home talking about applying to a Harvard pipeline program, she dismissed the idea. "You're not doing it," she'd said. "I ain't got no Harvard money." But he'd secretly applied behind her back.

Though Osazi had applied to the Harvard Diversity Project, he had no intentions of applying to Harvard College for undergrad. One day, during class, I told him and his peers to aim higher and dream bigger. He did not take it kindly. I later learned of a rant that he went on when we broke for lunch.

"I'm not listening to that crazy man," Osazi said to his peers. Other students agreed, saying that my advice contradicted what their school counselors were telling them.

"Uh-uh," Maya interjected. "What y'all not gon' do is talk bad about Mr. Fleming. Not in front of me."

"I'm just saying," Osazi added. "I'm the one applying to these schools. Not Mr. Fleming. I'm gonna apply to schools that I know I can actually get into."

That was long before Osazi had become my right hand. Now he was always at my side, studying my words and body language—just as I once had as a college student aspiring to be the next Cornel West. After our historic win, we were invited to appear on national television and at conferences. The kids playfully teased Osazi and called him professor because he mimicked my gestures and appropriated my favorite sayings when he gave speeches. Invitations poured in for us to speak at events and conferences throughout the city. One of these was for the Democratic Party of Georgia, the same group that had once invited my RCA students to appear. But this time, they did not invite us to sing and dance. This time, my scholars were the keynote. And they set the room ablaze.

At the end of that year, in December, I was on my couch at home, waiting for my phone to ring. It was decision day, and at 7 p.m. Harvard would announce its early action acceptances for the Class of 2023. The probability of being accepted fell in what the university later called "likely the most competitive early admissions cycle in Harvard history."

We had been waiting for this moment for months. The email notification was scheduled to come through any moment now. It was about 6:30 p.m. when I called Osazi. "Listen," I said. "This admissions decision does not define you. Regardless of what happens, I am prouder of you than you will ever know. I love you, my boy." He said, "I love you, too, Mr. Fleming," and he promised to call me the moment the email hit his inbox.

Seven o'clock came and went. He still had not called at a quarter past the hour. I paced my living room, grabbing the phone and setting it back down, running various scenarios in my head. Was the email delayed? Was he too devastated by bad news to call? Was he cursing me for getting his hopes up?

Moments later, my phone rang. I dashed across the living room and scooped it off the couch. Osazi's name was backlit on the screen. My heart wanted to know but was afraid to hear. But the answer was waiting for me. So I slid my thumb across the screen and raised the phone to my ear.

It was Osazi's mom. "Ahhhhhhhhh!" she shrieked so loudly that I nearly dropped the phone. "Oh my God! Oh my God! Oh my God!" she repeated between jagged breaths.

"What happened?" I asked.

"Oh my God! Oh my God!" she wheezed. Then she began sobbing uncontrollably.

"Ms. Wu, calm down for me. I need you to tell me what happened," I begged.

She tried to speak, but she could not quite catch her breath.

"You cha . . .

"You cha . . .

"You cha . . .

"You changed my family's life forever."

EPILOGUE

My dear scholars, it's hard to believe that so many of you have gone away. You're now off at Ivy Leagues, HBCUs, and the most elite colleges and boarding schools in the world, where your indelible signatures will remain in perpetuity. No place will ever be the same after you've stepped into it. No person's life will ever be the same after you've entered it—especially my own. How privileged I am to have shared a brief moment in time with you. And how beautiful it is that the Grand Weaver saw fit to thread our lives into a tapestry of Black excellence. One that our community can raise high and wave wildly like a banner of pride.

Nothing brings me joy like the times when you come home. We break bread and laugh and fight back tears as we relive those moments that will live in our hearts forever. Each year brought new challenges that seemed insuperable. But those challenges were no match for your magic. When the inaugural class of 2018 shocked the world, many cheered but skeptics questioned. Black dominance in many sports is not surprising. But Black dominance in academic debate is not to be expected, and the prospect of its longevity was not easily believed. So it raised the question: *Could they do it again?*

Then along came the rolling class of 2019—with all of your grit and wit . . . and drama. This was the first year that your training became yearlong. The stakes were even higher. We had something to prove. And the spotlight seemed to singe. All year, you fretted—wondering if you could walk in the legacy of our alumni. But you did not. Because you created a legacy of your own. By the time the Harvard debate tournament came around, your dominance was so overwhelming that our team crowded the final rounds. We were forced to face and eliminate our own pairs. By the semifinals, four of our students had gone eight consecutive rounds with a perfect winning record. It was unheard of. Especially because two of those students were the youngest debaters on campus: the mighty force of Keanen and Isaac. They lost only to our pair of seniors, DJ and Keith, who brought home the championship for our team with a unanimous ballot—and the first undefeated record in Harvard Debate Council history.

Then came the vivacious class of 2020. My heart was so broken when COVID-19 struck us in the middle of your year. It was my responsibility to give you the most unimaginable and unforgettable experience. But you were shortchanged when we could no longer have classes in person. And you were robbed when you learned that you would likely be the only cohort to not step foot on Harvard's campus. But when the residency switched to virtual, you saw this as an opportunity to make history in a new way. And you did it. Madison and Christian brought home the three-peat with another unanimous ballot in the final round—Christian as the youngest Black male and Madison as the first Black female to win the tournament in Harvard Debate Council history.

But none of that is what matters most. Because it was never about debate. It was never about Harvard. It was never about winning. It was always about teaching you about your responsibility. In Langston Hughes's iconic poem, he said *today* I will eat in the kitchen when company comes, but *tomorrow*—tomorrow, I will eat at the table. I need you to understand that Langston's *tomorrow* is your *right now*.

Now that you've found your voice, what will you do with it? Now that you have access to networks and resources, what will you do with it? There's nothing wrong with privilege. But it is in vain lest you remember that with privilege comes the responsibility to serve. This is how we break the back of poverty. This is how we rip the seam of injustice. This is how we shift the balance of power. By building as we climb. By shattering every glass ceiling. By breaking down every barrier of opportunity. By bringing your own seat. By building your own table. By having the courage to blaze trails in the places where we belong. And by having the audacity to be intrusive in spaces that are not inclusive.

Across all industries, professionals use metrics to define how well we've done our jobs. There is only one way that I'll know I have done mine. It won't be an award. It won't be any recognition. It will be determined in about another decade when we reunite. You will boast of incredible feats. I will listen. I will smile. Then I will ask, "How did you make someone else's life better?"

In this book, I tell these stories and pen uncomfortable truths because it took me far too long to learn that where a man has no voice, he does not exist. He can even be present and not exist, because inferiority is an induced consciousness whose physical manifestation begins with silence. He is seen, but he is not heard. He is not understood. Because he does not matter. His humanity is debased, his identity is usurped, and he is subject to abuse—because he does not matter. But when he discovers his voice, he determines that he can sing and summon the sound of hope. A hope in resistance, a hope in resilience, a hope in revolution: this song.

It is not without pain but because of pain that he sings. And it was long before his discovery that he mattered. But it is because of his song that he cannot be ignored. He was invisible. But he is invisible no longer. Because his voice pierces the veil that makes his identity opaque, and his song commands others to see him the way he has learned to see himself: educated. It is then, and only then, that he sings, "I am here." Everyone has a voice. But no one has your song. Sing, in a room of conversations; their heads will turn, their hearts will open, and they will want to know your name.

I heard the song of Frederick Douglass, and I was freed. I heard the song of Brother Malcolm, and I was freed. I heard the song of Socrates and Confucius, Langston and Zora, Ella and Billie, Baldwin and Toni, Alice and Maya, and I was freed. They sang—so I, too, sing. I sing so you, too, will sing. And others will be freed, but if—and only if—you decide to sing.

ACKNOWLEDGMENTS

When I interviewed my mother for this book, she was not the least bit concerned about her depiction. She simply asked, "Will it help somebody?" I said yes. She said, "Then I want them to know the truth." My brothers and sister shared the same sentiment. And for this, I want to first acknowledge my family's courage. Recounting the events of our childhood required me to spend hours on the phone with my mother and siblings, revisiting our past, reliving painful experiences, and removing bandages from old wounds. For us, I pray it brings healing. For others, I pray it brings hope.

Miseducated was my thesis during the MFA program at University of Georgia. I am immensely grateful for the director of that program, Professor Valerie Boyd, who recruited me. A memoir is not what I intended to write. I wanted to write essays about philosophies of education—something so smart it might make the scholarly seraphim sing. It would have been filled with academic jargon and lofty language. It did not have plot. It did not have characters. It did not rise or fall. It sat still and stiff, with one leg crossed over the other. It did not move. It did not dance. I had big ideas and wanted to show the world that I had solved the troubles of our educational system—arguably one of society's most vexing problems. I had already started writing that book, and I entered the MFA program at UGA determined to finish it. Then I met Professor Pat Thomas, who convinced me to throw it away. Professor Thomas was my instructor and the first editor to embark upon this journey with me. She helped me understand that great books are not about problems; great books are about people. And if

I wanted to impact people through literature, I needed to understand that stories change people more than data ever will.

Trustworthy people are to be treasured. I am so lucky to be represented by Jessica Papin, my phenomenal literary agent. I feel the same about my acquiring editor, Lauren Marino, and the entire team at Hachette Book Group.

Most importantly, I extend my fondest regards to the Harvard community. None of this would have been possible without the confidence of Tripp Rebrovick, Sherry Hall, and Dallas Perkins at the Harvard Debate Council. Thank you for taking a chance on me.

In the first year of the Harvard Diversity Project, we were just trying to survive as a startup. But the following year, we were given the greatest gift in a brilliant business-minded Black woman named Kellye Britton. She is truly the backbone of our organization and the reason that I was able to step away for some time to write this book. Thank you for being a partner, a teacher, a confidante, and a mother to our beloved scholars.

To the parents in our organization, thank you for trusting me with your children. Thank you for believing in my unconventional methods, and for trusting me to love your children—no matter how hard that love can be.

And finally, my dear scholars: the reason for my second chance. You have taught me far more than I could ever teach you. Thank you for trusting me. I will always be of service to you, because it is for you I live. *Miseducated* is our story. But it is only the beginning. It is what you choose to do with your voice and your power and your privilege that will ultimately tell the rest.